My Two words that I Nov 23, 1994
Like i... 24
"TE [barcode]
沙羅様
Sarah, Thank's ...
Thank you for everything
you are a wonderful person
I appreciate how you share
your kindness, friendship, love.

When you read this book.
I want you to remember
our first month Aniversary
and to remember me when we
are not together.

You are now my great treasure.
of my life. You are my only
support. Thank you.

Sometimes you do not have to
say any words. Because what we
share every moment. tells everything..

The only two words I want to say
you is I love you.
I need you and want you by my
side. Please remember me when you read
This BOOK

田中
清明
上

Kiyoaki
Tanaka

I want our
friendship
and LOVE
Last forever
and ever.

愛
し
て
い
る
よ

ガ
ン
バ
レ

むりしないでね。

No matters what is going to happen I'll be always with you mentally and physically. I believe physically. Until the end of life separates us. And our future that will last for ever love.

TAKE CARE

THE JAPANESE WOMAN

THE
JAPANESE
WOMAN

TRADITIONAL IMAGE AND CHANGING REALITY

SUMIKO IWAO

THE FREE PRESS
A Division of Macmillan, Inc.
New York

Maxwell Macmillan Canada
Toronto

Maxwell Macmillan International
New York   Oxford   Singapore   Sydney

The Free Press
A Division of Macmillan, Inc.
866 Third Avenue, New York, N.Y. 10022

Maxwell Macmillan Canada, Inc.
1200 Eglinton Avenue East
Suite 200
Don Mills, Ontario M3C 3N1

Macmillan, Inc. is part of the Maxwell Communication Group of Companies.

Printed in the United States of America

printing number
1   2   3   4   5   6   7   8   9   10

Library of Congress Cataloging-in-Publication Data

Iwao, Sumiko
    The Japanese woman : traditional image and changing reality / Sumiko Iwao.
        p. cm.
    Includes bibliographical references and index.
    ISBN 0-02-932315-0
    1. Women—Japan—Social conditions.   2 Japan—Social conditions—1945–   3. Sex role—Japan.   I. Title.
    HQ1762.I925   1933
305.4'2'0952—dc20   92-24871
                                                              CIP

In memory of my mother
Iwao Saoe

CONTENTS

PREFACE

One of the heroines of my life and career thus far has been my paternal grandmother, who seems to have been, judging from the stories told by one of my father's closest friends, Araki Masuo*, the epitome of what I have come to think of as the double—edged strength of Japanese women. My grandfather, too, was a source of inspiration. In 1872, only a few years after the country had been opened to the West, he left Japan at the age of 18 to study at Yale University (where 90 years later I received my Ph. D. and met the man I was to marry). He later served as governor of several different prefectures in Japan and was among the lords who waited on the emperor in the palace. His diary of the ocean voyage to the United States records his memorable encounter with American women: "Quite unlike any Oriental woman, there are Western women who, while still in the bloom of youth, may be found laughing and teasing very dignified older gentlemen. The women of the East cannot possibly compare as far as physical agility and robustness of health. And they [American women] are exceedingly kind. Is this the result of custom or is it because of their religion?" This diary, which I read before going away to graduate shcool, sparked my interest in the differences in female behavior and sex roles in different societies, in how and why these roles are changing and what the implications of those changes are for society and the family. My years in

* In this book, Japanese names are written, as is customary in the case of Chinese names, last name first in the traditional manner. An exception has been made for the author's name on the title page. Authors, scholars, and public figures mentioned in the text are identified by their family name. Persons described more intimately are identified by their first name only.

ix

the United States coincided, moreover, with the beginning of a tumultuous period of change in female roles and behavior in the United States.

My grandfather married the daughter of a Buddhist priest, and my grandmother was, by all accounts, a classic example of cultivated, modest Japanese womanhood, but Araki Masuo used to tell me that she was, in fact, a formidable woman. Araki was a civil servant, like my father and grandfather, who later rose to the post of minister of education and became an influential politician. (He was also appointed chairman of the National Public Safety Commission, of which I am now a member.) In their youth he and my father often went drinking together after work, enjoying the town until the trains were no longer running. So Araki often ended up at our house for the night. Time and again, as the two badly hung over men tried to slip out to work the following morning, my grandmother, I was told, would appear silently in the hallway with my mother, eyes twinkling with barely suppressed glee, in tow. Serene and formal, grandmother would deliver a crisp reprimand: "Perhaps you two went a bit too far last night?" The sternness of her tone and the glint in her eye, Araki recalled, never failed to strike real fear into their hearts. What is this power, I have long wondered, that enables a woman to make two fine grown men cringe before her? Episodes such as this have convinced me that the strength and power of women, especially Japanese women, must be understood in terms of both their superficial qualities and their inner resources.

Following in my grandfather's footsteps, I went to the United States (in 1957) to study at Yale University; later, I began teaching psychology and doing research at Harvard. My life thereafter was very untraditional. I married a banker after returning to Japan and began teaching at Keio University in Tokyo. When my husband was transferred to Washington, D.C., I decided that I should remain in Tokyo to continue my work, and for five years I commuted to Washington, where our son was later born. Juggling a teaching load, research, child care, and community obligations, I have not only studied but also experienced in full measure the challenges, joys, difficulties, and anguishes of a modern career woman.

In 1977 I was involved in the founding of the International Group for the Study of Women and, with the cooperation of other members, led various studies on women (investigating, for example, the effects of mothers' work on children). We held international symposia, workshops, and lecture series on the results of our studies and invited to Japan speakers such as Matina Horner and Betty Friedan. Over the years I have lectured in different parts of the world on the lives of Japanese women, and my experiences and encounters have shown me how diverse the lifestyles of women are throughout the world and have convinced me that we cannot adequately understand any society without a fuller understanding of female attitudes and behavior. Particularly unexpected and intriguing was the observation made by several women attending a lecture I gave at the Royal Society of the Arts in 1991 in London that my analysis of Japanese women sounded just like the story of British women.

Internationally active Japanese like myself often struggle against images of Japan and Japanese that are either outdated or mistaken. We encounter many people with a serious desire to know what Japan is like, but there is never enough time to respond with an appropriately complete picture of its complex realities. This volume, although by no means comprehensive, is my attempt to help fill the serious gap in information on Japanese women and to depict in depth the true nature of their lives and roles. It is my desire that this be a book accessible to general readers rather than a study for a scholarly consumption, but it is based on reliable and up-to-date research data. A great deal of this data are not available in sources published in English. Much of my information comes from my own original surveys, interviews, and research conducted for this book.

Needless to say, it is extremely difficult to generalize about women, considering the diversity of both American and Japanese societies; yet even as we compare the two to the extent attempted here, we find both numerous similarities and a number of distinct differences. It is my hope that by introducing the patterns of behavior, thinking, and problem solving peculiar to Japanese women this volume will help unravel some of the mysteries and provide a more vivid portrait of my country women for overseas readers, as well as contribute to a better understanding of Japanese society and Japanese as a whole.

The publication of this book would not have been possible without the assistance and support of many people, more than I can possibly mention here. I would like to express special thanks to Daniel Bell and Bruce Stronach for their invaluable comments and advice; to Jacqueline Atkins for her careful reading and attention to the draft; to Kunihiro Yoko for her effecient help in library research as well as for providing the invaluable participant observation data cited in Chapter 9; and to Lynne E. Riggs for her editing, translation, and organization of the manuscript. Research help and critical insights were provided by Merry White, Hara Hiroko, Hironaka Wakako, Kobayashi Yoshiko, Ogawa Akira, Fukazawa Michiko, Susan Stehlik, and Susan Carvely. I would also like to thank Virginia Petree, Sugawara Mariko, and Susie Schmidt for their help. I am also grateful to editor Susan Arellano, with whose skillful shepherding the book took its final shape, and to agent Yamashiro Sakiyo.

I would like to express a special note of thanks to my husband, Furuya Kuhachiro, and my son, Furuya Obumi. Their inexhaustible good humor and patience as well as bemused curiosity about the project that has consumed my every waking hour not taken up by work made it possible for me to abandon my domestic responsibilities for the sake of this book. I am also grateful to my parents, Iwao Seizo and Saoe, who supported me in every ambitious project I have undertaken and whose unconditional love has been my constant source of strength.

THE JAPANESE WOMAN

1

MYTHS AND REALITIES

The kimono-clad, bamboo parasol–toting, bowing female walking three paces behind her husband remains the image many Westerners hold of the typical Japanese woman. Satellite communications and high-speed travel have not dispelled the exoticism that captured Western imagination in the 19th century when Westerners first began traveling to Japan in significant numbers or removed for them the mystery that surrounds the thinking and behavior of Oriental women. It is still possible to witness such a scene of traditionalism and apparent subservience on the streets of Tokyo today. But appearances can be deceiving, a fact that is all too well known among Japanese themselves. The traditional female is rapidly becoming but one of several breeds of women in a society that is growing increasingly pluralistic.

The persisting myths about its women are just one dimension of the general inadequacy of information Westerners have about Japan. Cultural and economic frictions continue to stir nationalistic emotions and fears of what seems to Westerners to be a monolithic society, closed and inscrutable to outsiders.

Although exposing outmoded myths and probing beyond the simplistic images of Japanese society would further the cause of mutual understanding, I believe an understanding of Japanese thinking and behavior offers much more. This study of Japanese women, as a case in point, not only illuminates many facets of their society but also opens up a trove of female wisdom and experience that offers valuable points of reference to help members of other cultures change their own lives for the better.

1

Perhaps the most fascinating dimension of this study is the way Japanese women themselves have been changing, winning an astonishing degree of freedom and independence quietly and unobtrusively, largely without the fanfare of an organized women's movement or overt feminism. I would like to present the case for this alternative process of change, which is happening despite the basically very compromising stance of women. Pragmatism, nonconfrontation, and a long-term perspective are the rules that govern this change, which I call the quiet revolution.

The performers in the most sensational dramas of Japanese society unfolding over the past two decades have been almost exclusively men, but a pervasive and dynamic transformation, unquestionably dominated by women, has been taking place backstage. The core of this backstage revolution is the generation born after the end of World War II, between 1946 and 1955, mainly those who are college-educated and live in urban areas. Educated under the postwar democratic constitution in predominantly coeducational institutions, these women, it can be argued, have set the stage virtually to their own liking. Although the entire spectrum of Japanese womanhood is naturally broader, my focus in this book is on this generation.

One of the main issues for women is equality. Because the United States came into being as a melting pot of ethnic groups, the differences among its people were tremendous from the start. A strong orientation toward equality and equal opportunity is part of what prevents the entire society from being broken up into countless pieces. Throughout Japan's history, on the other hand, it has been thought that "as long as the changing weather from year to year produces good harvests and bad, people are all basically equal."[1] And this perspective, some believe, is why the issue of equality has not received as much attention in Japan.

The demand for recognition of equality not only with respect to rights and opportunities but in terms of behavior and occupations has galvanized the American women's movement. Leading the way into this brave new world of equality between the sexes are the female soldiers of the U.S. military (who made headlines during the 1991 Gulf War) and the career women in America's big cities who are determined to do anything a man can do. It seems clear that the scale upon which these women measure equality is determined by what men do and have achieved. From the standpoint of the Japanese woman (which shall be explained later, particularly in the chapters on women and work), seeking equality on a scale where the mean is determined by male behavior hardly seems likely to offer women what they really want.

American acquaintances often exclaim to me that they cannot understand how Japanese women tolerate the blatant sexual discrimination evident in their society. Their reaction, however, calls attention to an important point: American and Japanese women differ in their view of equality. Equality is a laudable ideal and, obviously, a core concept of modern societies. On the level of law and institutions, equality is a basic principle for determining action. On the level of rights and responsibilities, citizens should be treated as equivalent entities, and the attempt to do away with inequities based on gender, class, race, creed, and so forth is one of the great movements of modern civilization. But on the level of the human animal, no one human being is as equally endowed as another. Debate over whether gender differences are inherent or environmental, swayed by each new set of scientific findings, has pulled the thinking of Americans this way and that over the past 20 years. Japanese thinking, whatever the scientists are saying, is based on the belief that even though men and women are different in disposition, behavior, and biology, they can be equal as humans, although that equality consists of a balance of advantage, opportunity, and responsibility achieved *over time*.

This view of equality, which may strike American readers as not being equality at all, is something I attempt to explain in this book. In terms of rights, Japanese women believe, as do their American counterparts, in equal pay for equal work, equal opportunity, and so on. What appears to be different in their concepts of equality is that in Japan equality is not sought on principle and part-time working women and full-time housewives in particular consider themselves equal to their professionally or vocationally employed husbands, at least as far as their status in the household is concerned. Not only do women see themselves as equal to their husbands but their husbands willingly admit their dependence on women (in a sense, their inferiority). This not merely private lip service but the stuff of public opinion.[2] Rather surprisingly, in fact, surveys show that 40 percent of full-time housewives think of themselves as economi-

cally independent (the figure is 70 percent for married women
who are working).[3] This demonstrates clearly how these women,
who may have no income themselves but who control the
household purse strings, see themselves in relation to men. The
role of the woman in the home is valued and her self-esteem is
high because the management of the family has always been
considered central to stability and prosperity in Japanese society.
Contrary to the image of subjugation outsiders seem to associate
with Japanese women, the latter often believe it is they who draw
the boundaries within which their husbands move, not the other
way around.

Technological change and economic affluence are transforming all industrialized societies and ushering in the postindustrial
age. Behavioral change in human societies is the natural consequence. Although women in Japan have been relatively content
as backstage shapers and observers of the unfolding events of
history, they are nevertheless changing rapidly in the face of new
developments and international influence, faster, it would seem,
than the men laboring out in the limelight. The uneven pace at
which male and female attitudes and behavior are changing is a
current source of stress in Japanese society.

The developments that have transformed women's lives are
beginning to trigger changes in the lives of men and in the entire
fabric of Japanese society and institutions. The structure and
functions of the family have been profoundly altered, the composition of the work force is being progressively integrated, the
economy is forcefully swayed by consumers who are predomi-
nately women, and a cultural ferment is taking place in response
to the exercise of female economic and other freedoms.

MEN SUPERIOR, WOMEN DOMINANT

The lives and attitudes of Japanese women have undergone
tremendous changes in the past 15 years or so. The younger
generations, in particular, enjoy unprecedented freedom and
diversified options, and the relationship between the sexes is
described by some as *"dansei jōi, josei yūi* (men superior, women
dominant)."* But this is nothing new.

Amaterasu, the Japanese deity of the sun in indigenous
mythology, is female (in contrast, for example, to the male

Apollo of Greek mythology), and women were considered from ancient times to have a special supernatural power, with which men were not endowed, to communicate with the divine. Moreover, until the beginning of the Muromachi age (1336) Japan was a matriarchal society. Among the farming, fishing, and merchant folk who made up 80 percent of the population throughout premodern times, commoner women enjoyed freedom (including freedom in such areas as love and marriage), equality, and power as they worked under much the same conditions as men. The lives of women of the elite (primarily samurai) classes were defined throughout many centuries by the Confucian ethic (in which women's lives were bound by the "three obediences": obedience to fathers when young, to husbands when married, and to their children in old age) and were subject to many other constraints. In the Meiji era (1868–1912), marking the beginning of Japan's modernization, however, the samurai class culture of premodern times penetrated throughout the entire society as rigid class distinctions were officially abolished. As a consequence, women as a whole lost the power and equality they had enjoyed. In other words, it was only quite recently, a little more than a century ago, that women lost their previous power and producer/worker status and became, especially in the cities, "unemployed" consumers.

With modernization, the integration and centralization of Japanese society progressed, and the male-dominated, vertically structured society became firmly established, leaving women out of the mainstream, although they continued to play a strong role in society. Analyses of Japanese society have tended to focus on society according to this predominant structure and often overlook women. Nakane Chie's classic work on the structure of Japanese society, for example, explains it as a highly integrated, hierarchical (vertical) society.[4] Her work is superb in its accounting of the workings of power as observed through male or male-dominated groups and organizations. However, it does not take into consideration women and female-dominated groups, which are horizontal and qualification- or task-oriented in structure (as described in Chapter 9). Because women make up more than half the Japanese population today, no complete understanding of this society can be achieved without taking them into consideration.

The central organizations and groups that make up Japanese

society are almost exclusively staffed and controlled by men. It was not so long ago that only men in Japan enjoyed the great breadth of opportunities in life and the freedom to savor a variety of experiences outside the home. But today opportunities for women to work and pursue careers have increased, giving them a whole new range of freedoms, economic and otherwise. This development has led to a reversal of freedoms, as it were. Men have become increasingly chained to the institutions they have set up, as epitomized by the corporate security blanket, namely, long-term employment and the promotional ladder determined by seniority. Their wives, on the other hand, once chained to home and hearth, have been set free by the development of home and other consumer conveniences, and now their energies are being absorbed by a waiting labor market and a broad range of culturally enriching activities. Not only can they work outside the home but they have great freedom to decide how, where, and under what terms they will work (as will be described in greater detail in Chapters 6 and 7). In this reversal of freedoms, the female side of society has become extremely diversified while the male side, trapped by inertia and peer pressure, has become more homogenous.

Fifteen years ago, for example, a typical 35-year-old woman was most likely a professional housewife with two children who devoted her life to serving the needs of husband and children. On the basis of the fixed set of roles (e.g., shopkeeper's wife, schoolteacher, mother) she assumed, each of which was clearly and narrowly defined, it was relatively easy to visualize how she lived. Today it is not so easy. Every role (even that of wife or mother) is much more loosely defined. She is equally likely to be single, married, living with a partner, or divorced; to have children or be childless; and to be working part- or full-time. And she is as likely to be a person who seeks self-fulfillment and devotes herself to personal goals as an "education mama," who pursues vicarious fulfillment through the accomplishments of her children.

The typical 35-year-old man today is apt to be, as he was 15 years ago, a company man (corporate foot soldier), devoting most of his life to his work-related activities and associations. The roles men are expected to fill are still quite limited and fairly narrowly defined, leading to more uniformity in their life patterns. In other words, the scope of a man's world is much smaller than that of a woman in terms of options, and this is a complete reversal of the situation in prewar Japan.

What ultimately provided Japanese women with increased options, ironically, was their position outside the mainstream of society. They have not occupied positions of significance in policy-making and business and their existence and voices have been pretty much ignored by men in formal arenas, but there has been some advantage in this state of "inequality." It has exempted women from having to fit into the frameworks set down by the public or private organizations (corporations) of society and has allowed them the margin of freedom to explore their individuality in ways not permitted to men. One manifestation of this is that outside the corporation one is more likely to find an adventurous or creative spirit in women than in men. Women are the intellectual and artistic upstarts of society today, exploring new endeavors and expressing their raw energies in diverse forms, while men remain largely confined to the old established norms and codes of traditional hierarchical society. Mature women are going back to school, entering universities and graduate schools; they are going to work for international organizations like the United Nations, leaving humdrum jobs to run for political office, and becoming successful as novelists, writers, and poets (a count of recent literary prizes in Japan shows that the majority were won by women).[5] There is nothing to prevent a mature woman from striking off in any direction that catches her fancy; after her children are grown, she can become a mountain climber, architect, businesswoman, volunteer worker among the poor. Her male age-mate would probably not have the courage to break away from his secure position in his company and the often-demanding expectations of his family (ironically, women expect men to be good and reliable breadwinners, which assures the economic leeway it becomes their prerogative to enjoy).

Today it is, in a sense, the husbands who are being controlled and the ones to be pitied. The typical Japanese man depends heavily on his wife to look after his daily needs and nurture his psychological well-being. The Confucian ethic of the three obediences formerly binding women could be rewritten today as the three obediences for men: obedience to mothers when young, companies when adult, and wives when retired. Recent television dramas have depicted the plight of salaried-worker fathers as their presence and power in the home fades; such men are estranged from their families by extended absences (e.g., work assignments abroad or in other cities) and suffer from a syndrome known as "involuntary incapacity to go home [*kitaku kyohi*]." Their plight is only intensified by the stronger position of women in the home. These recent phenomena lead us to wonder whether it is not men, instead of women, who are being exploited in Japanese society today. The vast majority of men, however, remain largely unaware of their own vulnerability as they cling to the illusion that they are the respected superiors of society and belittle women's voices as nothing but emotional, unrealistic "female logic."

With increasing articulateness, Japanese women are asserting the validity of a logic that measures priorities on a scale rather different from the efficiency/economics/success/power scale adhered to by men. They are calling attention to the need for a more humane life (*ningen-rashii ikikata*), one that takes into account the quality of life, human feelings, care for others, preservation of the earth, and so forth, as opposed to one devoted to striving for wealth and power. They are challenging, in other words, the priorities their society so far has followed. Women favor the pursuit of a humane and fulfilled life, with more sharing and enjoyment of home and family for both men and women. If such a goal is to be attained, the implication is, naturally, that the economic pie will be smaller. What degree of sacrifice either men or women will be willing to make is something we will be observing in the years to come.

NONCONFRONTATIONAL STRATEGY

The value system that guides Japanese women is reactive. Their responses and attitudes are strongly shaped by the conditions in which they find themselves. Pragmatism, rather than principles, guides their behavior, and this is a fundamental difference between Japanese and, for example, American society. In the United States principles come first, and practice must be made to serve those principles. If principles are not adhered to, Americans reason, they are made meaningless. Logic therefore demands strict adherence to principles. Perhaps because of the cultural, ethnic, and geographic diversity of the United States, principles are especially important in establishing a common footing for all and defining the means by which people can deal with one another. Of course, the roots of American culture in Western philosophical and religious traditions are the decisive factor shaping the principle-oriented behavior and thinking of Americans.

The idea of principle in the strict English sense, however, does not wholly conform with the conceptual language of Japanese. *Principle* has been translated into Japanese as *gensoku,* which is a guideline or precept to be looked to and abided by as much as possible. Actual practice, which has to serve the diverse needs of living, breathing human beings, cannot always serve principle to the letter. Both the principle-first and the pragmatism-first approaches have their fundamental weaknesses and fallacies. Over the centuries, Japan has tended to opt for those of the latter approach.

Because of the family- and group-centered norms that govern socialization in Japan, women (even more than men) fail to learn in childhood to think independently, and this gives them even fewer inner resources to lean upon when they reach adulthood. In place of independence, they develop and maintain a high degree of sensitivity to what their peers and other persons significant in their lives expect them to be and to do. This tendency is often expressed by the phrase *nagare ni mi o makaseru* (in today's idiom, "go with the flow"), which describes the behavior of persons who are at a loss to make a more autonomous and deliberate choice of options but who wish to ensure a harmonious atmosphere among their fellows. In the context of American society such behavior might be considered irresponsible or negative, yet in Japan deferring to others is positive behavior, especially for women.

On the positive side, the pragmatic approach allows Japanese women to adapt themselves in the most appropriate or advantageous manner to the situation at hand. It is easier for many to think about what kind of life they want for themselves by taking the lifestyle afforded by their husband's occupation as a starting point and considering their options from there. On the negative side, the pragmatic, situational approach to making decisions prevents women from establishing a clear identity and taking full responsibility for the various choices and decisions that must be made in their lives; as a result, they vacillate and have less drive in accomplishing goals. This is part of the reason it is difficult to establish solidarity among Japanese women.

Today, nevertheless, we do see more women who have awakened to the options before them and are seeking more active involvement and planning in their own lives; as they say, they are in search of themselves. Yet they have not completely shed their characteristic passivity and, to a certain degree, resignation to their fate.

There is a strong nonconfrontational tendency in Japanese society in general, and individual behavior, especially among women, reflects an aversion to absolutes. (In the United States, on the other hand, because of the orientation to principles, there is a tendency to stick to absolutes.) Dichotomous values or categories—private/public, good/bad, happy/unhappy, winner/loser, male/female—are not seen by Japanese as the only options: Between the two ends of a scale there is usually a broadly perceived zone of yet further options. Between absolute goodness and evil, for example, is a wide territory that contains both the good and the bad. Happiness is always marred by some difficulty or unhappiness, and unhappiness is never completely devastating. You may be a loser in one game but a winner in another, at a disadvantage on certain terms but at an advantage on others. For this reason, Japanese will persevere under very difficult circumstances, avoiding confrontation until the situation becomes absolutely intolerable. Also, there is the belief that perseverance makes one a stronger and better person, which in the long run can be an advantage.

Japanese women consider their own happiness to be closely tied to that of their families—so much so that they will restrain their personal feelings to an extent an American woman might not be able to tolerate. It is common practice to forgo personal fulfillment and desire for the sake of nurturing and maintaining the harmony and happiness of the group (usually the family) that is so highly prized. Maintaining interpersonal harmony may be an important concern for many Japanese women precisely because they have fewer opportunities than men in which they can be evaluated on their own merits and abilities. They are more likely to be evaluated for their compliance (*sunaosa*) and concern for interpersonal harmony (*ki-kubari*). Although younger Japanese women are more outspoken and direct than the older generation, they still show much greater passivity than most

American women. Rather than reacting spontaneously or acting immediately on their beliefs or desires, they take time making any given decision or embarking upon any action because they tend to wait and size up the judgments of others beforehand. They rarely take an extreme position or form of behavior, preferring to adjust what they do and think, to a certain extent, to other people's positions; they also tend to perceive of most things as neither 100 percent good (right) nor 100 percent bad (wrong).

Another element of the nonconfrontational tendency in Japanese human relations is the long-term perspective people take to gain and loss, happiness and unhappiness, satisfaction and dissatisfaction, which is constrained by a consideration of others and the surrounding situation. Happiness may not be possible now or even five years from now, but if one perseveres and endures, it will eventually be possible. The time frame in which Japanese women seek their goals appears to be much longer than that of American women, who seem to be intent on satisfying current desires and goals as soon as they possibly can. While confrontation is seen as necessary in the United States, in a close-knit society like that of Japan avoiding an outright clash opens a wider variety of options, protects human feelings, and preserves the overall stability of human relations. In the movement for higher status of women, which involves gain for women but not necessarily for men, the nonconfrontational approach helps ease social resistance as women shift away from traditional role expectations and can be a factor that prevents or deflects backlash.

THE QUALITY OF EQUALITY

One misperception often held by others is that Japanese women are far behind American women in the fight for "equal rights." It is true that women's rights were severely limited under the Meiji Civil Code, which upheld the old Confucian ethic, and were further curtailed under the patriarchal system. Women had no alternative but to follow age- and role-appropriate behavior and life patterns whereas men's lives were more varied, with more options and more freedom to make their own choices in life. The postwar Japanese Constitution, which shapes today's society, clearly stipulates that "all of the people are equal under the law" and that there shall be no discrimination on the basis of sex. Thus, the problem of gaining equal rights under the constitution is not the issue, as it has been in the United States; as we shall see in later chapters, the problem is one of *equal opportunity.*

Equality is an ideal, but the question of *what* women want to be *equal to* is crucial. Apparently, attaining equality with men has been the goal for American women. In Japan increasing attention is being focused on the "humane life," which transcends both men and women. The fact that such Freudian concepts as penis envy and castration complex (i.e., the sort of men-versus-women complexes) have stirred little interest in Japan may have contributed to this kind of thinking. The waves of the international movement for liberation of women from the grip of traditional roles lapped at Japan's shores in the 1960s but did not set many further waves in motion. It was not until the launching of the United Nations Decade for Women in 1975, which lent the women's rights movement mainstream dignity, that the Japanese government began to consider public policy measures to overcome the discriminatory practices preventing the improvement of women's status. By that time, too, the changes taking place in women's roles were slowly gaining momentum.

Meanwhile, as structural changes accompanying the shift to a postindustrial economy began to transform Japan, the overwhelming dominance of men in the labor force waned, and large numbers of women entered service industries (in which the caretaking skills and sensibilities women have long cultivated were in great demand). The first wave of women to enter the labor force were young, and their stay was brief, as they quit their jobs upon marriage. But gradually the number of career-oriented women has increased, and in 1986 the Equal Employment Opportunity Law went into force, removing the overprotective clauses of earlier laws that legally prevented women from working alongside men (as described in Chapter 6).

Different paths may be taken in achieving equality between men and women, and it would seem that they diverge quite a bit in Japan and the United States, although both are at least officially committed to the principle of equal opportunity for men and women in education, job recruitment, employment, training, promotion, and retirement benefits. In the United States the status of men is seen as superior to that of women and apparently is the target of women's struggle for equality. Women, we hear it argued, are able to do anything that men do, and we now read of the extreme care taken in some cases to avoid differences in treatment on the basis of sex. One result of this view of equality, for example, is the abolition of maternity leave for female faculty members at Barnard College, which produces many of America's best educated, most professionally accomplished women. While the college adopted a generous leave policy in 1932, a "minimal maternity policy" was readopted in 1985. We presume that the new policy was based on the assumption that women ought not to be coddled but should be ready to work under the same conditions as men and that eliminating maternity leave was viewed as a step toward greater equality between men and women.[6] But the new policy limits the freedom of female faculty members and administrators to have children. It is an illusion to think that men and women are completely and literally equal, at the very least on the basis of the biological fact that only women are able to bear children, and to draw up organizational rules on that basis. Today the legitimacy of gender differences is acknowledged to a greater degree in the United States, although we still hear of cases where the principle of equality is carried to the extreme as when a male nursing aide filed a sex-bias lawsuit against a nursing home that refused to hire him.[7] While opinion among Japanese women is diverse, the general view is that equality has to be considered within a broad framework that takes into account inherent sexual differences, personal preferences, and a balance of various factors.

It would seem that Americans judge the way they are being treated by considering their position at a single point in time. If in examining their situation they find themselves in an inferior position with others of equivalent credentials, they are quick to accuse others of treating them unfairly or unequally, without waiting to see whether the situation will balance out over a longer period of time. In Japan questions of fairness and equality are conceived on a much longer time frame and in a more multidimensional context. Although the husband and wife in a household or the coworkers in an office may not seem to be treated equally at any particular point in time, those involved consider the question in a very broad context: If on an overall balance sheet the advantages enjoyed on one side and the disadvantages suffered on the other over a long period of time can be considered to mutually balance out, then they are willing to accept the relationship as workable and practical, that is, as fair and equal *in the long run.*

The precondition for achieving such a long-term balance, of course, is a sustained and trusting relationship; otherwise, there is not sufficient time for the necessary give-and-take to balance out. In a society like that of the United States today, where divorce is common and people change employers often, it is not surprising that the demand for equality is more immediate and urgent, since the relationships that are set up do not last long enough to provide a more relaxed, long-term context for mutual give-and-take. The advantages of considering equality over the long term are that a more flexible position can be adopted, taking the complex realities of human relations into account, and that responses to issues of minor importance can be more relaxed and tolerant. A Japanese housewife, for example, measures her status vis-à-vis that of her husband by using various criteria, including not only social status but also available economic resources, freedom to determine disposal of time and money, and degree of personal fulfillment. If she values free time more than the professional challenges of a full-time job, she may opt to be economically dependent on her husband for income (in which case she will control the purse strings, thereby securing a solid source of self-esteem), but this does not mean her role in the family is any less important. Women handle family relations in the community, affairs related to their children's education, and home management, enriching the family also through their cultural pursuits of one sort or another. This often means that husbands and wives move in very different worlds, but, as we shall see in Chapter 3, Japanese born before 1955 and earlier find this distance comfortable. Power relations in the Japanese family are exercised on different levels by men and women; to the observer, men may appear to be the more powerful while, in fact, women are the ones who exert the strongest influence in the home and control the purse strings.

Japanese women also view the issue of equality in terms of the burdens and freedoms involved. Believing, for example, that women are biologically best equipped to shoulder the bulk of the burden of childrearing, especially in the early stages, they believe they have every right to take maternity leave and other special benefits related to childrearing without apology. And women are willing to grant a husband who provides the economic support

for the household exemption from the bulk of household responsibilities. In facing specific day-to-day situations, Japanese wom-
en tend to be extremely pragmatic; they are not necessarily
concerned with achieving equality with men in terms of disposal
of time and energy or even in terms of income or status rewards
for performance. More important, they believe, is whether a
woman is able to pursue her goals according to her individual
preferences. There are situations in which the issue of equality is
important and others where it is not. For example, career-
oriented working women do not want to be asked to serve tea to
their male colleagues just because they are women, but if they are
making coffee for themselves, they are happy to make extra cups
for their fellows, whether they are men or women. This is what
they consider the humane way of living. In any case, they believe
equality with men in the literal sense is a question of individual
taste, not a matter of principle, an attitude I will probe further in
coming chapters.

Another reason the women's liberation movement has been
muted in Japan is that when women wish to protest against
unfair treatment, they are less likely to seek a frontal confrontation, because in this society head-on confrontation can be so ugly
that it prevents constructive progress toward a solution. Women
will let their dissatisfactions be known in clear but indirectly
communicated terms (e.g., by curtailing the spending money
given to the husband—if, say, he spends too many nights out on
the town—on the pretext that their daughter is taking piano
lessons and she needs the money for that). No matter how noble
a principle may be, they firmly believe, if it does not make
people's lives better, it is in some way flawed.

A reflection of this belief is the reluctance of Japanese women
to pursue the career modes and goals of men today; equality is all
very well, but if it means having to work so hard that individual
pleasures and private fulfillment are not permitted, they are
content to do without it. Men's lives in Japan today are confined
and regimented by their jobs to an extreme; they are alienated
from their households and deprived of time to engage in
culturally enriching pursuits. This is not a model women think
worthy of emulation. On the contrary, they think that happiness
for both men and women would be better assured by a model of
equality in which men were given the same freedom, rights, and
options in the three main areas of life (work, family, leisure) that

women currently enjoy. In this model, women could fulfill fewer family duties and seek more responsibilities related to outside work while men could slacken their work commitments and take on more family-involved responsibilities. The ideal is for both men and women to be able to emulate the model of the other in some areas if not in others. The balance a couple ultimately maintains in the three areas would depend on the stage of life they are in and their own specific needs and tastes. This is an approach that treats equality not as a binding principle but a guideline and tool.

Admittedly, this approach to equality has its unhealthy side as well. By their less than eager pursuit of equal treatment with men, Japanese women know full well that having to bear equal economic responsibilities with men is by no means a situation that serves their best interests. True equality with men would pare down their current options considerably. There is a tendency to evoke the issue of equality only when it is convenient, such as when a woman, having been discovered in an extramarital affair, excuses herself by saying that her husband has had affairs of his own and that the rules go both ways. In any case, in contrast to the central position it holds in the American women's movement, equality is not an issue in the forefront of the inconspicuous revolution going on among Japanese women.

WOMEN AND MEN IN DIFFERENT WORLDS

Although it is not a formal dictum in Japanese society, the worlds of men and women are often miles apart in their daily activities, in spite of some acceptance of gray zones in the male/female dichotomy. Excluded from participation in the activities dominated by men, women have ended up establishing a separate world of their own. Both sides cultivate their own closely knit networks of social acquaintances. Communication among members of the same sex is quite dense, but that between the sexes is minimal, especially in comparison with such communication in Western countries. In the latter, the couple (married or not) appears to be a basic social unit, with each partner being continually conscious of the other's existence, opinions, preferences, and so forth. Western culture might be called a "couples culture," in contrast to the "singles culture" of Japan, where activities tend to revolve around members of the same sex and individuals appear to be much more concerned with gaining the friendship and respect of members of their own sex than with making an impression on the opposite sex.

In the United States both men and women appear to devote much more energy to cultivating appearances and behavior with respect to their relationship with the opposite sex. For Americans, such close relationships between men and women can be both very stressful and the source of great pleasure. Because the distance between them is so close and ego-involving, confrontations between men and women can be shattering, causing a breakup or divorce. From the Japanese point of view, it seems paradoxical that independence-oriented, individualistic Americans would emphasize so much sharing and togetherness between a couple. Especially in this age of extended longevity, a reasonable amount of autonomy for each partner would seem to be a precondition for a long-lasting marriage. As we shall see, Japanese wives often show remarkable autonomy in arranging their lives. They possess almost too much autonomy, sometimes inhibiting a closer relationship between husband and wife.

WOMEN IN THE VANGUARD OF CHANGE

One striking characteristic of Japanese men today is their lack of awareness, not to mention genuine understanding or appreciation, of the changes that are occurring in women, even though the status and roles of women are closely intertwined with those of men. The lack of communication between the sexes may be one cause.

Men and women are changing at different paces. If we compare the changes in attitudes and behavior demonstrated by Japanese men and women, we find that women have undergone much greater changes. Women—especially those in their late thirties and forties who are sometimes called *"genki jirushi no onnatachi* [energetic brand women]"—are known for the immense diversity of their activities, their self-determined lifestyles, and their devotion to the rich cultural life offered by Japan's cities.

Not only have women's lives become more diverse than those of men but they have also shown at times a propensity to change ahead of men. The opinion surveys widely conducted in Japan at various levels by all kinds of organizations, from government agencies, major newspapers, and television stations to private corporations, offer data on attitudes toward a wide range of issues, including divorce, care of the elderly, foreign policy, and education. The findings of such opinion surveys show repeatedly that women precede men in the speed of their attitudinal change on specific issues. For example, the results of the annual surveys on popular lifestyles conducted by the Prime Minister's Office indicate that the average Japanese man began to attach greater importance to spiritual fulfillment than to material affluence around 1982. For women, however, the trend was already apparent in 1978, four years before it was evident in male responses.

Unfortunately, many men continue to view women as not fully adult, an attitude that dominated the thinking of the old family system. Inasmuch as they completely monopolize responsible positions in politics, government, finance, and other national institutions, men continue to presume they are the sole responsible members of society. Since men do not see women as an immediate threat to themselves, they do not intervene in the affairs of women and do not know much about what women are doing, enabling them to become quite independent. Men's blindness in this respect has indeed been frustrating, but, at the same time, the practically minded Japanese woman has been able to take advantage of it. This, indeed, is why the quiet revolution among women is moving forward so relentlessly. Even women with substantial incomes of their own are not sharing the household economic responsibilities equally with men but are quietly enjoying a degree of freedom and fulfillment not available to men. What these unobtrusively occurring changes in women will bring in the years ahead is a subject of immense importance to Japan's future direction.

GENERATIONS OF CHANGE

It may be helpful here to chart the changes in Japanese women's lives in terms of the major roles they play, available role repertoires, role expectations, conflicts between their own sex role expectations and that of males, and the stress they experience as a result of conflicting role expectations. The model of the traditional woman is embodied in the old expression *"ryōsai-kenbo* [the good wife and wise mother]." The dynamics of change in female sex roles are vividly recorded by comparing three contemporary generations of women: the older generation, born before 1935; the first postwar generation, born between 1946 and 1955; and the younger generation, born between 1960 and 1969. The youngest group will be taken up briefly in the final chapter on the directions of change.

I have made no attempt to deal comprehensively with all age-groups, because this study is intended to highlight generational change. Partly because of the still considerable homogeneity of Japanese society, the life-cycle follows a predictable pattern for people of all generations: for women, typically, graduation from high school at age 18; entry into university, 18; graduation from university and entry into employment, 22; marriage, average age 26; childbearing years, 27–29; reemployment after children enter primary school, 36. Despite the recent trend toward diversification, a Japanese person can easily imagine what the life of any Japanese woman is like in her early, mid-, or late twenties, or in her early, mid-, or late thirties, and so forth. For the purposes of this study, I shall focus on the following age-groups: the older generation (born before 1935), and 56 years or older as of this writing); the first postwar generation (born between 1946 and 1955, and 36–45 years old); and the younger generation (born between 1960 and 1969, and 22–31 years old). Other age-groups will be defined when necessary. Women called "middle aged" in this book are those born between 1931 and 1955, now in their mid-thirties to late fifties.

The older generation

Women of the older group were brought up by parents with prewar values, namely, maintenance of the *ie* (household), the superior status of men, and the inferior status of women. They accepted the traditional "good wife and wise mother" model as their ideal. The repertoire of sex roles at their disposal was very limited, but they were quite content with the roles of wife and

mother. There were few individual differences in role expectations and role-relevant behavior because role-appropriate behavior was clearly prescribed. Many women did work to help make
ends meet, but no matter how much they contributed, their work
had nothing to do with personal actualization or fulfillment; it
was simply to support the husband's role as breadwinner. In the
minds of the older generation (born before 1935), important
interpersonal relations—those between men and women, husband and wife, mother and child—are characterized by a
vertical, not a horizontal, power structure. If a woman's expectations of her husband are unfulfilled, her impulse to find meaning
in life is transferred to her children.

What women expect of themselves as "good wives and wise
mothers" is also not much different from the expectations men
have of them, so conflict in role expectations is low. Yet the
worlds of men and women in the older generation are often far
apart. In their own world women have attained great autonomy
and independence. Over half of the men of this generation (52
percent) claim proudly that they have never helped with housework and regard themselves as the ultimate authority in the
home (*teishu kanpaku*).[8] Relations between these men and women
are maintained without tension because the formal superiority of
the men is matched by the informal dominance of the women.[9]

This generation was already over 40 when the effects of the
women's liberation movement began to be felt in Japan and the
UN-sponsored Decade of Women began (1975); it was too late
for them to be much influenced personally by these new trends.
Few questioned the legitimacy of the roles they were playing or
explored the possibilities of other options.

The first postwar generation

This generation is distinguished from those before and after by
the fact that they were reared and educated immediately after
World War II, when the ideal of sexual equality, as opposed to the
traditional pattern, was emphasized, especially in the schools.
These women grew up to think of sexual equality almost as an
obligation—they were taught that they *ought to be* equal (the
meaning of which has never been well defined)—regardless of

whether they thought it was right or desirable. This generation of women therefore sought husbands they could relate to on an equal basis, as friends, and rejected the lifestyles and values of their parents as outmoded and undesirable. Their ideals, it seems, were affected more by what they saw in Hollywood-made movies or American television programs broadcast in Japan than by the way their own parents lived. The women of this generation also differ from those of the previous one in that they are better prepared to articulate their doubts and arguments about the status quo to husbands or society in general.

After marriage the women of the first postwar generation quickly realized that the roles of wife and mother alone were not sufficiently satisfying. They began to question and attempt to redefine their roles, especially after their youngest children entered elementary school. Some found work as one path for redefining and diversifying their roles. Others, though still a minority, found new meaning in their lives by their involvement in groups of activist women and in other nontraditional pursuits such as continuing education. Expanding their activities outside the home was not easy. Society was as yet inadequately prepared (e.g., through equal employment opportunity legislation and the availability of day care and other services substituting for house-wives' work in the home) to fully support working or socially active women, and men were not interested in what their wives were doing. Men continued to expect their wives to play the traditional good wife–wise mother role. Women did not include men in their attempt to redefine their roles but worked around the old expectations and roles of men. Women were eager to relate to their husbands on a friend-to-friend basis, and many husbands who would have preferred the status of authoritarian male in the household had to defer to their wives' pleasure.

Many women of this generation tried to adjust themselves to meeting conflicting role expectations by juggling their activities, doing everything they had always done *as well as* what they wanted to do in their new roles. They felt the options available to them were limited. Many who had taken up employment before marriage left work during their first pregnancy and later, after their children entered school, returned to the workplace, where the available jobs were mostly of the support type (clerical, secretarial, office helper). Regardless of what these women earn, they continue to live primarily on their husband's income. This results in an economic inequality that the women benefit from— even though they may feel guilty about the inequality. And they continue to feel a certain amount of frustration when they seek literal equality with men, a striving that never touched their mothers' generation. Whatever frustrations they suffer, women of this first postwar generation find ample outlets for their energies in such diverse activities as work, hobbies, grass roots political activities, and community work (see in Chapter 9). Yet a major source of stress for these women, even after they have successfully redefined their roles and found some means of personal actualization, is their sense that they may be neglecting their children because of their attempts to fulfill their increased role expectations and the commitments they have made outside the home.

The main focus of this book is on the women of this first postwar generation, those born between 1946 and 1955. The lives of these women have been profoundly affected by postwar values and institutions and bear witness to the transition be- tween traditional sex roles and behavior and those of the "liberated" woman of the postindustrial age. Faced not only with caring for aging parents but also with finding new direction for themselves, these women often remain suspended between the old and the new.

Because it constitutes quite a large chunk of the population, the impact of the first postwar generation on society as a whole is frequently noted. It was the first to be educated in coeducational institutions from first grade; its oldest members reached college age in the mid-sixties and counted among their numbers leaders of the violent and memorable mass student movement that protested Japan's complicity in the Vietnam War and the authori- tarianism of the nation's leading universities. When they reached marriageable age, they produced the "marriage boom," which boosted all sorts of marriage-related businesses to unprece- dented heights. And between 1971 and 1975 they produced the second baby boom (the first boom started in 1947). Today the women of this generation make up the bulk of the part-time workers who have expanded the population of working women (see Chapters 6 and 7). They were the supporters of Takako Doi, the first woman chief of the leading opposition party, the

Socialist Democratic Party of Japan, and the leaders of citizens' movements for consumerism and environmentalism (see Chapter 9). The majority of people now taking advantage of adult or "lifelong education" courses are from this generation.

The story of Akiko Noda, recounted in Chapter 2, gives us a concrete picture of the first postwar generation. Born in 1948 and a resident of the suburbs of Yokohama, Akiko is typical of the college-educated urban woman of Japan today. Her story vividly reflects the changes in the lives and attitudes of postwar Japanese women. The story of this woman, her mother, and her grandmother provides a typical picture of contemporary Japanese womanhood that applies to millions of other women of their generations, women who are still affected by the traditional demand in Japanese society that women's lives follow patterns considered acceptable for their age. Demeanor, clothing, hairstyles, manners, and even some forms of speech are expected to change appropriately as a woman grows older. When young and unmarried, Japanese women may wear bright-colored clothing, keep their hair long and loose, and be somewhat spontaneous or flamboyant in behavior, but the older they grow the more modest and subdued they must become in behavior, dress, and speech. In a society where community and social pressures are strong, conformity to age-appropriate norms is the safest protection from criticism and eliminates the need to make personal judgments, errors in which can bring quite devastating social consequences (this was especially true in the past).

On the whole, women do observe these age-appropriate lifestyles; there was (and, to a lesser degree, still is) considerable uniformity in behavior according to age. Women who lived as they pleased irrespective of their age were censured or derided with catty remarks like "What a disgrace! She ought to know better, at her age [Ii toshi o shite mittomonai]!" or "She's trying too hard, considering her age [Toshi nanoni gambaru wa ne]." These expressions are typical of those used to discourage behavior that diverged from the norm or fostered individuality; women were (and, for the most part, still are) expected to behave in conformity to the norms and accepted roles of society.

What this kind of conformity means, particularly for a study such as this, is that a discussion of averages, such as average age of marriage, is even more meaningful here than in a society, like that of the United States, where individual differences have received more encouragement. The life course of the vast majority of Japanese women follows more or less the same progression at more or less the same speed.

THE CAUSES OF CHANGE

The revolution that has occurred in women's lives was both facilitated by and the inevitable result of tremendous changes in a number of areas: legal and governmental institutions, biomedical intervention in the life cycle of women, Japan's industrial structure, and the fundamental rules of household economics, to mention the most important.

Legal and governmental institutions

The postwar Constitution clearly stipulates equality of all people, and this has had an immense impact on the first postwar generation brought up and educated under its legal guarantee of equal rights for men and women. The older generation born before 1935 tends to regard the Constitution as imposed by the American Occupation (it is often referred to as the "MacArthur Constitution"), but the postwar generation thinks of it as its own and behaves accordingly. There has, however, never been a full discussion or debate over what equality between the sexes is or how to achieve such a state. Japanese society is not litigious, as is that of the United States, and Japanese tend to look to what is "on the books" mainly as the general framework or moral bulwark upon which they demand certain changes. In Japan rectification of laws and government policies to assure equal opportunity and status for women has generally been initiated by the government itself, rather than in response to direct pressure by women.

A major legal landmark was the shift from the overprotective labor standards law to the Equal Employment Opportunity Law (discussed in detail in Chapter 6). Further progress has been made with the 1991 child care leave law, although its effectiveness has yet to be assessed. The network of public day care and nursery facilities operated by local government authorities (ward, city, or village) under the guidance of the Ministry of Welfare has also expanded significantly, supporting the increased activities of women outside the home.

International influences

The United Nations–sponsored Decade for Women provided an important impetus for the sociopolitical changes concerning women in Japan. In response to the international call to promote the status of women, the prime minister became director of the Fujin Mondai Suishin Honbu (Headquarters for Promotion of Women's Issues) and set in motion a domestic action program aimed at eliminating the inferior status of women in the workplace and in the home.

This official recognition brought women's issues out of the shadows, demonstrating that they were the concern not just of a radical and verbal minority but of mainstream elements in society as well. The Japanese women who attended the Mexico, Copenhagen, and Nairobi world conferences on women (numbering altogether nearly 1,500) organized meetings to report on and discuss what they heard at those conferences, and various groups focusing on women's issues were launched. The assumptions of both men and women were brought into question and discussed, gradually and unobtrusively penetrating the minds of women of all ages, but especially the first postwar generation of women brought up under the new Constitution. Public policies were formulated to promote the visibility of women in the decision-making process and to otherwise keep pace with the UN programs.

Women's issues began to be discussed in the media more than ever before, greatly contributing to the arousal of interest among the general public and the raising of consciousness. The details of the women's liberation movement in the United States—the formation of the National Organization of Women (NOW), the bra burnings, the introduction of women's studies in the universities—were reported on but did not necessarily strike sparks among concerned Japanese women. Far from leaping into action, most Japanese women watched with some apprehension and were somewhat skeptical of the American women's approach: Would the radical steps being taken in the United States really lead to happier lives for women? Would the scrutiny and denial of traditional sex roles bring progress or retrogression?

The life cycle

Perhaps the two most significant changes in the life cycle of Japanese women since the end of World War II are the extension of their average lifespan and the drastic decrease in the average number of children they bear, a result of the widespread practice of birth control and the legality of abortion for economic reasons.[10] In 1935 the average lifespan of Japanese women was 49.6 years; in 1985 it exceeded 80 and has continued to rise to a record 81.9 in 1990 (75.9 for men). The average lifespan of American women was 78.3 (71.3 for men) in 1986. In the early postwar years the average Japanese woman gave birth to an average of four children; in 1991 the number dropped to 1.53. While the previous generation of women often devoted their entire lives to raising children, the last of whom might reach adulthood when the mothers were over 60, many women today are still in their late forties when their youngest child turns 20, giving them a full 30 years of life stretching ahead of them. Clearly, the role of mother is no longer enough to occupy their entire lives.

Not only has the number of uncommitted years in women's lives increased but the number of free hours in their day has also increased. Time- and human energy–saving household appliances and convenience foods and services have taken much of the drudgery out of housework and generated more free time for women, accelerating their search (already stimulated by rising educational standards) for individual fulfillment.

The greatly extended lifespan and the near-zero increase of the birthrate have greatly accelerated Japan's transformation into an "aging society." In other words, women (and, of course, men as well) in their prime today, while they must help take care of their own aging parents, cannot expect to be taken care of by their children. Members of past and present older generations (now in their late seventies and eighties) customarily lived with one of their three or four children. Their savings and old-age pensions were too low to do otherwise. Pensions and preparations for old age have improved, but the smaller number of children cannot adequately care for the growing number of parents who survive to advanced age. This has forced successive generations of elderly Japanese to become more independent of their children.

These realities have greatly stimulated the return of women to the labor force as well as the redefinition of traditional female roles. Increased involvement of women in volunteer activities and citizen's movements, as well as in "lifelong learning" (academic or vocational adult education classes), has broadened their outlook, enhanced their awareness, and provided them with expanded social networks with other women. These contacts help them obtain information needed to plan for extended life as well as to deal with the care of aging parents.

Industry and labor

Another important change that has accelerated the inconspicuous revolution in Japanese women's lives is the transformation of the industrial structure. Japanese industry has shifted into the postindustrial phase with the expansion of the service and information sectors. Although the assembly line and other routine jobs that once absorbed female workers in large numbers now use robots or have been scaled down by computerization, the service industry has created many new jobs that welcome women especially or that do not involve any sex preference.

The low birthrate has changed the composition of the Japanese population, resulting in a growing labor shortage, the acuteness of which is expected to grow more serious as the years go by. Business is clearly counting on women and the elderly to fill the shortage.[12] As long as women are eager to expand their activities outside the home, taking any job they are qualified to perform, there are many jobs to be had. If they seek jobs they truly consider interesting and challenging, however, their desires often go unfulfilled partly because of their own lack of skills and partly because those jobs are amply filled by men. The frustration arising from this situation has led many women to consider their options in terms of trade-offs.

Affluence

With independent incomes of their own, women have gained not only economic autonomy but confidence; they know they can support themselves and perform useful work outside the home. They do not have to marry to obtain a comfortable life economically or sacrifice their own desires or goals for the sake of a family; they can remain single and enjoy its freedoms if they so wish. Money has allowed them to pursue goals of their own choosing—everything from a doctoral degree to a carefree sex life. The expansion of the Japanese economy has provided women with greater job opportunities as well as conveniences that shorten housework. The worship of consumption (the pendulum having swung to the opposite extreme following the still-remembered hardships of the wartime and early postwar periods) has motivated many women to obtain an income of their own. This increased affluence has given other women the leeway and free time to think about and reflect on their purpose and goals in life.

Women born between 1946 and 1955 are in the vanguard of these changes. Their experiences have been molded not by the old framework of obedience, self-sacrifice, passivity, and resignation but by the framework of the postwar period, which stresses equality, freedom, self-fulfillment, and optimism. They are well educated and socially aware, the pivotal members of the consumer and environmental movements.

In order either to evaluate the results of Japan's postwar democratization or to forecast the future of women in Japanese society, it is especially important to examine the lives of the first postwar generation of women, who are the socialization agents of young people today. This generation is typified by Noda Akiko, a well-educated urban housewife married to a salaried company employee and described in Chapter 2. While their husbands propel and navigate the Japanese economy, these women have obtained freedom and diversified options far greater than those available to men. The following chapters will try to show that they are examining the meaning of their lives, setting their life's course, scrutinizing society's institutions, and studying the way they will spend their old age with admirable earnestness.

Chapters 3, 4, and 5 examine these women in the family: their view of marriage, their relationships with their children, and the new household roles they perform as a result of the aforementioned changes. In an age when female longevity has extended to over 80 years, Japanese women are faced with the need to reconsider the patterns of conjugal relations, to work out acceptable sharing when both husband and wife are pursuing careers outside the home, and to achieve well-balanced lives for themselves and their husbands, permitting the fulfillment offered by family, work, and leisure activities. Perhaps the thinking and choice of options Japanese women display can offer food for thought for women in other cultures.

The discussion in Chapters 6 through 9 of women outside the home, at work, in politics, and in the community shows the way Japanese corporations have responded to the greatly diversified needs and work patterns of today's women and the extremely realistic, pragmatic attitudes and strategies women display toward those aspects of society that are slow to change (like the male-dominated corporate and political structure and the nonparticipatory stance of men in family life). We can also see the disparity that is growing within the ranks of women.

The story of former Socialist Party chairperson Doi Takako (see Chapter 8) recounts both what she contributed and how her contribution was constrained, throwing into sharp relief that most complex and also most tradition-bound realm of contemporary Japanese society: national politics. Doi's brief and frustrating term in the limelight demonstrates the tremendous obstacles that lie in the path of women's advance into national politics. At the same time, the fact that women, who constitute the majority of Japanese voters, did visibly redirect the course of politics, through the 1989 House of Councilors elections, suggests that the same sort of thing could easily happen again. Perhaps an even more fundamental dimension of the quiet revolution, however, is the achievements of the first postwar generation of women in initiating grass-roots political and civic endeavors by cultivating horizontal networks. The deepened awareness and know-how that these experiences are providing women are bound to have profound repercussions on the development of Japanese society in the future.

Not surprisingly, the changing roles of women are having an epochal effect on the qualities considered feminine and on the images of womanhood. What is happening as women pursue new identities? The reaction of men to the changes in women is also complex.

In attempting to present an objective view of the lives and behavior of contemporary women from a variety of angles, this book inevitably goes beyond the subject of women. At a time when much about Japan remains a perplexing and uncharted jungle as far as the outside observer is concerned, it is my hope that this book may light the path toward a better understanding of the thinking and values of Japanese as a whole, their strengths and weaknesses, original insights and fundamental flaws, as well as of the conditions and future of Japan's society, economy, and politics.

2

THE STORY OF AKIKO

Akiko was born in 1948, a member of the first baby boom generation. She lives with her husband, who works for a trading firm, and their two children in an apartment they own in a suburb of Yokohama. In contrast to the prewar household, which included three generations, theirs includes only the nuclear family and is typical of the majority of Japanese households today (the average size of a family has decreased to 2.95 persons as of 1991). Akiko, like some 90 percent of Japanese, thinks of herself as a member of the middle class, living a life "as contented as any one else's [*hodohodo ni shiawase*]." Being like most other people gives the conformist-minded Japanese a sense of comfort and security.

PARENTS AND CHILDHOOD

Both of Akiko's parents were born and reared in communities far from the urban centers of the country. When World War II ended, her father was 24; at 25 he wed Asako, Akiko's mother, then 22 and a high school (*jogakko*) graduate. The marriage was arranged by a go-between who happened to know both sets of parents and was decided on after only one meeting. Dating and romance did not generally precede marriage at the time, and this procedure was common. The term *miai* (arranged meeting of a potential couple) is still used, but by the time Akiko's generation reached the prime age for marriage, it represented a very different

31

process. The majority of marriages today, as in the case of Akiko herself, are love marriages. *Miai* continue in common practice, but the "arrangement" is generally limited to the first introduction only (in contrast to earlier days, when it referred to the entire process of matrimonial decision making). In the contemporary *miai*, an initial meeting between two candidates for marriage is arranged through a third party, either a relative or a friend. If both sides are favorably impressed, they can continue to date and form a deeper understanding and attachment.

Akiko's parents are a relatively harmonious couple; they depend upon each other and made a warm household for Akiko to grow up in, but they have never expressed overt affection for each other. Akiko's mother sometimes protests in front of her children, "If I had known your father was like that, I'd never have married him." To this her father retorts, "Same goes for me. You're just lucky I was good enough to accept you!" They grumble about each other in this fashion, but Akiko knows that a close bond has grown between them over the years, whether or not it can be called love. Expressions of affection between husband and wife are rarely seen in Japan, even by their children (as discussed in Chapter 3), since married people find it embarrassing for their mutual feelings to be openly revealed.

Akiko's mother lost her first child, a son, soon after birth; after Akiko was born, her mother gave birth to another son. Akiko's mother never worked outside the home. When the children were small, she took in sewing for the neighbors and later began to teach *kitsuke* (dressing in kimono, now taught formally because many Japanese women no longer know the intricacies or proper way of choosing, putting on, and wearing kimono), which brings her a small income for discretionary purposes. She is skillful with her hands, taking pride in her ability to do fine, detailed handiwork and speaking always of how she loved to please and be of help to her neighbors. (The fulfillment found in being of help to others is what Japanese women traditionally lived for; it was the only medium through which they could find identity and meaning in their lives.) The money, too, was obviously a valuable addition to the family budget, for which she held sole responsibility, as in most Japanese salaried-worker families. Yet she was always careful to charge her neighbors less than the going price for sewing. She was thrifty and careful with money, but always told her children that *"kane wa tenka no mawari mono* [money is for circulation]," the implication being that money may flow out of your purse but because it will flow back to you when you need it desperately, you should not cling to it.

Akiko recalls of her childhood that her mother was always busy, mostly with household chores, from early morning until late at night. Her mother would be up by six, before anyone else in the family, and it was to the sound of vegetables being chopped on the cutting board that the children awoke each morning. No matter how Akiko's mother felt, she woke early to prepare a hot breakfast of fragrant miso soup and steamed rice for the family and clearly took this to be an important responsibility. Her father never fixed his own breakfast, and Akiko cannot imagine him doing so.

Akiko, like many other women her age, often does not get up until after her husband, who sometimes fixes his own breakfast, leaves for work, which is quite early (6:30 or 7:00). The difference between Akiko and her mother is that the latter would not feel comfortable sleeping late, even if her husband was willing to fix his own breakfast, and, in fact, could not sleep late. Akiko, however, can sleep soundly without feeling the least bit guilty. She does, of course, get up to wake and fix breakfast for her children.

The average time Japanese women spend daily on housework has shrunk considerably. In 1959 food shopping, meal preparation, and dish washing took an average of 191 minutes, care of clothing 127 minutes, cleaning 87 minutes; and other housework 37 minutes, adding up to 7 hours and 22 minutes daily. Twenty years later, the daily average had decreased to 6 hours and 14 minutes and in 1989 stood at 5 hours and 55 minutes.[1]

Japanese eating habits also underwent a revolution during these years. In place of the unvaried diet of rice-centered, traditional-style meals, Japanese began to eat more bread and meat prepared by Western-style recipes, thus lessening the time women spend cooking. By the time Akiko was in high school, her normal breakfast had changed to toast, eggs, salad, and tea.

Akiko's father, as far as she can remember, never worked in the kitchen. He might be the one to determine the flavoring of the sukiyaki bubbling in a pot on the dining table with soy sauce, sake, and sugar, but only with condiments brought from the kitchen by her mother. There were some jobs requiring physical strength in the home that men were not embarrassed to undertake, such as moving furniture or doing house repairs. In 1976 the average time married men spent on housework on weekdays was 8 minutes per day; in 1986 it had risen to 11 minutes. Akiko now wonders why her mother had to plead with her father to do a household chore when it seemed obvious that he shared household responsibilities as a member of the family. She herself need only mention to her husband that something has to be done; she certainly does not have to beg. Still, he does not voluntarily involve himself with household chores; he simply complies with requests as they are given.

Akiko's mother used to sew all of her children's clothing as well as her own everyday clothing. Women either made their own clothes or paid seamstresses working in their own homes to do it for them. It was not so long ago that women's magazines regularly featured sewing pages and gave detailed instructions for making various kinds of apparel. Today they tend to feature ready-made apparel, which can be ordered by telephone or mail and paid for by bank or postal transfer. In 1965 women spent an average of 50 minutes a day sewing or shopping for clothing, but once ready-made clothing began to become widely available in the '70s, this figure fell to only 10 per day in 1989.

Akiko's mother devoted her life to the care of her children and husband. If it started to rain after Akiko had left for school in the morning, her mother would bring her galoshes and umbrella to the school by the time classes let out. Such attentions were a sort of symbol of the devoted mother and of close ties between mother and child. Today mothers are busier and less self-sacrificing, and they tend to expect their children to look out for themselves more (by keeping an extra umbrella at school, for example). Many mothers of Akiko's own generation work; some attend adult education or hobbies classes while their children are at school, so they have less time to look out for sudden showers or forgotten pencil boxes.

Like many households of the time, that in which Akiko grew up included three generations. After the death of Akiko's paternal grandfather, her grandmother came to Tokyo to live with the family. (As the eldest son, Akiko's father was responsible for caring for elderly parents, a tradition that was encouraged in the absence of an adequate social security system. This situation has recently improved.) Akiko's upbringing, therefore, was affected both by her grandmother, whose thinking reflected prewar values, and her mother, who was somewhat more liberal and modern. Her grandmother's chidings were usually framed by the custom of "shaming" (as discussed by Ruth Benedict[2] and others); thus, she would say, "Act like a respectable girl [*Onna no ko desho*]!" or "A good girl wouldn't do a thing like that [*Onna-rashiku nai*]!" Discipline was aimed less at discriminating between right and wrong than at showing what expected behavior was to be. Grandmother was most concerned that Akiko and other members of the family not act in such a way as to incite ridicule or censure, a concern that was crucial for survival in the village-centered society of prewar times.

Akiko's mother deliberately distanced herself from interactions between Grandmother and Akiko in order to avoid trouble with her mother-in-law, feeling that the gap in values was often impossible to bridge. For Grandmother, a young woman's goal in life was to get married and anything that might endanger her prospects was "lamentable." Akiko's mother, however, did not press her daughter to behave according to the traditional female norms and manners (partly, we may surmise, as a serene way of countering the influence of her mother-in-law). Instead, she would say, "A woman should get a good education and acquire some skills of her own," not forgetting to add, "Of course, a woman should get married. If you stay single, you might be regarded as not quite normal."

Although Akiko's mother did not encourage her in so many words, it seemed to Akiko that she wanted her to acquire the capacity for independence, perhaps reflecting her awareness of the experience of widowed women who had no social security at all if they lost their husband.[3] If such widows had formal training in a genteel or acceptable profession such as teaching the tea ceremony or flower arranging, they could support themselves and their children in a respectable fashion. Of those who did not, many had to submit to an unpleasant or forced remarriage in order to survive. In that sense, much of the training (*hanayome shugyo*) prospective brides received, such as in the tea ceremony or calligraphy, served as a form of economic protection at a time when no government social security was available to them. These forms of premarital training flourished because they suited both the practical mentality of Japanese and their love of beauty and aesthetic refinement.

Indeed, the position of a woman of Akiko's mother's generation vis-à-vis her husband was very weak, since she lacked any substantial economic power. The husband was unquestionably the head of the family. He was served an extra dish at dinnertime and was held in somewhat fearful respect. His moods affected the entire family. If Akiko's father had a hard day at work, he might be grumpy and temperamental; everyone would treat him with kid gloves so as not to irritate him unnecessarily. When cornered, his habitual retaliatory retort was, "Who do you think is earning the money in this household?"

No matter how unreasonable a father's demands or remarks, children were not to talk back. Akiko never questioned her father face-to-face, and when her brother once dared to, he received a very memorable corporal reprimand. Nevertheless, when in good humor, their father was kind and tolerant with the children, bringing them presents when returning from business trips and treating the whole family to shopping sprees when he received his twice-annual bonuses. He never struck Akiko, and though he quarreled with their mother, he never showed strong emotions in the children's presence. The incidence of conjugal violence is lower in Japan than in the United States, perhaps because there is often a third adult present or in close proximity (in-laws or neighbors), which tends to inhibit extreme acts.

In 1957 three revolutionary appliances—the television, the washing machine, and the refrigerator—made their debut, quickly establishing themselves as the "three sacred treasures" (sanshu no jingi, which refers to the three sacred regalia of imperial rule—mirror, jewels, and sword—handed down by the emperors of ancient times as symbols of hereditary power) of the household. These modern conveniences spread rapidly into Japanese homes, as they did in Europe and the United States, rescuing women from a great deal of household drudgery and providing entertainment.

Until 1959 one of the most exciting days of the week for Akiko was the day she and her brother went to their next-door neighbor's house to watch "Lassie." After her family purchased its own television, she was able to watch many more programs, many of them American (such as "Father Knows Best"), which left long-lasting impressions of the United States on her and her brother. Akiko was enchanted by scenes of the children's rooms, with their double-decker beds, and of outings in the family car, as well as by the democratic atmosphere that seemed to infuse the American family.

EDUCATION

Akiko went to kindergarten at age 4, entered a local primary school at 6, moved on to junior high school at 12, and completed compulsory education at 15. She then entered senior high school at 15 and went on to the university at 18, graduating at 22. The schools she attended were all coeducational and, except for the university, public and close to her family's home in suburban Tokyo. At the time Akiko entered senior high school, there were still more boys going on to secondary school than girls, but both figures stood at around 70 percent (the figures have reached 95 percent for girls and 93 percent for boys in 1990). In elementary and junior high school, girls and boys were treated on much the same footing (except that in some schools boys' names were called before girls' during roll call), with one each always elected as class representative, although the boy was always the leader and the girl the deputy or vice-leader. At the time, Akiko did not question the inconsistency with which the noble phrases "equality of the sexes [danjo byōdo]" and "equal rights [danjo dōken]" were applied; nobody else seemed to object, and no girls ran in the elections for class president.

In the senior high school Akiko attended the situation was rather different. The school had been a girls' school until the end of the war and was made coeducational during the period of postwar educational reforms, but there were still more girl than boy students. The girls therefore tended to be the center of many activities, a situation quite new to Akiko. Nevertheless, the required vocational subjects were home economics for girls and industrial arts for boys. Later, this discrepancy became a political issue raised by feminists (starting 1993 boys and girls have to take both subjects), but when Akiko was in high school, no one seemed to question the clear distinction.

Akiko attended a coeducational university, where, again, women "naturally" fell into supportive positions behind men in college politics, sports, and other activities. Although she had heard the phrase "equality of the sexes" often in primary and secondary school, she realizes that she never did hear any of her teachers or any other adult explain why such equality was necessary or important or what it actually meant. It was essentially the sharing of the same pie by a boy and a girl, but cut into two different-sized pieces.

In 1955 the proportion of women who went on for higher education was 2.6 percent for those entering junior colleges and 2.4 percent for those matriculating at four-year universities; these percentages have increased steadily. By the time Akiko entered the university, the figures (for 1965) had risen to 22.4 and 11.3 percent, respectively. Akiko's father reflected the typical double standard of the time in his objection to having her go to a four-year university: "A woman who is too smart can't find a husband [Atama dekkachi na onna wa yome ni moraite ga nai]." However, he insisted that her younger brother go on to a four-year university even though his grades were not as good as Akiko's, declaring that "a man without a university degree is worth nothing."

The results of a survey conducted by the Prime Minister's Office in 1976 depicts the kind of education parents wanted for their sons and daughters at the time: 41 percent wanted their daughters to attend high school and junior college, but only 25 percent supported the idea of giving them a four-year college education. However, 57 percent of parents wanted to send their sons to four-year universities. Clearly, advanced education was considered much less important for daughters than for sons, and the same attitude continues today, although the percentage of people who put their sons' education before that of their daughters has grown smaller. The reasoning is a pragmatic acceptance of norms: Men have to support the family, and the education they receive makes a big difference in the kind of job they can find and the caliber of life they can achieve. For women, it is more practical to find a promising husband who can guarantee her a comfortable situation than to invest inordinately in her own education.

Although Akiko's father objected to her going to the university, her mother stood firmly behind her. It was one of the rare occasions on which her mother took a definite stand and showed no signs of giving in to her usually domineering husband. Still, rather than confronting her husband (which would unpleasantly disrupt family harmony), she adopted the common tactic of undermining his opposition by indirect means, such as by openly encouraging Akiko and telling her, "If you want to study, you should go on to university. If necessary, I can pay your tuition with my own earnings" (from her piecework sewing). Akiko went ahead and did as she wanted, and eventually her father's strong objections evaporated.

The trend for a much larger proportion of girls to major in the humanities or in education than in the sciences continues today, but the bias was even greater in the 1960s. In 1967, when Akiko began her freshman year, 47 percent of the female students in four-year universities majored in the humanities while only 6 percent majored in the social sciences, such as economics, political science, or sociology.

Akiko, like her female classmates, thought that her grades were at least as good, if not better, than those of her male classmates. There seemed to be a shared understanding among girls that boys were equipped with greater potential and that if they studied seriously, they could easily surpass women. Generally speaking, however, the women tended to be more serious in their studies and attended lectures more regularly than men, and their grades tended to be better. Male students often asked women, including Akiko, to lend them their notes on the lectures, but the reverse was rarely true.

Akiko's college days coincided with the student movement. Helmeted students demonstrating against the Vietnam War or against rising tuition fees were a common sight on her campus. Akiko herself was against the Vietnam War but could not go along with the movement's violent tactics or the way activists tried to take over the podium in lecture classes every day. But even among the progressive students, clear-cut sex roles prevailed. The women students prepared meals for their male comrades at the barricades. Akiko and most of her friends wanted normal college life restored and became less and less sympathetic toward the activists. Her parents encouraged this sentiment, telling her repeatedly how nobody would treat her seriously if she became involved in the movement. The aversion she developed toward political activism on campus at that time may have contributed to her general political apathy, a trait typical of many of her generation, although the student movement produced some of the country's most committed feminists and women activists of today, such as those involved in grass-roots politics (as discussed in Chapter 9).

JOB HUNTING AND EMPLOYMENT

Akiko graduated in 1970, but there were not many job openings for female graduates of four-year universities at that time. Graduates of two-year colleges were said to have better chances of getting jobs, partly because they were younger and partly because they were thought to be more malleable. Except for women pursuing professional careers in teaching or civil service, higher education appeared to be more of a hindrance than an advantage for women looking for jobs.

Some of Akiko's more able and highly motivated friends were trying for jobs at the few corporations—airline companies, the mass media, and foreign companies with offices in Tokyo—that actively sought out female university graduates. The examinations for employment in these companies were extremely difficult, but if the girls were not successful, they hoped to use personal connections to at least find jobs as assistants to professors or as secretaries in some kind of office. Jobs such as these were considered perfectly acceptable as ways for women to learn about the world *(shakai benkyō)* before marriage.

When asked what kind of job she wanted, Akiko gave the answer most other women students gave: a job in which she could use her abilities *(nōryoku o ikaseru shigoto)*. Actually, what Akiko and her peers were thinking about was probably less actual ability than potential ability or aptitude, for they did not possess any specific skills or know-how. Their male peers entering the work force, meanwhile, were looking for jobs in which they could *develop* their abilities, not just put to use abilities already acquired. That difference in orientation may have a lot to do with the gap in advancement between working men and women after five years or so on the job.

Akiko herself looked for a job in publishing or among the newspaper companies, thinking (naively) that women would be treated more equally with men by such employers. She found the competition very keen, however, and was not successful. Then, through a connection provided by an uncle, she was hired to work in the public relations division of a large textile manufacturer as an editor for their promotional magazine. At her job interview, when asked how many years she intended to work she answered, "Three." She had no particular reason for giving such an answer but thought it would be unfair to the employer to think of quitting before that. Nor did she think they expected her to work longer than that. Her job hours turned out to be irregular, demanding that she work until 10 P.M. several nights in a row just before the deadline for each issue of the magazine. Her male colleagues, nevertheless, often stayed even later. She found the work taxing but thought it suited her temperament well and soon found herself wanting to continue working as long as she could.

Akiko was free from all housework save for cleaning her own room, as her mother, like most Japanese mothers of young, unmarried working women, prepared all her meals for her and did her laundry. Akiko's mother was content to keep Akiko dependent on her; by so doing she felt needed, and it also bolstered her identity as a "wise mother." She had begun to take *kitsuke* classes toward obtaining a license to teach, but this was only a small accompaniment to her main source of joy and purpose in life: caring for her children (grown-up though they might be) and her husband. She would say that her responsibility as a mother would not be over until both children married. Akiko handed over one sixth of her salary to her mother, who deposited it in the bank as savings for her wedding. Other than bringing home occasional gifts for the family, Akiko was free to use her salary as she pleased, for example, for clothes or ski trips with her friends and colleagues. And Akiko dated, something her mother approved of and seemed to take pleasure in, having been deprived of the experience herself.

ENGAGEMENT AND MARRIAGE

Akiko met Kazuo, three years older than she, at the university. They had dated for some time and reached the understanding, but without any specific discussion of the subject, that they would eventually marry. Whatever the private conversations of the couple were like, their references to marriage are certain to have been indirect, as is typical of Japanese-style conversation. They knew without saying so that they were in love and would eventually get married, so they quite naturally fell into discussions of what they would do "when we get married" or "after we are married." They were content with that.

At first, Akiko felt that she and Kazuo were totally equal. They discussed things easily and shared ideas. Kazuo was the eldest son of an old family living in the vicinity of Kyoto in the western part of Japan. Since graduating from the university, he had been working for a large trading company in Tokyo. Sometimes Kazuo would inform Akiko of messages from his mother that clearly showed that she expected Akiko to submit to Kazuo's judgment on everything. This caught Akiko by surprise, but she would not say anything to them in protest as she was determined to play the role of good bride and avoid the certain discomfort resulting from confrontation, therefore minimizing her interaction with them as much as possible.

After the engagement meeting, Akiko and Kazuo went to a jewelry store to exchange gifts as a token of their engagement. This became common practice after World War II and replaces the former custom of exchanging cash. Kazuo bought Akiko a diamond ring for which he spent three to four times his monthly salary (the average amount spent at the time), and Akiko bought him a pearl tie tack costing about one fourth what he paid for the ring.

As soon as Akiko began to wear her engagement ring to her office, she realized how much it changed things. The other young women in the office were full of envy that she had received a diamond ring. Her boss had always been ready with patronizing remarks like, "A girl should marry by 25, or she'll go to seed" (i.e., her beauty will fade) or "So-and-so is a bit hysterical these days because she's still single" (implying that she is sexually frustrated and unfulfilled) or, using the familiar and diminutive *chan*, "Akiko-chan, you'd better get married before you get to be an old maid." When he finally recognized that she was wearing an engagement ring, his first response was to congratulate her and his second was to ask her when she planned to quit work, as if he had absolutely no doubt that she would resign. Caught off guard by the second question, all Akiko could do was murmur an acknowledgment of his good wishes.

Kazuo's family lived in a part of Japan where it was customary to hold large wedding receptions, especially for the first son. Having lived away from home for several years and being somewhat liberated, Kazuo was insistent that their wedding not be turned into the old-fashioned "marriage of two families," that it be kept their own wedding. His idea was to hold a party at the university reception hall and to ask for a donation from each guest in place of the usual wedding gift. His parents were firmly against this, however, declaring that they would be laughed at by the whole clan if they agreed to such a plan. Akiko thought Kazuo's idea had been a good one, but when she saw how adamant his parents were in opposing it, she, for the sake of good relations with her future in-laws, convinced him to concede. Ultimately, their wedding ceremony was held at a shrine in Kyoto, and a dinner and reception were given for 80 guests at a nearby hotel. The two families divided the bill; it was very costly, but both sides were satisfied that they had been able to give their children an "average (hitonami no)" wedding.

Akiko had asked Kazuo whether he would mind if she continued working after marriage, and he had answered, "No, I don't mind. Do as you wish. You don't seem like the type to be satisfied with just staying at home." He recognized that a woman with a college education was different from one without and indicated that he was also different from the ordinary company employee in understanding her desire to work. None of the other women in Akiko's office stayed on the job after marriage, and when others, especially the men in the office, found out that she would stay on, they were incredulous, asking her repeatedly if her husband really did not mind her working. The single women would make insinuating and envious remarks like, "Are you sure your husband won't mind?" or "Aren't you lucky to have an understanding husband." (I, too, have been treated to such comments countless times. We never hear people praise a wo-man for being understanding of the demands of her husband's job; it is taken for granted.) Akiko's case was obviously consid-ered an exception in her office, and most of the men probably wanted to keep it an exception, as we shall see in Chapter 6.

Akiko's company did not have a formal rule that women had to resign upon marriage, but Akiko was the first married woman to continue working there. Some who had been unable to find a marriage partner by the time they turned 28 or so, ended up leaving the company anyway, as they were made to feel un-comfortable among the other, much younger, women in the office.

Akiko and Kazuo found a two-room apartment not far from Akiko's place of employment. When Kazuo's parents learned that Akiko was not going to quit her job, they were apparently displeased and concerned as to whether Akiko could take proper care of their son, especially since his mother regarded Akiko more as her son's housekeeper than as his life companion. She and her husband did not express their feelings directly to Akiko, but her parents were put in a vulnerable position and felt apologetic to Kazuo and even more to Kazuo's parents for the behavior of their daughter. Akiko did not think it was any of either of their parents' business, and as long as Kazuo did not mind, she intended to keep on working. She felt lucky and grateful that Kazuo's parents did not live in either Tokyo or Yokohama.

Feeling responsible for Akiko's decision, her mother tried to help mend the situation by bringing cooked or ready-to-cook dishes to the couple's apartment from time to time. She thought Akiko was not being quite as devoted a wife as she ought to be. Akiko felt her mother was being rather old-fashioned but appreciated her concern and help.

Akiko did not tell either of their parents that Kazuo had promised to share the housework as much as possible. It would have irritated his parents especially, since they already thought he was not standing firm enough and appeared to spoil his wife too much. Akiko's mother and father, on the other hand, were more concerned about whether the couple was happy than whether or not Kazuo was properly controlling Akiko.

In reality, Akiko soon learned, Kazuo's good intentions regarding the housework would not be carried out. The demands of his job kept him at the company long past the workday's formal end at 5:00, and he arrived home after midnight almost every day. Akiko's job finished at 5:00, and, like the other women, she left immediately and arrived home by 6:00. This allowed her time to prepare a normal meal by a relatively normal dinner hour, though she soon found that her husband would rarely be there. Akiko did all the housework herself. She purchased a large refrigerator and spent Sundays shopping and preparing meals for the following week while Kazuo slept most of the day to make up for the sleep he missed during the week. They did not have much opportunity to talk or enjoy their lives

together. It was not what she had expected, but Akiko gradually
became accustomed to the stable but rather distant relationship.

Work and contacts with her many women friends kept Akiko
busy enough that she did not have time to complain. She made
and cultivated many friends and enjoyed herself. She was happy
enough to use the time in the evenings while waiting for Kazuo
to come home for reading or watching television. They lived on
Kazuo's income alone, putting most of hers into savings in her
name and using some for special expenses, such as occasional
trips. In fact, Akiko believed from the beginning that the household had to be run on Kazuo's income alone. She knew that she
could not possibly expect Kazuo to help with child care once a
baby arrived and that she would have to quit her job then; she
wanted at least to prepare for the time when she would have no
income. Kazuo seemed to share her ideas on running the
household finances and never raised the issue of putting both
their incomes together. Since husbands still do not demand that
their wives share the financial burden of supporting the household, the economic freedom Japanese women enjoy is remarkable.

Akiko married at 25 and became pregnant when she was 26,
more or less the average age for Japanese women to have their
first child. When she gave birth to a son and two years later to a
daughter in the mid-1970s, it was common to give birth in a
hospital. In her mother's time, it was usual for a woman to return
to her parental home for childbirth and to be assisted by a
midwife. The rates of infant mortality and mortality of the
mother during pregnancy were much higher then; in 1947 they
stood at 76.7 per 1,000 and 16.8 per 1,000, respectively. Both
rates have steadily decreased, reaching 10.0 and 2.9 per 1,000,
respectively, in 1975. Akiko was careful to make sure she did not
become pregnant by mistake and has been spared the experience
of abortion so far. Many of her friends, including some unmarried ones, have undergone abortions, some as many as three or
four times. Akiko thinks that if she gets pregnant by mistake, she
would be willing to bear a third child but that a fourth pregnancy
would have to be aborted because education costs are high and
she does not want to be tied to home indefinitely by the care of
small children. She feels the decision is hers, not her husband's.
She is familiar with the feminist claim that women should control

their own bodies but thinks an argument is hardly needed. After all, it is the woman who carries a child, and, reflecting the independence and autonomy of Japanese women, she thinks she has the right to make the decision.

The most widely used means of contraception in Japan (about 70 percent) is the condom. Birth control pills were not sold over the counter in drugstores for a long time owing to the Japanese government's claim that it had too many potentially bad effects. Abortion for economic reasons has been legal in Japan for a long time, its acceptance stemming from a history during which infanticide was forced on people by the demands of survival; the practice of *mabiki* (literally, "spacing" children) was the people's way of limiting the number of mouths families had to feed before contraceptive methods were known. In prewar days, especially among poor farmers with many children born in close succession, infanticide was often facilitated by midwives, who would put their hand over the newborn's mouth upon birth "by mistake." According to traditional folk belief, the soul of a child thus denied life would depart from the flesh but remain within the village to be born again as a baby of another family. *Mabiki* was thus not considered in the same category as *kogoroshi* (child killing), and infants subjected to *mabiki* were known as "returned children *(kaeshikko)*." The souls of these returned children were enshrined in statues of Jizō, the bodhisattva protector of children, which are found in every community in Japan, even in the big cities today.

This history may have made Japanese women more accepting of abortion when modern medical methods were introduced. It is still within recent memory that women bore children one after another, often as many as 10 or 12 within their then relatively short lifetimes of less than 50 years (49.6 in 1935). Sometimes several in one family would die naturally, in infancy or later, and surviving children were considered treasures and received all their parent's devotion. But if disease or hunger took away small children, women simply bore more, as long as their health and economic situation enabled them to do so. Since a fetus is not considered distinctly human until it reaches three months, it arouses no strong sense of guilt, and miscarriage and abortion in general was, and is today, viewed in very practical terms. In the pragmatic Japanese tradition, priority has been attached to the health of the mother. Although many women know full well the trauma, both physical and psychological, that abortion brings, they often do not take sufficient contraceptive precautions. A survey conducted in 1982 by the Kyodo News Service reported that 60 percent of the college graduate women with husbands in managerial posts in this sample had undergone abortions.[4] The ratio was as high as 75 percent for older women in their fifties and lower for younger women who take advantage of contraceptive methods.

THE HOME AND MOTHERHOOD

Akiko was of the firm conviction that a mother should devote full time to raising her children. The widely held theory or, rather, myth in Japan is that the close physical contact and interaction between mother and child—usually called "skinship" in Japan —between birth and the age of three has special and long-lasting significance. This theory formed the basis of Akiko's approach to her childrearing responsibilities. She left her job when she was seven months pregnant. One of her senior female colleagues remarked on her leaving with genuine regret because Akiko had accumulated valuable experience during the five years she had worked. But Akiko, believing that no work could possibly be as important as rearing a child, resigned happily without giving it a second thought and with great expectations for the child to be born. At the time, she had no thoughts of the more distant future. It never occurred to her that someday she might regret having left such an interesting, not easily found job with its pleasant work environment; the notion that she might want to work again once her children were in school never entered her mind.

Since Akiko no longer had to commute, the couple moved to a larger apartment in the outskirts of Yokohama, and the following year they bought an apartment in a newly built complex in the neighborhood. It was Akiko who took the initiative whenever they decided on a change of residence. She would collect as much information as she could on possible choices, work out the details of loans and other business, and take Kazuo to look at the sample apartment. Kazuo's role was perfunctory. He would listen to the reports of her findings and survey the possibilities she presented, but mostly he left everything to her to decide. Akiko had the freedom to choose a residence to suit her own tastes; Kazuo would indicate his approval briefly, but he seemed satisfied to leave affairs of home and family to Akiko, as his work preoccupied most of his waking hours. Virtually all aspects of management of the home were under Akiko's control. There were times when Kazuo felt having to move was too much bother, but Akiko always seemed to have a good reason for the move and her judgment was generally sound. Thanks to her foresight and good judgment, they now live in an apartment with 90 square meters of space, spacious by Japanese standards, and now extremely valuable owing to the recent skyrocketing price of real estate.

Today Akiko's children are 16 and 14. When they were small, their father was among the middle-echelon managers of his company and was often absent on business trips abroad. At one point, when his son was three and his daughter an infant, he spent 18 months in the United States. Today we might call their marriage at that stage a "commuting marriage" (see Chapter 4). It was a rule of Kazuo's company that if an employee was stationed overseas for a year or less, he did not take his family along. Kazuo's original assignment had been for a year, but it had been extended; during the 18 months he had been able to come home only once for two weeks.

As a mother, Akiko's life was not much different whether Kazuo was abroad or in Japan. She trained and lavished affection on her children according to her own childrearing policy, with little participation or intervention from her husband. Her son and daughter doted on her and rebelled against her authority in the same way that children do in any other country. When they were very small, she indulged the majority of their whims while firmly guiding them in the direction of expected norms.

The older they grew, the more strictly the children had to toe the line, as society expected of them. Akiko's daughter became helpful around the house at an early stage, quickly absorbing the model of caretaking behaviors exhibited by her mother and other females surrounding her. Mother and daughter have a close rapport, appreciating the same pleasures and enjoying each other. Akiko's daughter is instinctively neat and aware of her surroundings. Her son was never expected to perform any chores voluntarily, but beginning when he was 10, Akiko made a deal with him to clean and fill the bathtub every day and put out the trash in the morning in exchange for his weekly allowance. Akiko lavished physical affection on her son in his preschool years, but by age 7 or 8 he had become more distant and there were frequent battles of wills. Akiko has difficulty in understanding his needs and in getting him to cooperate with family activities or to attend to personal hygiene, like brushing his teeth and taking a bath. They often clash over routine matters, like unfinished homework, a messy desk, and the way he treats his sister. By the time he entered junior high school, he had become somewhat more responsible about his own activities, but Akiko is worried that she has not made her son help more with household chores and that he depends on her too much for his daily needs. She knows that males of his generation are growing up with females who expect men to be more involved in domestic matters and feels that he ought to learn to cook and take care of his own personal needs. Kazuo has very little involvement with the daily lives of his children, although he helps Akiko make important decisions involving their schooling. When the children were small, he was a very indulgent and doting father, often behaving more like a big brother or playmate with them than a father. The older they grew, the more stern he tended to become. Now he is concerned mainly with whether they are studying properly and in good health.

Akiko at times feels like a single parent. Unlike her stoic mother, she sometimes complains openly both to Kazuo and her own parents of the difficulties of never being free of responsibility for the children. Save for an occasional Sunday, the family rarely eats a meal at the same table. From time to time Akiko cannot help asking Kazuo which is more important to him, his family or his company. Kazuo's reply is always the same: "Of course, it's my family. I am doing my best at the company for the sake of my family, even doing things I don't enjoy." Akiko realizes that Kazuo's situation is not easy; he cannot enjoy his family as much as he would like, and he puts up with a great deal of stress. She wonders whether Japanese women are not better off than men, since they not only hold the purse strings but have time to use as they please and can spend a great deal of time with their children. She does not often say this to Kazuo because he alone cannot change the system, but she seriously doubts whether all the time he puts in at the company is really worth the sacrifice.

When the children get sick, Akiko's anxiety is very great. She is generally alone with the toil, the worry, and the responsibility, and then she grows angry with Kazuo's company and thinks it inhumane to run an enterprise in a way that takes fathers away from their families for virtually all their waking hours. Her mother is always willing to help out, but Akiko tries not to impose on her, feeling that her mother has sacrificed enough of her life for her family and should be allowed to enjoy herself.

Caring for an infant was a wholly new experience for Akiko. She and her brother were born only two years apart, so she had never had the experience of helping to raise a sibling. Although anxious about whether she could take proper care of her baby, she felt that her children's well-being was mostly her responsibility. She depended on various child care books, the primary one being the Japanese translation of Dr. Spock's *Baby and Child Care*, which most of her friends were using. She read these books over and over before her first baby was born, until she had practically memorized them. As is practically established custom, her mother came to stay with them for about a month to help care for the baby and Akiko.

With an infant in her care, Akiko became concerned with the additives in prepared foods and the insecticides or chemical fertilizers used in growing vegetables, things that she had hardly paid any attention to at all before giving birth. She stopped using chemical detergents and switched to old-fashioned powdered soap, and she cut down on instant or commercially prepared foods as much as she could (this has become an important trend among young mothers, as we shall see in Chapter 9). There is a growing amount of information on the deleterious effects of food additives, and Akiko's determination to protect her children as much as possible has helped heighten her awareness of environmental issues as a whole.

Akiko joined a cooperative consumer group that ordered fresh food for members from farms that raised organic produce. The group is run by women and holds monthly meetings to study various topics such as recycling of wastes and purifying drinking water. Akiko became increasingly involved in the recycling and consumer movement and made an important discovery: Most of the members of the cooperative were only interested in the movement in order to protect their own family; in other words, their interests and perspectives were quite limited. They did not think of the group as part of a social movement to protect children or people in general; nor did they relate their activity to a political movement that would make it more effective. This is the unfortunate result of the tendency among many Japanese women to act on the basis of practical advantages rather than firmly held principles.

Kazuo was actually glad to hear that Akiko was again becoming involved in an activity outside the home. He was relieved to find that she had found something outside the home to absorb her energies and express her abilities. Yet, like many Japanese husbands, he did not particularly encourage her. Husband and wife seem to tacitly agree that it is up to her to decide what she will do with her free time, just as they have always agreed that she is completely in charge in the home.

When Akiko quit her job and became a full-time housewife, she spent a lot of time associating with other women in the neighborhood. She learned that most of the husbands of Kazuo's age who were employed in large companies were not home much. Some of the women seemed to interpret the fact that their husbands were so busy and that they came home late every night as a sign that they were part of the corporate elite. The wives themselves kept busy enough, for their husbands' long workdays left them considerable freedom to attend adult education classes provided by local government agencies or by commercially run "culture centers." There was a wide variety of subjects from which to choose, from jazz dance or pottery making to Greek mythology and foreign languages. There were even lectures in how to find a meaningful life as a woman. Many professional housewives were already saying that they wanted to find a goal of their very own in life (apart from raising children and keeping house), but they did not know quite how or where to look for it.

BEYOND MOTHERHOOD

Few of the women Akiko knew thought much about creating a meaningful life themselves, but they had gone one step further than Akiko's mother's generation, when women never questioned the meaning of their own lives but simply accepted and followed with courage and endurance what they considered their fate. The first postwar generation of women was groping toward something new, although their husbands did not seem to understand what they were talking about. Indeed, most men merely thought their wives should be more appreciative of the regular increases in salary they were getting and could not figure out why women were dissatisfied.

For Japanese women, one of the most distinct markers in their life course is the age or school year of their youngest child, rather than their own age. They therefore plan to start new activities, like work, when the youngest child starts kindergarten, primary school, or university. Akiko began to consider what kind of work she could do, in addition to her volunteer activities in the recycling and cooperative groups, once her children entered school. At the same time, she did not feel tied down by the children. Although not in a hurry to go back to work, she did begin to look around for employment opportunities.

There were not many kinds of work Akiko could do at home while keeping an eye on the children. She wanted something she could put down when the children needed her and resume when she was free. She found a job grading and correcting the examination papers of a *juku* (preparatory or cram school) for junior high school students. She could do the work at home; it was a more or less automatic job, checking against a master answer sheet. After ten months, however, she realized there was little intrinsic satisfaction in the job and decided not to continue. Since the household budget was not dependent on her income, she was free to quit as she pleased. Her job had brought in some income, but it had also cut into the time she had used before for cooking or interacting with the children. The mechanical work of grading papers, despite the income it produced, she decided, was not worth giving up activities she treasured. She decided not to work again for money until her younger child entered elementary school, but she was determined not to drop out of a nature lovers' group she had joined and asked her mother to take care of the children while she attended the meetings.

Observing nature and bird-watching had been Akiko's hobbies since high school. She sometimes spent household money for equipment or books, but Kazuo made no objections as long as she balanced the family accounts. One day she wrote a short essay on the wildflowers that grew in the area and sent it to the editor of a neighborhood newspaper. The editor thought it had some fresh insights and asked her to contribute regularly to his paper. Although Akiko was initially pessimistic that her rusty brain could produce anything original, the editor's encouragement gave her confidence. With this small job, she began testing the waters of the working world.

Like most of the other mothers in the neighborhood with children the age of her own, then 13 and 15, Akiko was anxious to start doing something "meaningful," although she was not sure what that would be. There was a whole rainbow of options at her disposal. Her friends had started to move back into the work force in various kinds of part-time jobs: receptionist at a local dentist, department store salesperson, piano teacher, home tutoring for schoolchildren. Some, called "part-time gypsies," changed jobs every three to six months, trying such jobs as cash register work at a fast-food outlet, home sales for insurance companies, and home visit sales of lingerie in the hope of finding the ideal occupation. They were free to leave jobs they did not like. Housewives who until yesterday had worn out-of-fashion skirts and shabby sweaters as they busied themselves with volunteer and child-related activities were busy transforming themselves into smartly dressed, high-heeled middle-aged working women, part of a dynamic work force that was vigorously stimulating the Japanese consumer economy.

After observing her friends for nearly a year, Akiko began to feel left behind. At the same time, she did not actively look for a job, having seen some of the unhappy experiences of her acquaintances. One friend had filled up her time by teaching patchwork quilting, joining a chorus, studying English conversation, and taking other courses at the adult education center where she taught quilting. Her busy life was her way of remedying the boredom of being at home; then she had an affair with one of the teachers and was eventually divorced. Another friend lamented how she would find an interesting job and get involved in other absorbing community activities only to be uprooted when her husband was transferred by his company every three years or so to a different city. Akiko knows it is possible that her husband might be sent overseas or to a branch office in another city in Japan, and she, too, might have to give up everything.

While Akiko was vacillating over what to do, she received an offer from an association of local shop owners to edit their quarterly public relations magazine. The magazine, a small-format 30-odd-page publication, mostly made up of advertisements and articles about local stores, their history, or the personalities of their owners, was distributed to the customers of the member stores of the association. Akiko's editorial and writing experience was known to her associates in the coop, some of whom had apparently mentioned it to some of the leaders of the store owners association when they were looking for an editor. The offer was a godsend for Akiko, since editing was a job she knew and felt confident in. She now works for the magazine three days a week, sharing the job by her own choice with another part-time woman, and she is quite content. Her coworker is not as happy as Akiko because she really wants to work full-time, despite her husband's vehement objections. The pay is low but Akiko does not envy the women who make much more money by working full-time or nearly full-time, for she feels she has attained a good balance between family, work, and community involvement.

When Akiko resumed working, she splurged on new clothing and accessories like a starving person after years of deprivation; once that hunger was assuaged, she began to save for her dream—a family trip abroad—which she hopes to realize while the children are in high school. For her, providing memorable experiences for the children is more important than giving them quantities of playthings or luxuries, but she has a feeling that her savings may actually end up being spent for more immediate needs, such as special study school fees for her daughter, now a sophomore in junior high school.

Akiko would be delighted if both her children could succeed in entering the university that she and their father graduated from, but which school they select is ultimately their own choice. The competition in the Japanese educational system is very intense, however, as they discovered when her son tried to get into a prestigious private high school. He failed to pass the rigorous entrance examination and ended up at the local public senior high school. Akiko simply thought that he had not been lucky and had not studied hard enough for the entrance examination. She thought that he had only to work harder to meet the next challenge, the university entrance examination. His grades might not have been the best, but what concerned her more was that he was caught smoking cigarettes at school with two others. It troubled her that Kazuo's only comment was, "Oh, he was probably teased into it by his friends," but, then, Kazuo tends to be much more concerned about his son's academic standing than anything else.

Ordinarily a very understanding and supportive husband who tried his best to make up for his long absences, Kazuo became emotional about their son's poor academic performance, blaming Akiko for not doing enough to prepare him for the entrance examination competition. He and Akiko had a bad fight when he made it sound as though their son's failure was solely her responsibility. She had been furious but was unable to counter Kazuo's charges of inadequate attention to their son's preparatory study because her mother had been hospitalized and a great deal of her time had, in fact, been taken up with care of her father, who was helpless without his wife at home, and with visiting her mother at the hospital. Akiko does not want to go through a similar scene with her husband again, so she plans to send their daughter to an expensive but highly reputed preparatory school.

Akiko has no intention of pressuring her children to aim for employment in the so-called prestigious companies but does hope they can find work that they find interesting. She definitely does not want them to end up like their father, sacrificing their private lives for the company they work for. She knows that Kazuo thinks differently, however. With many families it is the mother who is more concerned with getting the children into good schools, but in her family it is the father. If Kazuo is so worried about their education, Akiko thinks, he ought to spend more time with them, helping them study. In any case, her observations of others tell her it would be a mistake to push her children too hard in the race for educational credentials.

The average lifespan of a woman in Japan is now over 80, and Akiko, now in her early forties, knows that she cannot depend on her children in her old age. So, instead of investing inordinate sums on the children's education, she has decided to save steadily so that she and Kazuo can live comfortably and independently in advanced age. They will take care of the children until they finish college, but then they must support themselves. Akiko is looking forward to doing many things with Kazuo that they have put off over the years. Will they be able to fill the communication gap that has grown between them since they first married? Akiko realizes that it will take considerable effort on the part of each of them, and she has begun to explore hobbies that they could share. Kazuo, meanwhile, does not seem to think about postretirement much and shows little interest.

A more immediate concern is the care of her own and Kazuo's parents. So far, except for her mother's hospitalization, they have been healthy, but should any of them become bedridden again, as they age, she and Kazuo will face serious problems. Their parents invested heavily in their children's education and marriage, putting relatively little aside to take care of themselves in their old age. Akiko's parents have suggested that Akiko and Kazuo try to move to an apartment that is close to their house—"close enough to get to before a pot of soup cools," as the expression goes. Akiko knows that she won't be able to count on her brother to share the care of their parents because his wife's mother, already suffering from senility, is living with them. Furthermore, her sister-in-law and her mother do not get along, having almost completely opposite personalities. And if Kazuo's parents need Kazuo and Akiko's help, they will have to be brought from Kyoto to live with them.

Some of Akiko's older friends have recently given up jobs and hobbies to take care of aging parents, and she knows the time may come when she must do the same for either her own or Kazuo's parents. Having her mother in the hospital a little over two months was a hard enough burden while juggling a job, preparations for her son's examination, household chores, and volunteer work. The greatly extended lifespan has presented Japanese, especially women, with a whole new set of problems. Today, the care of both infants and the elderly rests almost solely on the shoulders of women. With so many women working, a new system may be needed in employment practices that allows not only for maternity or parental leave but also for temporary leave for the care of elderly dependents.

When the average lifespan stood at under 50 in prewar times for both men and women, many parents died before all of their relatively numerous offspring reached adulthood or became independent. They could die filled with the dreams of what their children might become or accomplish. Those who lived to an advanced age were taken care of by their children at home until they died. But now the older generation lives to see how their own children will treat them in old age, and children find the idealized image of their parents as the incarnation of love and selfless devotion hard to sustain as they care for parents afflicted with senile dementia and other ailments. A change in the parent–child relationship is unavoidable when members of the older generation live into their eighties. Generally speaking, the extended lifespan is more of a double-edged sword for women than for men: First, women do live longer than men, and second, it is women who must take care of the elderly. Akiko is determined to be well prepared for her own old age and do her best not to depend on her children. How successful can she be? No one can be certain.

WOMAN IN TRANSITION

Akiko is very much a woman with one foot in tradition and the other resting uncertainly on completely new ground. Her thinking and behavior are still largely affected by the old norms, namely, that women should take primary responsibility for the family and home while men work outside the home and that the husband's role in the household is first and foremost that of the breadwinner. Her commitment to her family is unshaken, and she takes immense pleasure in her role as mother and housewife, adoring her children and eager to create the kind of warm and comfortable home she knew as a child. She believes that these things are more important to her than the fulfillment to be found in a career.

What is new about Akiko is likewise clear. She relates to her husband on a far more equal basis than her mother did to her father. She does not slavishly attend to his every need but leaves him to fix his own breakfast, get out his own clothing, pour his own beer, and put his dirty clothes in the laundry basket. She also believes that Kazuo should help around the house. Although she can see that he cannot fulfill that expectation because of his job, she hasn't abandoned the idea. Her son, she realizes, must be more self-sufficient than his father is. How to train her son and convince him of that need, however, is a subject on which she has yet to formulate clear answers. The society around her remains quite traditional as far as the upbringing of boys is concerned, providing too few clues and too little support Akiko's new childrearing norms. She is well educated and knows how to think for herself, and her husband, although he might not be willing to admit that she is his intellectual equal, recognizes her abilities and judgment.

In the areas in which her thinking has been traditional, Akiko's awareness is gradually changing, as is the awareness of her peers and the society as a whole. The generation younger than Akiko's, especially those in the urban population, has already begun to question many of the norms women in their forties take for granted. How or whether Akiko will change further, after her children have left home, is only a matter of conjecture, but the way her life cycle thus far has coincided with changes in postwar Japanese society has forced her to confront and consider options that were not permitted to her mother and that her own daughter may not find nearly as troubling.

3

MARRIAGE AND THE FAMILY

The story of Noda Akiko introduces many issues relating to female identity, the status of women in work and family, and the role of women in society. It illustrates how the lives and attitudes of well-educated urban women of the first postwar generation remain firmly oriented to marriage and the family. At the same time, Akiko's life up to the age of 42 traces the path of those substantive changes in the attitudes and status of women in the family that are subtly transforming Japanese society as a whole. In this chapter, we shall look at the way women today marry, what they look for in marriage, what the limits of their expectations are, and how traditional relationships with spouses are changing. (Since Akiko's generation is already married, we shall also look at the younger generation now in their twenties and early thirties, born between 1960 and 1969.) In addition, we will learn about the woman's position in her marriage and in the family and the sources of her strength therein. An understanding of these issues helps us grasp what the changes in women's lives mean for Japanese society as a whole.

FROM DESTINY TO OPTION

Thirty years ago, a young woman was expected to marry between 20 and 24, and those still single at 25 were often pitied or disparaged as *urenokori* (unsold merchandise) or *tō ga tatsu* (overripe fruit). Perhaps the main reason was because, for that

59

generation of women (now in their fifties), marriage was a must. It was the source of economic power. Men, on the other hand, were untrained in domestic arts and needed a person to run their households as well as bear children to carry on the family name.

Women who did not marry were sometimes thought to be cold or unattractive; even men could not afford to ignore marriage. A man who remained single past his mid-thirties was considered not quite fully adult (*ichininmae*) and was presumed to be eccentric in some way, although men seem to have been spared being thought cold or unattractive (indeed, sometimes a man's inability to settle down was attributed to his being *too* attractive).

For the first postwar generation of women (born between 1946 and 1955, now in their mid-thirties to mid-forties), the situation was somewhat more relaxed. Many of these women received a university education and took a job after graduation. Their resultant economic independence permitted them more options and a greater diversity in lifestyle. Today, with marriage no longer necessary for social and economic survival, the marriageable age extended considerably and marriage became a less pressing concern for the women themselves. In 1990 the average age for a first marriage was 25.8 for women and 28.5 for men, one year later than the average 10 years earlier.

The urge to marry (*kekkon ganbō*) has been found to peak at around age 24.[1] The idea of getting married in a gala wedding with all the frills and settling down with a handsome, gentle husband of respectable background in a charmingly appointed little apartment in the suburbs has irresistible allure for the relatively indulged, sheltered young women in their twenties today. Accustomed to dependence on their mothers, as well as to affluence and a protective environment, they have little experience of the real difficulties or complexities of life and little confidence in their own ability to cope with obstacles; these young women pursue an ideal of happiness largely made up of surface images. They vacillate between the fear that they may never find a better candidate for marriage than the perhaps less than ideal individual immediately at hand and their fantasy of falling in passionate, permanent love. In all their relationships they tend to keep a tight grip on their emotions, fearing above all the fate of a broken heart. The number of women who actually do marry in their early twenties (20–24) is small, only 14 percent in 1989 (in 1965 it was 32 percent), while the majority pass the age of 25 still single. Interviews conducted in 1991 show that these young women have been largely freed from the traditional confines of female destiny and have grown up with the same individualistic and hedonistic values as the men of their generation. Little concerned with the ideals and sense of responsibility to social causes felt strongly by the members of the first postwar generation when they were in their twenties, the current generation of young adults is a product of the consumer culture. They tend to act less on the basis of some future goal or strongly felt commitment than on the basis of feelings, and this affects their work patterns, family relations, and thinking in general. Unlike their seniors, they work less for work's sake than to be able to play.

Once young women today pass the first age hurdle, around 25, without successfully finding a marriage partner, they begin to divert their energies to other things and find interest and challenge, as well as gain, in work or hobbies. As a result, marriage ceases to be an obsession for them.

The recent Japanese tendency to marry late may reflect the fact that marriage in Japan, in contrast to the United States with its emphasis on romance and love, is generally contemplated in objective terms based on practical considerations (e.g., economic stability, social status, and family relations). Unlike most Americans—who marry as long as they feel they are in love, regardless of age—Japanese (except perhaps today's youth) tend to think that marriage and falling in love (ren'ai) are two different things. They consider marriage a long-term arrangement that entails (ideally) permanence, commitment, and (whether they like it or not) a great deal of unexciting day-to-day toil. To the practical-minded Japanese, romance is a fleeting thing and is not expected to last throughout the many years of marriage. Japanese consider themselves quite lucky if love and marriage turn out to coincide. There is also a belief, inculcated by the older generation of women, that once two people start living together in marriage, love will grow between them. Japanese of the middle and older generations tend to see the relationship between husband and wife, like so many other things, in a long-term perspective, extending into old age, and to anticipate it as a developmental process throughout life.

Once women pass 30, they pay (or pretend to pay) less attention to their age and its social implications and appear to be more relaxed—in spite of growing, although often unspoken, concern on the part of their parents. Although their chances of meeting a suitable man decrease, since many of the men they meet are either married or younger, these women feel they should marry only if someone comes along who is appealing enough to merit giving up the freedom they have come to enjoy. By this time, a working woman's salary has generally reached a point at which she can live fairly comfortably on her own. Although women age 30 and over do think it would be nice to be married, they do not want, having waited this long, to settle for a man who does not meet their qualifications in educational background, salary, and occupation (income).

By this stage, too, many women have established their identity in a particular job or career and are actualizing themselves in an occupation other than marriage. For them, marriage has definitely become only one of several options. It offers social and economic security difficult to obtain otherwise, but some women find it hard to forgo the freedom of the single life, which the mass media now glorifies as the destined path of the independent, self-reliant woman of the 1990s. Today, a career-oriented woman can enjoy the company of many other still-single women friends her own age, with whom she can share various pursuits and diversions in a sort of companionship that is an important psychological support in this collectivist society.

The past-30 career-oriented women have redefined their roles, but social norms have not caught up with them. One single woman in her early thirties reported her experience when interviewed for a job: "I was asked whether I was single or married, whether I intended to marry or not, and so on. Why is being married or not an issue? Is it so important to the company?"[2] Her annoyance stems from the lag between women's attitudes, which have drastically changed, and social norms, which remain largely unchanged.

Many single women over 30, who probably hoped to live with their parents until marriage, eventually move into their own apartments in order to escape their parents' prying eyes, although they may try to live nearby in order to indulge as often as possible in meals and the other accustomed comforts of a mother's care. Attaining independence is not a goal in itself; young people are practical enough to want to take life as easy as possible for as long as possible. And parents often become lonely when their offspring—only one or two in number—leave the nest, so they are happy to have them living nearby.

Today's young women, therefore, will only marry if the right man appears. Many are careful to prepare for a possible spinsterhood, and consequently, sales of insurance and commercial pension plans for such women are reported to be flourishing.[3]

WHAT'S BEST FOR A WOMAN

Though the marriage age has moved upward, 63 percent of Japanese do get married at least once before they reach 30, and 88 percent marry by the time they reach 35. The number of women who choose to stay single, with or without a partner, is expected to grow, as suggested in public opinion surveys.[4]

Women now feel less eager or compelled to marry than men or than was exhibited in earlier periods, a tendency that is strongest among highly educated women in their twenties with professional skills. A growing number of of women young people (28 percent of men and 37 percent of women surveyed) agree that "women should not necessarily get married if they can get along on their own." Among single women (invariably in their twenties and early thirties in Japan), 41 percent responded affirmatively to this statement, a remarkable change from the days when marriage determined destiny. These attitudes, in fact, add to the reasons men have been finding it harder than ever to find marriage partners, and they have serious implications for society.

The first postwar generation of women differed from their mothers in that they did not want to lower the level of qualifications they desired in a husband even if they passed 30; they preferred to remain single. They are fully capable of supporting themselves economically, if necessary. As witnesses to the self-sacrifice and subservience of their mothers to husband and family (including in-laws), they are not anxious to follow in their mothers' footsteps.

What sustained the hopes and expectations of this first postwar generation of women were the obvious changes in the social climate that had occurred by the time they reached 30. Single working women over 30, though still a minority, were no longer subject to the pity of those around them. On the contrary, they were often called *tonderu onna* (flying women), a term that appeared first in the media in 1977 to describe the progressive, career-oriented women who enjoyed attractiveness, vitality, and independence. Society could not quite decide whether such women were to be abhorred or admired. Their parents, though concerned, had ceased attempts at matchmaking, defeated by their daughters' unbudging requirements. Many mothers were secretly proud and even somewhat envious of their daughters' economic capabilities and freedom. Marriage for this generation became a matter of individual choice, although figures show that the majority eventually did marry.

For men and women born after World War II, the largest difference from their parents' generation is that there is greater equality in relations between husband and wife. This generation was, after all, taught since primary school that men and women are equal—at least as far as the Constitution goes. Until the first postwar generation, women generally had to be accepted (*moratte morau*) by the bridegroom and his family, and in the extended family their status was very low until the mother-in-law passed away. Today, young women can count on more equal treatment, and they anticipate the far more appealing prospects of "going to become a bride (*yome ni iku*)." For young women currently entering marriage, who have their pick of a large number of men, the tables are turned; it is they who do the men the favor of marrying.

FINDING A SPOUSE

The way people find their spouse has greatly changed since the mid-1980s. The majority of urban young people meet the person they eventually marry in their university or after graduation in their place of work. Such natural meetings now often lead to love and marriage, but a sizable number of young people, especially men, are too shy, inhibited, or uninterested to put together a lasting relationship with a member of the opposite sex on their own. Here the age-old system of arranged meetings (*miai;* explained in Chapter 2) often comes to the rescue, although the number of those who claim to have married through *miai* has been decreasing (now down to 24 percent). Of young people married since 1980, the number who say they married after finding a partner by chance and falling in love (*ren'ai*) has increased to 74 percent.[5]

Miai in the contemporary sense is by no means regarded with contempt. It comes to the aid of eligible persons who do not have adequate opportunities to meet members of the opposite sex or are too shy or inhibited to approach them. If the go-between is a trustworthy person who knows the two parties and their families, a *miai* provides an acceptable, reassuring backup for nervous candidates. It has great value for Japanese, who often tend to be overly resigned to fate and passive or accommodating about what life brings but who are also practical. In their passiveness, they believe that the web of *karma* will bestow upon them the required *en* (relationship), but being pragmatic, they realize that *karma* sometimes needs a little nudging.

Arranged meetings are especially important in Japan because of the separation of activities of the sexes (described in Chapter 1). Young people often pursue hobbies and recreation in all-male or all-female groups, and this tendency does not encourage familiarity with the opposite sex or confidence in dealing with it. Not only go-betweens and friends but professional marriage brokers (public and private) and computer mating agencies have entered into this breach.

NOT FINDING A SPOUSE

Many people who would like to get married are not successful in finding a satisfactory spouse. A growing number of men in their thirties, in particular, are having a very hard time finding partners. Men still feel the urgent need for a helpmate and permanent companion, and they often need, at the very least, a partner to help shoulder the responsibilities of inherited land or property or a family business, which impose a considerable burden on younger generations in Japanese society even today. They cannot afford to follow the example of a growing number of women who would rather become spinsters than undergo the hardships of an undesirable marriage situation at the expense of cherished freedom.

The shortage of brides began in rural areas, where the sons of farming families, no matter how attractive or wealthy, had trouble finding brides because of the hardships of a farming woman's life and the many old-fashioned customs still binding in rural life, customs that hardly appeal to today's young woman who greatly prizes her freedom and autonomy. Farming mothers, not anxious to submit their daughters to a fate like their own, do all they can to avoid marrying them off to farmers, and this tendency in turn has created problems for their sons. The lack of suitable partners for young farming men led to an influx of women as brides from Korea, the Philippines, Thailand, and as far away as Sri Lanka. Although this phenomena has suddenly exposed the basically very conservative rural people to the shocks of international encounter, the shortage is being met to some extent, despite many language-related and other cultural problems, through this method. Rural men, however, have the older generation to help them search for brides and therefore have a fair chance of finding a mate. Their urban cousins have a much harder time; single men in the cities have to hunt on their own.

Where can the urban bachelor turn for help now that the volunteer go-between has nearly vanished? One place is the flourishing marriage broker/computer mating business, now with more than 5,000 enterprises crowding the market. Some companies, in hopes of increasing their appeal among women, will register only men who have graduated from the most prestigious universities or who are employed in such high-income occupations as medicine or dentistry. This leaves the nonelite majority out in the cold. Some large corporations, concerned about the growing number of male employees who are unable to find wives, have set up special departments to organize social events and other functions to promote the mixing of single men and women in their employ. Here again, however, the old patterns of corporate paternalism and male-dominated thinking persist, but with little success. This sort of paternalism infringes upon the need of today's young people to keep their private lives to themselves. Far more constructive would be a policy of curtailing overtime work so that their young employees could date more easily and pursue hobbies that might enable them to meet young women after hours.

So hard-pressed have men become in finding marriage partners that a lecture series called the School for Bridegrooms (*hanamuko gakkō*, a take-off of *hanayome gakkō*, a school that offered classes for young women in such arts as cooking, flower arrangement, sewing, and the tea ceremony) came into being in 1989. Although the idea sounds absurd to the older generation, married in the days when marriage was a "bridegroom's market," the mass media has made quite a fuss over the series, noting that it is indicative of the 180-degree about-face in the expectations of men and women. The lectures are intended to help men train themselves to become "good husbands and wise fathers," just as women once studiously pursued the requirements of the "good wife and wise mother" tradition. The lectures showed men how to see things from the woman's point of view and to grasp the changes women's lives have undergone. They also offered hints on ways to establish good relationships with women. Those lectures appear to represent the modest beginnings of a new industry.

The competition among men to capture a willing woman while they can has grown intense. Those who are able court women with costly baubles, expensive meals, and attentive services (like driving them around town or accompanying them on shopping sprees) and generally go to extreme lengths to please them.[6] But do they really have any clear image of what kind of woman they want to marry? Other than the requirements that she be supportive and companionable, and relatively good-looking, their image is somewhat hazy. These young men tend to be rather unimaginative as far as their vision of what they want in a wife, and they are intimidated by a woman who has a high income or an outstanding academic pedigree or is physically tall. Yet the shortage of women makes men fear that if they demand too much, they might lose out completely. This can be frustrating for women, who come to the marriage counter with a shopping list of specific requirements.

The causes of failure in finding a spouse are several, but the crucial factors appear to be the changing attitudes of women toward marriage and men's inadequate appreciation of those changes and their failure to alter their own attitudes and behavior. The tendency among women to feel, as they get older, little urgency to marry can make them seem unapproachable, and their demands are hard to live up to. Women are said to hope for the "three highs" in the man they marry: high income (at least ¥5 million or $35,000 annually), higher education (graduation from a prestigious university), and physical height (at least 175 cm, or 5 ft. 10 in.).[7] They objectively appraise any man suggested as a marriage candidate with regard to how comfortable or enjoyable a life he can offer; if he does not measure up, they may refuse even to meet him. Because their own economic earning power has given them a taste of the material luxuries and comforts available, they have set their sights too high for many men to meet.

Another major reason for the failure of men to find a spouse is the demographic imbalance. Since the end of World War II, with the end of war and with improvements in medical care, the survival rate of male infants (generally more frail at birth than females) has radically increased. For the generations of men 40 and under, the number of men today exceeds the number of women. There are approximately 2.5 million more single men than single women 20 to 39 years of age. In Tokyo alone, 500,000 men are destined for possible permanent bachelorhood.[8] Women are distributed unevenly among the professions (as well as among major fields of study in the universities), thus making it very difficult for some men to meet women on a casual basis.

A further stumbling block is filial responsibilities. Men who are only children, the population of which increases every year, have heavy family obligations. Women are reluctant to marry only sons or eldest sons because of the generally accepted duty that accompanies such a marriage, namely, the duty to help care for the husband's parents in advanced age (which can be quite a burden now that the lifespan in Japan has extended to about 80). For women who themselves are only children, the prospect of their burden being doubled can cause them to turn down an otherwise very attractive proposal of marriage. Women tend to postpone marriage, feeling that marriage will force them to give up much of what they enjoy doing. Men believe the sacrifices required in marriage are surpassed by the value of the support system thereby acquired, which will make it possible for them to continue doing what they want. Again, this discrepancy in attitudes adds to the odds against marriage.

Of course, there must be frequent cases in which the actual chemistry between the man and woman cancels out all these objective demands and practical considerations. The reason women post such high demands in the first place may be an indication of their frustration with what they feel is the unwillingness or inability of men to adjust to changes in female lives. Women also decry the tendency among those men who hope to make up for their ineptitude in the social graces to follow the book (there are, in fact, many how-to books sold to help men master the arts of courtship) when it comes to dating, entertaining women, or even giving compliments. The pitiful ineptitude of many men in these areas may be the result of their loss of confidence as women have grown more assertive and articulate.

EXPECTATIONS OF MARRIAGE

What do Japanese women expect from marriage and what factors are the measure of their satisfaction or dissatisfaction in marriage? In 1990 studies of fairly large samples of both married and unmarried men and women over age 18 in the United States and Japan conducted by Roper and Dentsu (hereafter referred as the VSR Survey) showed extremely interesting differences between Americans and Japanese in what they consider conditions for a good marriage.[9] Clearly, Americans expect much more from a marriage than do Japanese. (It should be noted at the outset that this survey was originally planned for American respondents and that its questions therefore reflect a peculiarly American orientation.) Thirteen different conditions (see Figure 3–1) were listed, and respondents were asked to rate each on a scale from "not at all important" to "very important."

In both the United States and Japan, men tend to consider almost every condition to be slightly less important than women, which may be a reflection of the greater expectations women have of marriage than men. Americans rated 11 of the 13 conditions significantly more important than did the Japanese. The two exceptions were "financial security" and "having children," which more Japanese than American women rated as very important. The most important conditions of marriage for American women, in order of priority, were the following: "being in love" (87 percent; Japanese, 68 percent), "sexual fidelity on the part of the spouse" (85 percent; Japanese, 46 percent), and "being able to talk together about your feelings" (84 percent). This last condition was rated as very important by 73 percent of Japanese women of all age-groups (and more so with older

Figure 3-1 Conditions for a Good Marriage, 1990

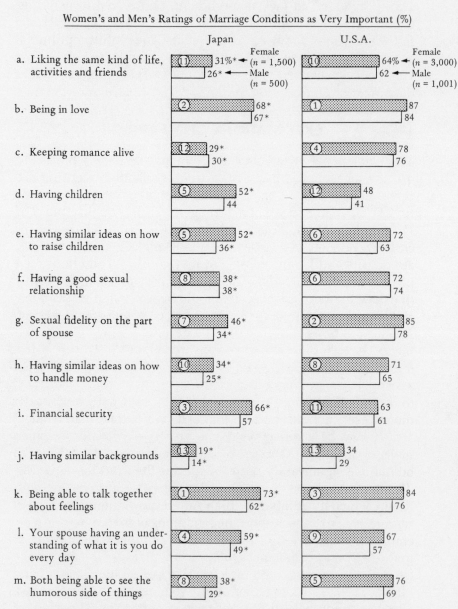

Women's and Men's Ratings of Marriage Conditions as Very Important (%)

Japan / U.S.A.

a. Liking the same kind of life, activities and friends — Japan: ① 31%* Female (n = 1,500), 26* Male (n = 500); U.S.A.: ⑩ 64% Female (n = 3,000), 62 Male (n = 1,001)

b. Being in love — Japan: ② 68*, 67*; U.S.A.: ① 87, 84

c. Keeping romance alive — Japan: ⑫ 29*, 30*; U.S.A.: ④ 78, 76

d. Having children — Japan: ⑤ 52*, 44; U.S.A.: ⑫ 48, 41

e. Having similar ideas on how to raise children — Japan: ⑤ 52*, 36*; U.S.A.: ⑥ 72, 63

f. Having a good sexual relationship — Japan: ⑧ 38*, 38*; U.S.A.: ⑥ 72, 74

g. Sexual fidelity on the part of spouse — Japan: ⑦ 46*, 34*; U.S.A.: ② 85, 78

h. Having similar ideas on how to handle money — Japan: ⑩ 34*, 25*; U.S.A.: ⑧ 71, 65

i. Financial security — Japan: ③ 66*, 57; U.S.A.: ⑪ 63, 61

j. Having similar backgrounds — Japan: ⑬ 19*, 14*; U.S.A.: ⑬ 34, 29

k. Being able to talk together about feelings — Japan: ① 73*, 62*; U.S.A.: ③ 84, 76

l. Your spouse having an understanding of what it is you do every day — Japan: ④ 59*, 49*; U.S.A.: ⑨ 67, 57

m. Both being able to see the humorous side of things — Japan: ⑧ 38*, 29*; U.S.A.: ⑤ 76, 69

Note: Circled figures indicate ranking of women's responses. *Statistically significant difference between Japanese and American responses.

age groups), although in reality their marriages are known for their lack of communication, one of the problems faced in Japanese marriages.

Less than 70 percent of Japanese women rated the other conditions covered in the survey as very important, with the following three conditions (in descending order of priority) cited as very important: "being in love," "financial security," and "your spouse having an understanding of what it is you do every day." The results for some of the other conditions show striking differences between the attitudes of Japanese and Americans. They include, for example, those conditions related to the romantic or sexual side of marriage, such as "keeping romance alive" (Japanese, 29 percent; Americans, 78 percent), "having a good sexual relationship" (Japanese, 38 percent; Americans, 72 percent), and "sexual fidelity on the part of the spouse" (already noted in the preceding paragraph).

Clear differences are also observable for conditions related to communication and sharing, such as "liking the same kind of life, activities and friends" (Japanese, 31 percent; Americans, 64 percent), "having similar ideas on how to handle money" (Japanese, 34 percent; Americans, 71 percent), and "both being able to see the humorous side of things" (Japanese, 38 percent; Americans, 76 percent). Among Japanese, young, single, and highly educated women tended to regard the romantic aspects of marriage as more important while older, married women showed a tendency, although considerably less than among Americans, to regard having children and confidence in the sexual fidelity of the spouse as very important for a good marriage.

As detailed in Table 3–1, Japanese women's expectations of marriage have changed in some respects and remained stable in others. "Having similar ideas on how to raise children" and "financial security," for example, continue to be important. Regarding what Japanese women consider most important for a successful marriage, on the other hand, we can see a clear emphasis among those in their thirties and younger, in contrast to those over age 40, on "being able to talk together about your feelings" and issues centering around companionship with the husband. The figures also show that the younger generation does not necessarily place great importance on sexual fidelity (this trend is supported by other surveys, which are introduced in the following chapter). Comparing the generations over 50 and under 30, we can observe a difference of more than 20 points for the items on "being in love," "keeping romance alive," and

Table 3-1
Items Considered "Very Important" Rated by Japanese Women of Different Age Groups (in percent)

	Age Group			
	20–29	30–39	40–49	50 and older
Liking the same kind of life, activities and friends	37	38	29	24
Being in love	80	75	67	58
Keeping romance alive	43	35	26	20
Having children	45	50	50	57
Having similar ideas on how to raise children	51	51	54	52
Having a good sexual relationship	44	38	40	34
Sexual fidelity	35	43	44	53
Having similar ideas on how to handle money	38	35	31	34
Financial security	68	64	70	64
Having similar backgrounds	17	16	17	22
Being able to talk together	83	81	69	65
Your spouse having an understanding of what it is you do every day	73	66	58	49
Both being able to see the humorous side of things	40	39	37	38

"your spouse having an understanding of what it is you do every day," showing how much greater the demand is among young women for affection and involvement with their husbands. These data suggest a clear trend away from the old-fashioned cool and distant relationship between husband and wife toward a closer relationship involving more intense feelings.

The items in this survey are based on the many conditions Americans seem to feel are necessary for a marriage to succeed. If any of the conditions considered very important by Americans are not met or maintained in an American marriage, there is a great danger of the marriage breaking up. Japanese, on the other hand, appear to be more lenient about the conditions for marriage and about what it takes to make a marriage last. The conditions they consider very important may not even be included in the VSR Survey, for it appears that marriage itself is defined differently by the Japanese and that it involves a rather cool, practical relationship. In any case, Japanese do not stake all their expectations on marriage; they look to friends, relatives, parents, co-workers, bar hostesses, and others to fulfill their various needs for sharing, moral support, and enjoyment. A marriage as conceived by Americans cannot be sustained as a lasting relationship without constantly pouring tremendous amounts of energy into it. It should also be noted that most Japanese men and women are convinced and resigned to the belief that romance ends with marriage, and especially after the birth of children; as a result, much of the joy and magic of a relationship tends to be lost once a family is begun. Yet most Japanese, young people included, seem content if marriage and home provide creature comforts and close bonds. The basic expectations we have observed do not differ much from one generation to another. Now let us look at some of the features that make up successful or good marriages in Japan.

CLOSENESS WITHOUT COMPLETE SHARING

A good (i.e., stable, happy) Japanese marriage, as far as the first postwar generation is concerned, could be likened to a pair of cars traveling through the landscape. The two cars may at times take different turns and often remain far apart even if they are on the same road, although they may make the same pit stops from time to time. It is recognized and accepted that the two cars are of different make, power, shape, and so on and that the distance they have to cover is very long; a mutual appreciation of their differences will help to facilitate the journey. They drive along with the understanding that neither will abandon the road or the other in mid-journey. Because they are different, each will have its advantages in different circumstances or conditions. With the mutual confidence based on the trust they have from their long-term commitment, they can continue their journey with a strong sense of security, even though they may be, at times, so far apart that they cannot see each other on the road. The relationship between a husband and wife, therefore, like the question of equality, cannot be evaluated adequately at any one point in time but must be taken in the context of their whole lives.

In this way, a bride and groom begin their married life with the understanding that since each has spent over 20 years in a different family environment, they will naturally be incompatible in some ways and come into conflict over some issues. This prior assumption of their differences makes them relatively relaxed with each other and mutually tolerant. American newlyweds, on the other hand, seem determined to share everything in their lives. A Japanese couple starts out with lower expectations of each other and a hopeful feeling that the shortcomings they find in each other will be made up for or corrected over time. Partly because of the relative separation of male and female lives throughout society, complete sharing is not expected.

Married people also become more accepting of human weaknesses and foibles the older they become. Certain traits are considered in the folk culture to be part and parcel of the male or female sex and not worth struggling against. This attitude, often described as *otagaisama* (it goes both ways), recognizes that there may be fault on both sides and that it is best to be mutually forgiving. A woman will tolerate the klutziness, grumbling, childlike playfulness, and hopelessness at domestic tasks of her man as the "nature of the beast." A man might dismiss his wife's emotional reactions to crisis, love of gossip, obsession with social appearances, and excessive domesticity as female tendencies. Neither is inclined to think that any other woman or man would be basically much different in nature. In contrast to Americans, who are more inclined to focus on the individual differences from one man or woman to another, the Japanese think that whatever people are like on the surface, physically or in terms of personality, underneath they are all basically the same human animal. However their marriage begins, most Japanese develop a certain objectivity and resignation toward the disagreeable qualities of their spouse, and, as in any close association, both sides learn to see beyond those faults and recognize the good qualities as well.

A RELATIONSHIP LIKE AIR

Middle-aged or older Japanese often say that a good relationship between a married couple is "like air." This is not to say, as we might first think, that it is lightweight or empty. On the contrary, the expression implies that the relationship, like the air we breathe, is vital for the survival of both sides even though its presence is hardly felt. If we find ourselves gasping for air, it is usually indicative of a serious crisis; if a couple begins to feel the weight of their bond, it may mean they are having trouble. This sort of stable and reliable relationship does not take shape immediately. It evolves over the years out of the autonomy, acceptance, and forbearance of the partners as well as from the mutual recognition of the need for a supportive relationship, commitment to the family, and genuine affection.

If a relationship is not palpable and vibrant, Americans are likely to think there is no point in maintaining it. And even Japanese women of the generation born between 1956 and 1965 (following the first postwar generation) are not fully satisfied with a relationship that is to be taken for granted in the traditional mold; they expect and want their relationship to their husband to be based on friendship and to be more sharing and alive than that of their parents. In this sense, some changes are occurring, and yet on the behavioral level the difference between generations turns out not to be so very great once married life actually begins. Younger people, like their parents, are forced to make compromises in the face of reality, and husbands are just as absent from the home today (though for different reasons) as they were a generation ago, as in the case of Akiko's husband, Kazuo. As the years go by, the limits of sharing become manifest, and the couple develops a practical, expedient division of responsibility, care, and labor. As long as this accommodates their mutual needs and does not generate stress, the relationship becomes exceedingly stable—like air.

One reason for this stability is that once married, Japanese exert relatively little conscious or deliberate effort to enhance the relationship with their spouse. This continues to be true of the first postwar generation. They cease to use honorific language with each other, rarely comment on or compliment each other's appearance or activities, do little to remember birthdays or anniversaries (although children's birthdays are the center of great attention); the verbal expression of feelings of affection or attachment is practically taboo. These customs may be changing among younger couples to a certain extent, but the old saying "You don't proffer bait to a fish once caught" still guides behavior among married couples and symbolizes the great confidence they place in the marriage relationship.

In the home, both men and women are completely relaxed in the presence of their spouse; the tension and formality of the male–female relationship they felt before marriage falls away from their interaction completely. One might add that this is especially important for Japanese because other social relationships are fraught with tension, formality, and concern for appearances. A Japanese woman of the first postwar generation and older does not think of putting on makeup and changing into a nice dress to greet her husband upon his return from work, although she dresses meticulously when going out to a wedding or to chitchat with her female friends. If his wife is in nice clothes and careful makeup, a husband would want to know where she is going off to. As far as both spouses are concerned, they do not have to prove their attachment or faithfulness to each other through words or appearances, only through actions. Many women are actually discouraged from trying to look nice in front of their husbands because in the privacy of the home husbands take little overt interest in how their wives look and rarely comment on a change of hairstyle or new clothing. For their part, men do not feel called upon or comfortable with verbalizing appreciation for their wives.

As will be discussed in detail later, verbal communication between husband and wife is minimal; compliments and expressions of fondness tend to be backhanded and indirect, sometimes covered up by teasing or negative comments made to a third party. Sometimes, in the presence of others a man may order his wife around and complain about her as a means of demonstrating his male superiority—and many men are less than sensitive about whether this kind of treatment hurts their wife's feelings. Although wives know their husbands care about them in their own way, men are not socialized to be sensitive about feelings of women, and it is considered "unmanly" to coddle or humor wives. Many men nevertheless do care intensely about their wives. The husband–wife relationship is unique in Japanese society in that it is the only one in which two people can tacitly and effortlessly depend upon each other and be totally at ease with one another. Certainly, it is all the more prized because of the great pains that must be taken with other social relationships.

The contrast with the high expectations maintained throughout marriage that we observe in the United States is remarkable: Not only does an American couple want to love and provide emotional support to each other, but they also want to share each other's feelings and activities "in joy and in sadness," have a mutually gratifying sexual relationship, and know and understand what the other is thinking, feeling, and doing—*all the time.* They also want their relationship to grow. Expecting all that from a marriage must take great effort. It must make the time spent with one's spouse full of sustained tension and energy, which could become quite strenuous. Perhaps the Japanese-style marriage, in which sharing takes subtler forms, has something to offer America's individual-centered society.

The attitude toward the marriage relationship among Japanese is much more passive and exacts a lesser degree of involvement. There seems to be little constructive struggle on the part of either spouse to make the marriage more than simply what it is. One reason for this is because of the long tradition, which prevailed even in the West, in which women persevered through any difficulty in a marriage. Even today, when faced with some unpleasant behavior on the part of their husband, many Japanese women of the older generation still say, "We'll get over it, if I just put up with things for now [*shibaraku gaman sureba*]." Perhaps this stems from the willingness to take the long view of life. Good or bad periods in a relationship, victories or failures at one time or other in life, are difficult to judge or identify (e.g., a failure in one thing could easily lead to a better outcome in the long run). There is an understanding and acceptance that life has both ups and downs, and Japanese tend to cleave to, rather than try to control or vanquish, those changes. In a relationship, this attitude means believing that although things may not be going well right now, they may improve sooner or later. Since one never knows the future, one does not leap into combat but endures the situation for a while to see what turn matters take.

From my observations in the United States, people seem to be thoroughly success oriented regarding others, even family members, viewing them either as winners or losers, and to be less willing to settle for mediocrity or compromise. For all their competitive spirit, Japanese are realistic; they will aim for an average goal if it seems more likely to be attainable rather than press for the top if it seems beyond their means. In the United States winning or losing is felt to be basically up to individuals and their ability to control their lives. If a situation is unsatisfactory and has enough counts against it, a person is expected to remove himself or herself from it. Perhaps this is why much more concentrated effort is exerted by Americans than by Japanese—even to the point of creating stress—to make a success of marriage and everything else about one's life. For Americans, the expectations and demands made of life are very high; if those expectations and demands are not fulfilled, the individual experiences hurt and disappointment to the point where a relationship or a marriage may be terminated.

Americans may seem to expect too much of marriage, but Japanese appear to expect too little. Japanese, who have many other cherished relationships in their lives to rely on, may be all too accepting of whatever might happen to a marriage—yet are less likely to suffer intolerable disappointment—while Americans are more likely to face disappointment and struggle against it, sometimes with success, sometimes in vain. The relationship between a Japanese husband and wife is almost too distant, with too little sharing; in a sense, the two parties are too far apart for collision to occur. By contrast, the relationship between an American husband and wife may be too close (and they may try to make it closer, depending on their image of a successful marriage), interfering with the independence and freedom of each party and thus producing stress. (It seems ironic that the close sharing and companionship that Americans emphasize in marriage conflicts with the individualism and independence to which they also attach high value.)

For the individualistic American, curbing one's autonomy is something one does only when the cause is important and the returns are certain. This must be related to the high demands they make of marriage. But here the Japanese pattern may have something to offer, for it would seem advisable for husband and wife to keep a safe distance from each other in their journey through life, to return to the metaphor of the two cars driving along the highway, just as do two cars headed down the same road. They can move along side by side at the same pace, or one can move ahead at one time or another, depending on the condition of their vehicle or the destination to be reached.

In marriage, as in other aspects of contemporary Japanese society, we can observe the strong orientation to efficiency that is in fact, behind the economic success Japan has accomplished. Now that the present level of affluence has been attained, however, it could be damaging to both the individual and society to cling too tenaciously to this orientation. Traditionally, the husband–wife team was ideal if it functioned efficiently, and this could be best achieved through a complementary relationship and a separation of roles. The postwar generations, however, have been reared to believe in equality of the sexes, and they (especially women) are finding the lack of sharing and companionship in marriage frustrating. Women think they started from the same position, although the reality is different. The distance that exists between husband and wife in contemporary Japanese society is most pronounced in urban families, where the men are employed far away from home and are in the home for relatively few hours each day. In such a situation it is often impossible for a couple to have a close sharing relationship even if they want one.

One reason Japanese women are less angry than their American counterparts about the fact that their husbands do not share household and childrearing tasks may be that, unlike American men, Japanese husbands are often not present in the home when they are needed. In other words, their lack of cooperation is not because they choose not to, but because they are simply not there enough of the time. Their absence helps to prevent the inequity of the burden-sharing arrangement from becoming an immediate source of tension between husband and wife, as vividly illustrated in the book *Second Shift*.[10] Since women exploit that absence instead of resenting it, tension from the unfair distribution of domestic burdens is dispersed.

ROLE AND STATUS IN THE FAMILY

Japanese women of all ages, whether they work or not, consider their home and family as important as their activities outside the home. In contrast to the large number of women in the United States who sometimes implicitly assume that endeavors in the world outside the home are more significant and important than taking care of home and family, Japanese working mothers repeatedly say they strive for a healthy balance among their identities as mother, wife, worker, and individual.

To sustain these diverse identities, women also maintain a balance of skills and strengths. Although they may excel in one particular profession, skill, or pursuit, they tend not to become totally absorbed in any one but to prefer a balance, concentrating their greatest attention on the basic or core tasks at hand and disposing of peripheral tasks efficiently.

Some urban American women tend to look down upon the full-time housewife/mother or to deprecate themselves as "only a housewife." A working woman visiting a friend who is a full-time housewife/mother is apt to ask her, "What are you going to do?" as if she cannot imagine that being a housewife/mother would be enough for an intelligent woman.

Japanese women's priorities are the opposite. For them, family and home life continue to be the center of their identity as women. Home management and their children's education make heavy demands on the energy and intellect of Japanese women. If they work, the majority choose and go about their work as much as possible at their family's convenience. If their employment should prove detrimental to family or home life, it quickly becomes the object of reconsideration, even if the work itself is appealing or rewarding.

Many extremely able and well-educated women continue to opt for the full-time mother/wife role while children are small despite the very attractive opportunities for fulfillment outside the home. There are very cogent reasons for this, for the home offers them several sources of power and fulfillment. First,

Japanese traditionally associate home and family with warmth and comfort while the outside world is viewed as cold and often indifferent; this gives the family great intrinsic importance in the eyes of Japanese, especially women. The society is intensely competitive and achievement-oriented, for children and young people in the academic realm and for adults in their professional lives. It is widely believed that unless individuals are part of a family that is stable, they cannot fulfill their full potential, whatever their chosen pursuit. Since family members can ultimately bring back to the family the best rewards society has to offer, maintaining the home as a solid, nurturing base is an occupation that can offer great material as well as personal fulfillment, as women long engaged in that profession can readily attest.

Second, women monopolize management of the home. To a large extent, of course, this happens by default. If a Japanese man is asked which is more important to him, family or work, he invariably professes it is the home that matters most; in his actual behavior, however, he is essentially subject to the will of his employer. As long as he can leave the affairs of the household up to his wife, a Japanese man puts his work first. At least for men employed in business and industry, the home is important because it is their only place to rest and rejuvenate energies depleted by long hours of work and work-related activities. They therefore lay little or no claim to control or power in the home, as long as it fulfills their needs as a refuge. Women, meanwhile, do not share home management with other members of the family, nor do they make much effort to do so. While some men who are home enough hours of the day to help with housework do contribute, the majority cannot, as the story of Noda Akiko demonstrated. Children may be given certain regular chores, but for the core jobs of cooking, laundry, and cleaning, family members depend entirely on the housewife; this makes a woman virtually indispensable to the survival of other family members. Housework itself has become much lighter due to the availability of household conveniences, but women continue to excuse husbands and children from participating in home management, thereby preserving certain prerogatives for themselves as the one who satisfies daily needs.

Third, the home is the woman's territory. Women design the home to their own tastes and exercise full control there. Urban housing is very cramped, and storage space is minimal. Usually, the housewife is the only member of the family who knows where things are kept. She organizes the household and dictates the way it runs. If she is efficient, she often has considerable time left over after she completes the household chores. She knows that as long as the basic housework is done and the children are taken care of, her husband will not be much concerned about how she spends her free time. Her freedom as well as economic stability are therefore guaranteed. A housewife is nevertheless careful to maintain an equitable balance of performance in relation to her husband, who shoulders full responsibility for earning the family income, making sure that her contribution to the family in other forms does not fall short. Knowing that income alone does not make a family, women consider what they do to be just as or more important than what the breadwinner does.

Fourth, a housewife has the option to augment personal and family income by working part-time or even full-time outside the home. If she works full-time, in addition to managing the home, she may have to cut corners in her housework and may not perform 100 percent in her job, but by performing 70 or 80 percent of both roles she reaps a total reward that exceeds the benefits of only one role (she would not even try to perform 100 percent in both roles, as an American woman might). Japanese women place their performance aims deliberately low (at 60 to 70 percent of the ideal), and this makes it possible for them to achieve a sense of satisfaction and even the admiration of others, which would be impossible if they tried to aim for 100 percent.

In Japan the basic assumption behind marriage is the creation and nurture or support of a family, a project to which both spouses contribute a great deal. The traditional pattern, not much changed today, is for the man to be the breadwinner (or "rice winner") and the woman the homemaker. Some women do have the option of seizing the breadwinner role for themselves, but if a woman devotes herself entirely to outside work, she can no longer make her contribution to the household in other ways. And unless she has special skills, her earning power may remain low. If she both maintains the household *and* works, she can contribute in the financial realm as well as in her role as homemaker, and earn the right to do something extra for herself from time to time.

Someone has to do the housework, Japanese women figure, and it does not have to be drudgery. Housework can be a great way to relieve stress, especially that accumulated in the workplace.[11] In the United States when women began to work, household work was drastically devalued and women began to consider it a waste of time. Family tensions and difficulties emerged because there was apparently little or no discussion of who would do these still very necessary tasks. Once housework was devalued instead of regarded in a positive light, men could not realistically be expected to want to share in it or to approach it with alacrity. At least in Japan, household work has not been devalued; those who enjoy it are not looked down on, thus leaving open to both men and women the option of devoting time to housework.

In a way, the American women's liberation movement seems a misnomer: Women may have been liberated from the household, but the vaunted career woman seems chained to her professional pursuits and her options have narrowed instead of expanded.

Today the lives of urban male employees can be quite drab. They work regular hours (usually nine to five) at least five days a week, plus overtime, to complete the heavy workloads imposed by inadequate staffing and the pressures of corporate competition, and must also engage in after-work socializing, all of which keeps them away from the home or from any other sort of pursuit not connected with work. Watching their menfolk over the decades, wives see how much of the joy and richness of life can be lost by becoming preoccupied by only one sphere of work; they see the risks and the distortions of the single-occupation life. When faced with difficulty or disappointment, men in the corporate employee rut may feel there is nowhere to turn, and they have no alternative form of fulfillment from which to seek consolation or psychological relief. A failure or disruption in expected patterns can cause intolerable isolation. Women, on the other hand, with their diverse social networks based on family, sports, recreation, and, often, work are assured of moral support from one direction or another. This is one reason women do not necessarily aspire to be like men and do not envy men's lives.

Profound changes have taken place in the functions and significance of the family in postwar Japan and, in turn, in the roles of both women and men. Nuclear families have become much more private and self-contained in some respects; interdependence and the resultant psychological bonds among family members have weakened, leading to a greater reliance on social institutions (for education, child care, care of the elderly). Many women are still in the process of redefining their roles in the family and therefore have mixed feelings about the changes in which they are caught up. They certainly welcome the lessening of household burdens but realize, at the same time, that their position as the pivotal member of the family may be weakened. Keeping the family stable and its bonds strong is one way women can continue to enjoy both power and freedom.

The changes in the family (including the stronger status of women, women working outside the home, absence of the father) are often exaggerated by the mass media as constituting a crisis or foreshadowing the breakdown of the family. Still dominated by male-centered thinking, the media invariably associates the causes of these changes with the changing attitudes and lifestyles of women. Women themselves, on the other hand, do not feel that what is happening is anything like a crisis. It is simply, they are convinced, the product of men's inability to recognize fully the changes that women have undergone and to respond to those changes in a constructive way.

PURSE STRINGS AND POWER IN THE HOME

The fact that Japanese women hold the purse strings of the household and manage the home with great freedom and autonomy is a major factor in the continued pride they take in the home and in the profession of housewife. If they did not hold the purse strings, their freedom and autonomy would be extremely limited and husbands would have far more control over their activities. This household power has given Japanese women tremendous psychological freedom, which American women perhaps never had. Without it, the Japanese women's liberation movement would probably have been much more active. I like to compare the Japanese housewife to the pivot of a folding fan. She serves as the fulcrum upon which the rest of the family—like the leaves of the fan—can expand, functioning smoothly and happily yet united at the pivot she provides.

The quite strong position in the home Japanese women enjoy

has a long tradition. During the long centuries of Japan's agrarian history (until a little more than 100 years ago, 80 percent of the population lived on farms), the housewife was responsible for the distribution of food to every mouth in the often-large farming family and for assuring that the entire family could survive until the next harvest. Women tended to be thrifty while men could not be counted on not to spend money extravagantly on food, sake, women, and other temptations. Invested with this heavy responsibility, women had to be prepared for any eventuality, especially a poor harvest. They learned to scrimp and save, putting away extra for emergencies and bad times. These traditions have been retained throughout Japan's industrialization period, and women are still responsible for handling family finances and food. Their propensity for saving and frugality also continues. Husbands still turn over their salaries intact to their wives, and wives dispense them a monthly allowance. If a man's salary is not sufficient, it is the wife's responsibility to manage, making up the necessary amount with earnings of her own or by borrowing money, cutting down on expenses, pawning her personal valuables, or doing whatever else she can think of. In the days when women could not easily find work, this custom imposed great hardships on poor women, forcing them to make all kinds of sacrifices, from which women today are, fortunately, exempt.

Women save money regularly in household accounts, insurance plans, and so on, but they also know the wisdom of secret accounts, the famous *hesokuri* (belly button savings, a term that comes from the custom of keeping funds in the sash of a kimono, next to one's belly), which are put away for those times when extra funds are urgently needed. In modern times, wives can save in their husband's name or their own and can disburse those savings at their own discretion as long as the household account is balanced.

Among the younger generations, no less than the older, the wife takes over family finances after children are born. Husbands often refer to their wives as the "household minister of finance *[uchi no Ōkura Daijin]*." If they need extra spending money or want to buy one of the children a costly plaything, they must consult the exchequer. The fact that the husband is the one bringing home the money is superseded by his wife's control of the purse strings. And if a wife contributes income of her own, her power in the household is even more stable than when it depended only on income earned by her husband. Her confidence and insistence on enjoying certain freedoms within the marriage is further strengthened by this independent income.[12] However, a kind of threshold may be reached beyond which increased income does not correspond to greater freedom and autonomy for the wife; beyond that income level a wife may enjoy less freedom because the household may come to rely on her contribution or because her husband may become more interested in her activities as a result.

Japanese women enjoy more economic independence than meets the eye. If they need a new appliance, they shop for it on their own; if they want a new dress, they consult their fund for extras, not their husband. These freedoms mitigate their often subservient, inferior status in Japanese society. Although the battle for economic independence for women in the United States has been overt and often bitter, Japanese women have exercised great autonomy in this realm for a long time. No doubt this unheralded realm of power and freedom has been an element that has kept the women's movement dormant in Japan.

The VSR Survey reflected this vast difference in the roles women (of all ages) play in handling family finances in Japan and the United States. American women's responsibilities are primarily limited to handling daily expenditures, such as shopping, and paying utility bills and rent. Their Japanese counterparts handle almost every aspect of family finances, including setting up and maintaining the household budget (true of 70 percent of Japanese women in the VSR Survey vs. 23 percent of American women) and overall financial planning (Japanese, 46 percent; American, 20 percent), both of which are done jointly more often than by women alone in the United States. When it comes to buying property in Japan, the final decision is made either by the husband alone or the couple together, not the wife alone. But decisions regarding once-in-a-lifetime purchases of this sort do not much affect the sense of power women have over family finances.

Japanese women are now earning substantial incomes, but, as noted earlier, the majority of working women do not contribute monthly to the household budget. The amount of money a working woman has free access to per month is about ¥85,000 ($650.00) while that for a working husband is about ¥52,800 ($406.00). As long as their husband's earnings are sufficient to cover the bulk of household expenses, many women tuck away their income for other purposes. This is also true for younger women with children. (In young double-income households the couple contribute equally to household accounts.) Their contribution is most often used to support fees for tutoring or extra study classes for the children, luxuries (e.g., trips, special foods), and other expenses that are visible enough to be appreciated by the family. Nevertheless, husbands do not demand that their wives make an equal contribution to the regular budget. In the past the reason for this was that it maintained the man's superior status as the sole breadwinner and assured that wife and children would be duly grateful and respectful.

There was a time not long ago when men received their monthly salaries in cash. On payday they would return home directly and proudly hand over the precious envelope to their wives. The wife would await her spouse's return with a specially prepared meal and would receive the envelope in front of the children, lifting it gratefully to her forehead in the time-honored custom and thanking him for his hard labors. When computer networks facilitated banking by electronic tellers, this custom soon became a thing of the past. Salaries are now transferred directly into household bank accounts, from which housewives withdraw cash or remit payments for rent and utilities by electronic transfer. The children do not see much of their father, much less the fact that he is making money; they see their mother withdrawing money, paying the bills, worrying how to make ends meet, and earning enough herself (often in jobs at home or near home) to treat them to luxuries that were impossible when there was only one source of income. The children become keenly aware of their mother's economic power, while the father and his economic power are distant and out of touch.

The significance of the changes brought about by electronic banking should not be underestimated. They are undermining the status of fathers and their authority within the family without any compensating change in the awareness and behavior of fathers themselves. Without being aware of it, these men become virtual outsiders in their own households. Only a few Japanese men are recognizing what is happening and making an effort to expand their role within the family on an everyday basis.

GOOD HUSBANDS ARE HEALTHY AND ABSENT

Although the male tendency to share little with their wives is a problem, men are not wholly to blame for the lack of communication in the home. Women are at least partly responsible for the reluctance of men to share in household affairs.

When first married, a Japanese woman of the first postwar generation (and the same is true for many younger women, too) is often lured into the habit of lavishing care on her husband by playing the role of the traditional ideal wife (the *sewa nyōbo*, who was famous for helping her husband dress and undress, handing him his underwear as he emerged from his bath, serving him tea as he stretched out his hand toward the table, making exquisite and delectable box lunches for him to take to work, and so on) and, before the novelty wears off, of devoting herself with great zeal to keeping a tidy and attractive home. With new furniture, new dishware, and shiny pots and pans, housework does indeed seem more enjoyable than it was back in her mother's home where everything was old, worn, and all too familiar.

The small, often brand-new apartments newlyweds move into, moreover, are relatively easy to care for, the seeming epitome of the "home sweet home" a bride dreams of. In these surroundings a young woman can easily become absorbed in a kind of "play house–keeping" and may come to deem any and all devotions to her husband a pleasure, regardless of the burden they impose. Young women's memories are imprinted with the efforts of their mothers to be of service to their fathers; that was the way the older generation of women found meaning in life. Then, too, there are the "maternal instincts" of these young women (also nurtured by their particular upbringing), which cause them almost compulsively to lavish care where it will be received. The domestically helpless husband—and some women do call their husbands "my big baby" or "eldest son"—is a prime target for such care. Japanese women give greater priority to their role as mother than to that as wife, but in fact the two overlap considerably.

A young husband, meanwhile, who long relied on the services

of his mother (perhaps with the exception of an animal-like existence while in college) very quickly learns to appreciate and depend on these wifely services, shifting adeptly from the indulged son to the indulged husband. Pretty soon he expects his wife to do all the domestic tasks and attend to all his needs; the sweet nectar of being tended hand and foot can be addictive.

Even today, under the total care of doting mothers, many young men have no opportunity to gain domestic skills. In households where the income of the mother is relatively large (equivalent to 60 percent or more of the father's), however, children have begun to help with the housework, so it is likely that the generation of men maturing in the 1990s will have better domestic instincts and skills than their fathers.[13] Some men of the younger postwar generation occasionally share in other tasks of homemaking, but their energy and interest flag quickly; in any case, they are not home much to help, as in the case of Akiko's husband. Japanese women, who are more practical than concerned with principles, find it easier and faster simply to do all the housework alone than to appeal to frequently absent, reluctant, and often clumsy husbands.

In Japan today, the traditional pattern whereby the wife alone does all the household chores is still quite widely supported, particularly by older and less educated women. A larger proportion of women in the generation that entered adulthood in the 1980s are of the opinion that husbands should share the housework; those who are married with infants and children under 6 are most adamant (65 percent) in their belief that a husband should help, since they have their hands full already. Yet, surprisingly, 45 percent of working women remain of the opinion that women *alone* should do the housework.[14] Behind this, perhaps, is the fact that their income is still much smaller than that of their husband, whose salary pays for most of the household bills.

Women still want to keep the home a place that they can control and manage to their pleasure, and husbands, taking advantage of this persistent female impulse, gladly and with clear conscience leave as much as they can to their wives. (That they are therefore depriving themselves of independence does not seem important to them.) For the first postwar generation 90 percent of household chores are therefore performed by women, regardless of whether they work or not.[15]

In the days when women's legal status was very weak and they could be easily divorced, one way they protected themselves was to ensure that their husbands could not lead healthy, decent lives without them. Japanese women of the first postwar generation, while outwardly demanding more communication and sharing, inwardly seem to strive to maintain separate territories of activity for themselves and their husbands just like the older generations (although for women the home is only one of their spheres of activity); they prefer complementarity to sharing, both inside and outside the home, because of the considerable psychological as well as physical autonomy and freedom it assures them. This proclivity is only strengthened by the fact that most company-employed husbands have to devote so much of their time and energy to their company and work-related activities, including social engagements or weekend golf with colleagues or clients.

When the domestically helpless husband is at home, the wife must be there to provide his meals, do his laundry, and otherwise attend to him, chores that can consume all her time and energy. As long as he is absent, a woman can dispense with the household chores quickly and use the remaining time as she likes—pursuing hobbies, volunteer work, long telephone chats with friends, and so on. She can invite her friends in or go out, and she can work as she pleases either at home or outside during the long hours when her husband is regularly and predictably absent. Her daily schedule is up to her alone. As long as the house is in order, expected meals are on the table, and his wife is at home when he needs her, a husband does not pry into what she does otherwise. Among women 50 and older (whose husbands are typically of this type and who therefore enjoy such freedom and autonomy) the common expression is, "A good husband is healthy and absent [Teishu wa genki de rusu ga ii]." The husbands of women of the first postwar generation, who are somewhat more cooperative, can be counted on to contribute in a new way: by getting them to look after the children while wives go out on weekends and in the evenings (Teishu wa genki de rusuban ga ii).

Women are skilled at building full lives of their own, which are adjusted to fit in with their duties in the home and toward the children but are otherwise free and independent. They may complain that their husband is not at home much (and that when he is, he lapses into utter inactivity and passivity), but they are openly pleased if they know he is to go away on a business trip. Thus, instead of welcoming more holidays, 70 percent of first postwar generation and older women were unhappy about the decrease in working hours and the shortening of the workweek.[16] Five reasons were given for their reservations and apprehensions about such a policy: their housework will increase, they cannot relax, they have to cook more full meals, caring for husbands takes time, and a husband's presence imposes various burdens (*wazurawashii koto*).

Japanese women, especially those of the first postwar generation, obviously enjoy great autonomy and freedom as well as economic prerogatives, a far cry from the stereotype prevailing abroad that continues to portray them as exploited and unenlightened. American friends, including Betty Friedan in a public speech given in Tokyo in 1980, have commented with sympathy on how Japanese women must feel being left at home with children all the time while their husbands go out to dinner parties and other entertainments.[17] In the American social milieu this is quite natural: People expect spouses to be invited to workplace-centered social gatherings, and both spouses may be annoyed if invitations exclude them—but it is dangerous to judge other cultures by the standards of one's own. In Japan spouses are not thus automatically included in such invitations.

For their part, Japanese women with children, especially those of the first postwar generation, are neither envious of the menfolk's activities nor anxious to attend parties or other recreational events with them. Interviews with women consistently reveal that, except for those who are tied down constantly by small children and totally deprived of other chances to get out of the house, Japanese women are perfectly content to be overlooked.

If a woman of the first postwar or older generation is invited to attend a function with her husband, her reaction is likely to go something like this: I have to go get my hair done (it costs money). What in the world will I wear (she may feel that everything she has is not quite right, maybe even out of fashion)? I have to be on my best behavior in front of my husband's colleagues and make a good impression on his superiors (very humiliating to a woman of pride who feels that having to be ingratiating with people she does not instinctively like is degrading and can be left to professionals like bar hostesses or geisha and that the occasion will be very tense). Whatever will I talk about? Furthermore, going downtown at night is exhausting (although she is always ready to go to the department stores there during the day), and (if the children are small) someone must be found to watch the children. All in all, the whole idea is *mendokusai* (too much trouble). Women want to go out but prefer their own friends, with whom they can relax and enjoy themselves; it is their pleasure to treat themselves (or their children) at a restaurant of their own choice. After their usually busy days, women are just as happy to spend the evening watching their favorite television programs or reading.

The younger generation (born after 1960) is gradually breaking away from this pattern. The increase of marriages based on friendship among women in their mid-twenties has led to more frequent inclusion of spouses on social occasions, such as the now-stylish "home parties."

As noted earlier, young women with small children living in small apartments in the cities are the ones who most want their husbands to be home to share housework and child care. A husband who needs constant attention is not welcome at home. In households where wives cannot work because they are tied down by small children, money for pleasures and luxuries is scant, and these young mothers often feel cut off and left out. They eagerly await the day when their children can go to day care or kindergarten and time to use freely will again be theirs. Ironically, the years of managing the home alone help Japanese women cultivate a resilient emotional independence and inner strength.

WOMEN AT THE HELM

In sharp contrast to their mothers, the first postwar generation and their younger sisters (born after 1946) are far more actively in charge of their own lives as far as marriage is concerned. Benefiting from better education, greater affluence, and demographic factors, they take a more active and thoughtful role in choosing or not choosing a spouse. More mature when they marry, they consider more thoughtfully the kind of household they want and what roles in choosing or not choosing a spouse. More mature when they marry, they consider more thoughtfully the kind of household they want and what roles they want to play. They can no longer be described as passive and submissive. If they marry, they may take a relatively laissez-faire approach to their husband's attitudes and lifestyle, garnering quite a large measure of freedom and autonomy. Meanwhile, the gradually eroding status of marriage as an institution is among the causes of a radically decreased birthrate and the vigorous advance of women into the labor force.

4

COMMUNICATION AND CRISIS

The norms of marriage and family life typically observed among women of the first postwar generation in Japan presented in the previous chapter can be summarized as follows: (1) couples hold a pragmatic, nonromantic view of married life; (2) emotional distance exists between the partners; (3) there is limited sharing; the wife's domestic role is unchallenged and the role of the husband in the home is marginal. These features possess the potential for great flexibility in a marriage—as well as for crisis and potential breakup. On the one hand, if it were not for these characteristics, the large number of "commuting marriages" successfully maintained by Japanese couples today would be impossible; on the other hand, these very characteristics—limited sharing, too much autonomy, and too little communication—are responsible for the rising divorce rate. The traditional forms of communication between men and women in marriage have produced both admirable strengths and serious weaknesses. In this chapter, we will look at how the Japanese marriage can allow for prolonged separation without rupture as well as the ways in which it is vulnerable at a time when female identity and attitudes are rapidly changing. New forms of behavior and new roles for men and women present difficult challenges to the institutions of marriage and the family. Some couples surmount the obstacles; others are plunged into crisis.

94

RAREFIED RELATIONSHIPS

Although the ideal image of marriage is of a couple who get along with such smoothness that their relationship is described as "like air" (as noted in Chapter 3), sometimes the air can be so rarefied that it becomes difficult to breathe. Many couples have minimal communication problems despite the reliance on tacit understanding, but among younger couples some partners, especially women, wish for more communication with their spouse. The women of the first postwar generation are not completely resigned to this situation. When they try to converse, they often find themselves up against a stone wall. Older women in their fifties and upward are resigned, as revealed in letters published in the *Asahi Shimbun*,[1] a mass-circulation national newspaper:

> On weekends, my husband and I drive to a sports club, two hours going and coming. I gaze out at the beautiful blue ocean and the scenery we pass with delight, exclaiming how splendid it is—to myself. I have learned not to try to engage my husband in conversation over such things as I am sure only to receive a thorny response. After some twenty years of marriage, we happened to join the same sports club and so we started driving together. Now I feel even more isolated from him than before joining the club because of these hours I have to spend with him without being able to communicate what I am thinking. (Housewife, aged 52)

In response, another woman in her fifties wrote of her own experience:

> I share the feelings of the woman who wrote about her silent two-hour ride with her husband. I am sure there are many women who feel just the way she does. If I say to my husband, just for the sake of conversation, "Sure is cold today, isn't it?" he is sure to snap back that "It's winter; it ought to be cold." If I say, "I would like to go on a trip with my friend, so-and-so," his response will be an indifferent "Do as you please." I have long since given up expecting thoughtful or gentle replies from him. Whenever I feel like vocalizing my thoughts, I sing a song or talk to the flowers or the sky. I am told that personalities never change. It is hopeless to try to appeal to your husband. I suggest that you simply disregard

him. Your husband may be satisfied simply to be by your side. (Housewife, aged 59)

Neither of these women mention anything about leaving their husbands or asking for a divorce. They make no attempt to change their husband or the situation but instead try to accommodate themselves, creating a situation common in Japan: the *kateinai rikon* or "divorce within the household." The last line in the second letter is an example of the way Japanese women try to see the positive side of an unsatisfactory situation—a typically practical Japanese way of dealing with the complexities of life.

Members of the first postwar generation, though passive, are not ready to give in so easily. Their feelings are expressed in the following two letters:

Why have things come to such a pass? It makes me so sad. When my husband and I were dating, he would *say* he was glad when he was glad; he would talk to *me*. I wish my husband would look at me now when he talks to me, instead of averting his gaze, and not call me with the domineering "Oi [Hey]!" After I go and look after his mother, he could give me maybe one word of thanks? I am tired of guessing from his expression that he is grateful. And why does he act so grumpy when we are alone? He demands, "Tea!" and I reply, "I'll bring it in a minute." But then he insists, "Why don't you have it ready the minute I sit down?" Then, if I do serve him immediately, he doesn't say a word in thanks. I just wish he would say once, "I love you." I never heard him say that, not even once. I want to hear him say so before I die. Otherwise, I feel as if I am already 200 years old. (Housewife, aged 37)

This letter shows how the changes Japanese women are experiencing in themselves are producing frustration in their relationships with their husband, but it also shows that they are still unwilling to take an aggressive approach (such as obtaining a divorce) to solving the problems from which their dissatisfaction stems and that they are as anxious as ever about threatening their marriage and will not squarely confront their husband with their most urgent needs. Another woman expresses the growing isolation younger women feel.

In the days when the entire family was engaged in production and thus shared a common goal, family members shared the joys and the agonies, and everybody's dreams, hopes, and values were the same. But today, everything's different. The husband is away and preoccupied at the company and has no leeway to listen to his wife when she wants to discuss with him matters of household business.

Many wives are afraid of what will happen when the children grow up and they are left alone with nothing to talk about in the company of their husbands. Many others submissively play the role of the obedient wife but complain constantly about their husbands behind their backs. True, men have their work outside the family and don't have the time to think about their families. I feel really frustrated, vacillating between a sense that everything will work out all right in the end and despair that there is nothing I can do. If my husband thinks his wife can fix up everything by herself, I want him to know that the burden is too much for her to bear. (Housewife, aged 39)

This generation of women, who were brought up to believe in sexual equality, are relatively more active in searching for a solution to their problems and in demanding a response from their husband rather than quietly retreating into the traditional shell of womanly stoicism and passivity of the older generation. These letters suggest that the authors are on the verge of taking active steps to resolve their frustration.

The typical Japanese husband's habit of showing little explicit sign of his concern for his wife's happiness or well-being can be very frustrating for women, and this apparent unwillingness to express feelings is often carried into the workplace. According to a recent study I conducted of white-collar American women working for Japanese corporations in New York, one of the problems for these women is that they do not receive enough feedback (negative or positive) from their Japanese managers (all male) or any words of appreciation for favors done or services rendered.[2] The same may well be true for the male employees who work under these managers. While the managers do suffer somewhat from the language barrier, they do not seem to be aware, simply because such feedback is not needed in the Japanese workplace, of how this lack of what their American employees consider common etiquette contributes daily to their growing frustration. They apparently expect their employees to serve them on the job without any words of recognition or thanks. As more businesses become internationalized and frictions grow, Japanese men will no doubt find themselves required to change in many ways.

MARRIAGE AND THE MASCULINE MYSTIQUE

According to the Japanese traditional ideal, the most manly of men was a man of few words, one who did not reveal personal weakness by complaints or lay bare his innermost thoughts and feelings, least of all to his wife. Why do men not see the need to talk with their wives?

First of all, part of the Japanese ethos is the belief that the closer the relationship between two persons, the greater the expectation that understanding without recourse to words will be possible. Kazuo, for example, never proposed to Akiko in so many words; Akiko just knew that she had been proposed to. A husband and wife in Japan are expected to develop a relationship known as *isshin dōtai* (one heart, one body). A couple that does enjoy this kind of relationship manages with relatively less overt communication—and is by no means unique to Japan.

There is an unspoken belief among Japanese in general that putting deep feelings into words somehow lowers or spoils their value and that understanding attained without words is more precious than that attained through precise articulation. Interpersonal communication is based on a great deal of guessing and reading between the lines. In a culture where directness can seem ugly and repulsive, being able to guess the feelings of another and correctly grasp what she or he wishes to say without verbal expression is considered a sign of closeness between two persons. Therefore, between husband and wife, supposedly the most intimate relationship, verbal communication is thought to be unnecessary for the things that count most.

Television dramas aside, few Japanese tell the people most dear to them that they love them in so many words. The expectation of complete tacit understanding works to discourage the verbal expression of deep or important feelings. If a Japanese woman were to get up the courage to ask her spouse if he loved her, he would become profoundly embarrassed because saying so would seem to him to spoil the tenderness of his feeling; if so confronted, he would bluster: *"Iwanakutemo wakaru deshō* [You know even if I don't say it, don't you]!" When a Japanese man is forced to be explicit about his feelings or opinions with a person ordinarily expected to know them without asking, he is apt to become annoyed and demand, *"Sonna koto made iwaseru no ka* [Do I have to go *that* far in explaining]?"

Of course, thorough tacit understanding can be genuine and beautiful. It can also be an illusion. Sometimes a husband and wife may think they are in perfect accord when in fact they are not. Husbands are accustomed to expecting their wives to know what they want to say without having to say it in so many words. But women have been changing. Women now think that that sort of tacit understanding ought to go both ways and that their husband should make more effort to be perceptive in return. So far, few men are ready to respond to that expectation.

This cultural climate of interpersonal communication does not encourage people to hone their skills at verbal expression. Some outside observers as described in a book by Ogura Kazuo, call Japanese culture a "culture of no words (*mugon no bunka*),"[3] but this too (like the Bushidō tradition and the cult of efficiency first) may be a product of the masculine norms that have dominated the culture. Japanese women, like those anywhere, tend to be the more garrulous (both the Chinese and Japanese character meaning "noisy" or "talkative" is composed of three parts, three small characters meaning "woman"). But men were traditionally aloof and silent; it was acceptable to be unresponsive to a wife's talk, sometimes even shutting her chatter off with a gruff *"Urusai na* [What a noise]!" In marriages between Japanese men and American women this sort of behavior is often the root of serious frustration on the part of the wife, and there are frequent cases where it leads to crisis between the couple.

A Japanese man, especially one of the older generation, usually does not discuss his work much with his wife, except perhaps unimportant tidbits of gossip, as there is a deep-rooted belief that women and children (*onna kodomo*, long considered one category) cannot possibly understand the complexities of a man's world. If a man feels unhappy or frustrated about work or colleagues, he stops at a pub, bar, or even a temporary street stall (*yatai*) and pours out his woes to the bartender, hostess, or stall keeper before returning home. Men tend to forget that women today are better educated and more experienced (many wives have had work experience) than in the past and are fully capable of understanding the complexities of the "man's world." Since

women, especially those with a college education equivalent to
that of men, consider themselves the intellectual equals of men,
they find it frustrating to be thus dismissed as confidantes.
Lacking rapport with their spouses, women avoid feeling isolated
and lonely by channeling their energy into communication with
children and friends.

Men regard the home as a place to rest and recuperate, a refuge
where they can enjoy the luxury of not doing anything they do
not want to do. They do not feel any compulsion to make an
active contribution to the functioning or activities of the household or to the disciplining or education of the children. Activities
as strenuous as playing with the children or taking the family out
to dinner at a restaurant, known in the man's world as "family
service [*katei sābisu*]," they consider extra effort. They are not
much concerned about the physical condition of their home as
long as there is space and quiet enough to sprawl on the tatami or
couch with the newspaper or to watch the baseball game on
television. They also expect to receive the further comforts of
being served tea or beer and snacks without having to ask.[4]

The number of husbands who help with housework and care
of children has increased, but they still remain a minority. The
contrast with the contemporary American male is striking. Even
the most recent crop of Japanese men has not acquired much
domestic aptitude; it remains to their wives, even if they are
employed as well, to hang out the futon to air, do the laundry,
pick up after the children, do the shopping, fix the meals and
snacks, and so on.

The Japanese male has a far easier time in the family than his
American counterpart. Discussing problems of the household
(such as the education or discipline of the children, or the
handling of daily problems) he also considers beyond the bounds
of duty, preferring in his exhaustion from overwork and daily
commuting just to leave these matters up to his wife's best
judgment. Men say that they do not want to be bothered by
household matters and that they trust their wife's judgment, little
realizing the serious gap that such an attitude creates between
them and their families. They seem hardly aware that this
attitude has made their wives very independent and that it is
slowly undermining their own place and position in the home.

Indeed, a serious gap has existed for a long time in the average
Japanese family,[5] and it is becoming more obvious that men are

not aware that women today have developed a totally new outlook on life. Even if men are aware of the changes, they are not ready to respond to women's strong need to communicate, as substantiated by the data compiled by the VSR Survey. A large proportion of Japanese women think that "being able to talk together about your feelings" is very important for a good marriage, but men do not consider communication between husband and wife to be quite as important. Yet men do seem to sense women's dissatisfaction; when questioned about six aspects of their relationship with their spouse that they would like to improve (1. financial rewards; 2. childrearing practices; 3. communication; 4. sex life; 5. burden of household chores; and 6. length of time spent together), the largest proportion of subjects (and somewhat more men—38 percent—than women—32 percent) mentioned communication.

Such men, however, remain the minority; the majority do not even realize that communication needs to be improved. Many still labor under the illusion that husband and wife can fully understand each other without verbal communication. Although the world we live in has become too complex to understand without verbalizing, the thinking of some men is still shaped by the traditional idea that women are intellectually inferior to men and therefore not capable of meaningful and serious thought or discussion.

Until men are raised who do not believe that communication is unmanly, what recourse do women have? Basically, there are two outlets for their frustration: (1) their network of women friends and relatives and (2) their children (to be discussed in Chapter 5). Women have ample opportunity to satisfy their needs to communicate and do so at least as much as men do among themselves; these avenues include ladies' choral groups or volleyball clubs; lessons in tea ceremony, flower arranging, and other arts; and classes at continuing education centers. Women nowadays even go out to bars or taverns together, something they never did in the past.

When husband and wife do find themselves alone together, the main topics they feel comfortable talking about are matters involving their children or mutual friends and acquaintances. The issue of children's education is the most common source of disagreement between husband and wife.[6] This reflects not only the importance of children to Japanese couples but also the fact that they are one of the few matters of their common interest and concern. But even when communication centers around the topic of the children, it generally consists of an almost one-sided report by the wife. The typical scene is of the husband relaxing at home after work by reading the newspaper or watching television. While he feigns concentration on what he is doing, his wife tells her story. He briefly acknowledges her remarks and, if he hears something that displeases him, is quick to criticize, reproach, or blame her for bad judgment. He rarely listens attentively or offers advice or support, simply grunting assent or approval. Thus, there is not much conversation in the true sense, not much equal or forthright exchange of views.

COMMUTING MARRIAGES

In today's Japan during any one year, one in every three male company employees, or some 175,000, is living apart from his family because he has been transferred (for stints of from one to three or more years) to a distant branch of his office.[7] Because such transfers are often short-term and return to the home office is assured, many of these men opt for *tanshin funin* (i.e., the option of moving temporarily to their new post alone, leaving their families behind). With children in school and, often, elderly parents to be taken care of, the logistics of moving an entire household for a two- or three-year stint in a city out of daily commuting distance can sometimes be more of a burden than sticking out a period of family separation.

The most frequent reason a husband may opt to relocate alone, no matter how much he dislikes the idea, is his children's education, especially if his children have gained admittance to a private school. Relocation to a different city would remove them from the advantages of such a school and the track it paves to a position among the elite of society. Uprooting children in school can impair their achievement or bring on adjustment problems that are likely to interfere with their performance in the entrance examinations they must take to get into good schools.

The second most frequent reason is reluctance to give up a family home. If the family owns their own home, they are reluctant to close it up or rent it out for the duration of the posting. Caring for elderly or bedridden parents may be another reason prohibiting the family from easily moving to another part of the country. Seldom does the matter of the work or career of the wife enter the picture. Women are generally against having their husbands posted elsewhere; the prospect of being left literally with all the responsibility for family affairs is one thing, but they are also concerned for the husband, who must shift for himself in a strange place despite his lack of domestic skills and general indifference to looking after his personal health. A study by Iwao, Saitō, and Fukutomi of 216 cases of husband-alone transfers conducted in 1989 found that 70 percent of wives hoped, upon first learning of the transfer, that their husband would go alone, although they were greatly concerned about their husband's health.[8] The reluctance of the wives to relocate is understandable, considering the autonomy they have established in their lives and the networks in the community they have built up over the years. Moving to a different city every so many years would mean discontinuing activities, including work, and abandoning community and other social contacts, which must be cultivated through considerable effort in Japan. The emotional satisfaction and daily interaction with their husbands may not be sufficient to compensate wives for the greater comforts they receive in the social circles they have painstakingly cultivated in their own community. Furthermore, Japanese women consider marriage a long-term commitment based on trust and do not think that a temporary separation will threaten that commitment.

Whatever the reasons men use in deciding to relocate alone, the study showed that they are compelling enough that the decision does not take much time. Some husbands even decide without consulting their wives. Twenty percent of the sample in the study had been living away from their families for more than three years (and a few had been away as long as seven years). Families keep in touch by telephone, and some even find that the distance actually promotes more closeness. In nightly or frequent intercity calls, husbands can sometimes achieve better communication with their wives than when they come home exhausted every night and depart early every morning from the same abode. They experience for themselves something of the feeling wives and children have when the father is away from the home most of the time. Returning home once or twice a month for weekends, a husband's time with his wife and family can sometimes be qualitatively better than when he is ostensibly living at home but absent so many of his waking hours.

In some cases, relocation of the husband gives the couple an opportunity to see each other more objectively and appreciate each other more; in others, the husband finds that upon returning from a distant posting he feels estranged from his family, whose members have developed an extra measure of closeness in his absence. Men who experience separation from their families because of work transfers express greater appreciation for their wife's contribution than those who have not had such an experience.

Now that women with careers of their own are beginning to work internationally, we can expect to see the gradual increase of wives as well as husbands in commuting marriages, especially in the younger generations. In one case covered in the above mentioned study, the wife (age 29) was posted to Singapore by her bank employer at the same time her husband (age 31) was posted to the Philippines by the large trading firm for which he works. Married only recently, the two began with this situation as part of their lives and have yet to live together on a regular basis. They meet once a month for weekends and call each other almost every day. The wife is now pregnant and plans to join her husband when her maternity and child care leave begins. She has not decided what to do after her leave period is over. She wrote that the big adjustment for them may be in actually living together, although she is not of the opinion that a married couple has to live together.

This kind of couple is still a novelty, however, for the general climate of opinion in Japanese society does not support women moving out of the home for a work transfer, as it does such a move by husbands. No matter how attractive an offer his wife might receive to transfer elsewhere, a man would never think of quitting his job to move with her. It would be far too great a blow to his pride, not to mention his career. The earlier cited VSR Survey scrutinized this very issue, and the results highlight the differences in husband–wife relationships in Japan and the United States: In response to a question asking what a husband should do if his wife is offered a very good job in another city, nearly 30 percent of American men and women said the husband should quit his job and move with her, but over 30 percent of Japanese men and women supported the wife relocating alone to the new job.[9] The American responses indicate the fundamental belief, shared equally by both sexes, that a married couple should, above all, live together, a belief that would seem to conflict with their belief that both husband and wife should be free to develop independent careers. The kind of commuting marriages that have become common in Japan offer one resolution to American career-oriented couples—if they can accept a lesser degree of emphasis on sharing, extended celibacy, and more emphasis on a long-term trusting relationship.

In households where fathers are often absent, regardless of age, Japanese women function in the roles of both mother and father, assuming both so-called masculine and feminine roles in the family. The same sort of adaptability is beginning to develop among men who take job transfers alone as well. In Japan today both men and women, perhaps not as the result of conscious choice but in response to current circumstances, are gradually being nudged away from traditional male and female behavior and toward androgynous, flexible, and situationally adaptable behavior and roles.

VIRGINITY AND SEXUAL FIDELITY

Japanese women today, for all their freedom and autonomy, want above all to have the companionship and caring of their spouses, but with husbands largely away and increasingly alienated from the home and from caring relationships with their wives, it is not surprising that the frequency of extramarital relationships has increased. Once, the guarantee of economic security was enough to assure wifely obedience and fidelity, but today women are more independent both economically and psychologically.

Surveys on conditions respondents give for a good marriage show that Japanese do not consider sexual fidelity or the maintaining of a good sexual relationship with their spouse to be of critical importance. In the prewar period there was a clear-cut and mutually accepted double standard regarding sexual norms binding men and women. Women were expected to be virgins upon marriage. Divorced women therefore found it very difficult to remarry; they were known as *"kizumono* (damaged)." Virginity was never a requirement for men. On the contrary, men who had had sexual experience were supposed to be more desirable because they knew how to treat women. Society condoned the practice of keeping a mistress, and prostitution was legal. Existing in the ethical no-man's-land between men and women were prostitutes and geisha of various classes, women who provided sexual services to men for money in what was euphemistically called *mizushōbai* (the water trade). By virtue of their calling, they were subjected to an entirely different ethical standard and held none of the rights of ordinary women.

Legalized prostitution (not outlawed until 1956 after great effort by the women's movement) encouraged a separation in sexual behavior in men between the pursuit of pleasure and the procreation of children, with the prostitutes enjoying the benefits of the former and the wives, the latter. Relationships with mistresses or prostitutes were thought of as *asobi* (play or frivolity) and were kept separate from the world of respectable society, and involvement with a prostitute was not supposed to be a threat in any way to a man's household or relationship with his wife. This dichotomy in behavior was encouraged by the importance of maintaining the family line (the *ie*). A man had to marry a respectable woman of good family regardless of personal feelings, and children had to be produced, even if the wife was barren. There were occasions when the child of a mistress was adopted into the household to carry the family name.

Sexual infidelity on the part of the wife, on the other hand, was sufficient grounds for divorce. The Confucian ethic, which governed morals roughly from the 19th century until after World War II, demanded that a wife be obedient to her husband no matter what he did. Subject to this unqualified rule, women came to passively accept loose sexual behavior on the part of men and developed a passive and restrained attitude toward sex, which had not existed in earlier centuries.

After the war the legal and social situation was completely different: The male-dominant, family-centered Confucian ethic was discarded, monogamy was backed up by the law, and contraceptives and medical abortions became widely available. Sex is, nevertheless, not a matter discussed openly (despite the sensational and often pornographic material to be found in the mass media), so it is difficult to assess relevant behavior and attitudes.[10]

However, accounts that are available indicate that the days of highly valued female virginity and sexual fidelity are clearly gone. According to surveys conducted by a women's organization, Group for Wives (*Grupu Waifu*), for the prewar generation of women (born in or before 1945), some 32 percent were reportedly virgins at marriage, 27 percent had had premarital sexual relations with their future husbands, and another 30 percent had had a premarital sexual relationship with a man (although predominantly only one) other than their future husband. Premarital sexual activity is less restrained for the postwar generations, among whom an even smaller number of women are virgins upon marriage (20 percent); 40 percent have had sexual relations with their husbands before marriage, and another 39 percent have had affairs with one or more (many with two or three) men.

The desire to enjoy sex, which itself reflects changed attitudes, is more visible among younger women, even those who keep their virginity until marriage. More and more women are asserting that since many men, their own husbands included, have been involved in premarital sexual relationships, they feel there is nothing wrong with having had the same sort of experience themselves.[11]

Once married, the importance and enjoyment of sex in the relationship between Japanese husband and wife rapidly diminish. The 1990 VSR Survey showed that Japanese women and men considered a "good sexual relationship" equally unimportant for a good marriage, while the opposite was the case for American men and women. Some Japanese women, an average of 12 percent of surveyed women of all ages, even consider sex to have no importance at all in marriage, as reported in *Messages from Wives*.[12]

What is the reason for this apparent disinterest? The reports provided by married women of all ages as quoted in *Messages from Wives*, suggest that it stems from dissatisfaction in sexual relations on both sides. Their own enjoyment of sex suppressed by culturally ingrained passivity, women are often affronted by what seems a too-active desire on the part of the husband, while the husband is frustrated by his wife's apparent lack of sexual

desire. Their predicament is related, no doubt, to their overall
lack of communication and real closeness. Women are annoyed
by the generally one-sided sexual behavior of their husbands and
wish for more tenderness and companionship. But they are
tripped up by their own inhibitions; the majority of women
apparently cannot or do not tell or show their husbands what
they want or hope for sexually. Their desire for more companionship in marriage has increased, yet on the behaviorial level they
still do not indicate their desires.

Older women are more apt to accept unwelcome sexual
advances from husbands but remain completely passive; younger women are less willing to endure what is unpleasant to them,
feeling that they have the freedom to refuse what they do not
want. While a marriage (with children and family responsibilities) might have to be endured, they do not feel they have to
endure unwanted sex; this leads easily to the temptation to have
sex with other men, those who can be counted on to be more
romantic and caring. Japanese women do in fact refuse unwanted
sex with their husbands, thinking that it will not dramatically
rock the marriage boat. If an American woman were to do the
same, no doubt it would lead to a marital crisis; because sexual
compatibility is considered to be crucial in an American marriage, it is very difficult for sexually incompatible couples to keep
their family together.

In Japan today there are two types of extramarital affairs: One
involves prostitutes in the so-called pink districts that replaced
the official red-light districts of old in Japan and abroad (access to
which is gained, for example, by the infamous "sex tours," trips
to the Philippines, Thailand, Taiwan, and Korea organized
expressly to cater to men seeking sexual pleasures in countries
where prostitution is not outlawed). These can be assumed to be
transient relationships. The other type of extramarital affair is the
longer-term sexual relationship (furin). The latter is a largely
postwar phenomenon that has grown more common as a result
of the increase in opportunities for men and women to meet
outside the home, especially at work, the greater economic
resources of women, and the vast changes in the attitudes and
sexual behavior (more active, freer) of some women. Also, the
availability of contraceptives and abortion have eased some of
the risks of extramarital affairs. Another change in society is the

greater anonymity, especially in the big cities, permitted to individuals following the dissolution of the old close-knit neighborhood associations, which were a particularly strong force in maintaining the old moral order. With greater mobility of the participants and less social surveillance, affairs can go relatively unnoticed.

Messages from Wives reported that a small number (20 percent) of survey respondents (who, as the editors note, tend to be of a more serious type than the average) think that wives should not become involved in extramarital sexual liaisons. On the behavioral level, however, one in every six women admitted to having had extramarital sex, and of these women 30 percent had continuing relationships with other men. Contrary to what we might expect, the percentage carrying on extramarital affairs increases with age; for those born before 1945 the rate was one of every four women. This figure, backed by their written reports, suggests that extramarital affairs among older women result more from a poor relationship with their spouse than from a change in the moral code, which appears to be the main factor in the behavior of younger women.

Who are these sexually liberated women of the younger generation? The majority are working women with sufficient income to be economically independent if need be. Clearly, economic independence has given them the power to behave in accordance with their own inclinations. Their occupations, moreover, tend to be of a type that allows the physical and temporal leeway for involvement in a secret sexual relationship, that is, occupations such as free-lance reporting, home visit sales, and part-time high school or university teaching. Most of the relationships these women form are either with colleagues or with former classmates from their university, reflecting the wider contacts provided by coeducation.

The majority of the women involved with extramarital affairs appear to think that marriage is marriage and an affair is an affair and the twain need never meet. Sixty percent of those studied by the Group for Wives denied having any feelings of guilt regarding their extramarital affairs, offering comments such as, "It has nothing to do with my husband,"[13] which reflects the absence of emotional commitment between husband and wife. The atmosphere—the "air"—of the relationship between these women and their husbands may be so thin that the husband's feelings hardly seem to matter. Far more important to these respondents than sexual fidelity is the economic security marriage affords. Of those who did express some guilt feelings, only a small minority did so because they felt bad for their husbands or because they thought their behavior immoral; the largest group who claimed to have guilt feelings attributed them to the fact that "it is unpleasant to have such a secret."[14] This seems to be more egocentrism than guilt, however.

As for how husbands react, two thirds of the women surveyed stated that their husbands were unaware of the affair. Two examples illustrate this situation:

> In the fourth year of our marriage, I started having an affair with a married man I had first met at work. Our relationship is based on love (not just sex), so I have no guilt feelings. My husband has a mother complex and absolutely no idea I am having an affair. (Publishing firm employee, aged 32, two children)

And another women wrote:

> In the eighteenth year of our marriage, I ran into the man who had been my boyfriend before marriage and we resumed our relationship, meeting now for over a year. At the time we were married, my husband was very harsh when he learned of my premarital relationship with this man. Now (18 years later), he has no idea of the hours I am spending in that man's passionate embrace. (Part-time coffee shop employee, aged 43, three children)

Some husbands either know what their wives are doing or suspect them of such. They tend, however, to take a long, adult view of wifely infidelity as long as it is discreet, believing that their wives are committed to the family and that such a fling is bound to be transient, as the husband of the woman quoted in the following passage may well believe:

> In the fourth year of our marriage, I fell in love with a colleague five years younger at work. He is a very attractive human being. Our relationship has lasted on and off for the last 28 years. I am so irresistibly drawn to this man that I have no guilt feelings. My husband seems to have a vague idea of what is going on, but says nothing. I have a good sexual relationship with my husband, but

the relationship with my lover gives me a much greater sense of psychological fulfillment. I expect our relationship to last throughout my life. (Currently unemployed, aged 56, two children)

These stories suggest that many Japanese women (who are often not in love with their husbands, having married them for other reasons) do not feel an extramarital affair is morally wrong if they feel deep love for their partner. This lack of a strong sense of exclusive involvement and commitment in Japanese marriage reflects the negative side of the freedom women have won.

We can conjecture that most Japanese men would be much shocked by messages of this kind, for they remain conservative enough to refuse to accept their wife's extramarital liaisons even though they condone those of their own. Still, the price to be paid for pointing the finger at their wife could be a broken marriage, which many are reluctant to have happen. Their safest defense, perhaps, is psychological rejection, that is, a refusal to think that their wife would have an affair; and this fiction can be easily maintained because the "healthy and absent" husband may know little of his wife's feelings and daily activity.

So proficient are married women at maintaining their facade of the "good wife, wise mother," and respectable member of the community that the extent of extramarital sexual activity may be unknown even among themselves. Many respondents to the survey might have been surprised to learn how many other women were having such affairs.

We can only conclude that Japanese women (and men, too, of course) have not yet internalized the ethic of sexual fidelity. In the anonymity of urban life, therefore, where "the eyes of society" are not closely focused on individuals—as they were in Japan's old communal society, where social norms rather than morality acted to restrain people's behavior—many Japanese women simply fall back on their emotions to guide their sexual behavior. This is why when asked what they would do if faced with the temptation to have an affair, many answer that they do not know until they face the actual situation. Conventional morality, based as it is not on a religious creed or ethic but on what is socially acceptable, tends to be reduced to maintaining *sekentei* (appearances). The behavior of these women is striking in that it is guided not by rationally thought-out ethical principles but by situational conditions and considerations of maintaining the appearance of socially acceptable behavior. This, however, is not just a characteristic of a small proportion of women; it may be observed in Japanese behavior in general.

Wada Yoshiko, assistant editor of the Group for Wives' journal, speculates that the conspicuously loose sexual morals observed among women living in the big cities may be related to the fact that many are the daughters or granddaughters of farming families, among whom much free sex (meaning a sexual relationship in which spontaneity and fulfillment of natural desires on both sides is permitted) was carried out. She also believes there is some influence from indigenous religious beliefs (Shinto) in which female gods have several sex partners (although always one at a time), forming an undercurrent in popular behavior. Wada's hypothesis has yet to be tested, but historically, sexual behavior was left in the hands of the individual. It was expressed freely and openly, as clearly seen in the classic *Kojiki* [Record of Ancient Matters], which recounts the ways of oldest antiquity, and in the *Man'yōshū* anthology of poetry of the eighth century. Spontaneous sexual behavior was not suppressed in the popular moral code throughout Japan's premodern, agrarian history, as seen in the *wakashū yado* (young men's lodges) and *musume yado* (young women's lodges), which were part of village society, and premarital sex between occasional lovers was common. Only in the samurai class was the sexual behavior of both men and women tightly restrained.[15] Scholar of philosophy Umehara Takeshi notes that "Japanese have had a positive and accepting attitude toward sex since ancient Jōmon times. Worship of sex is, in fact, at the very foundation of Japanese culture."[16]

The alacrity with which Japanese leaders of the Meiji period, when the country launched its modernization drive, encouraged Confucian morals and the spread of samurai ethics throughout the society was in part inspired by the embarrassingly loose (that is, by the Western standards of the mid-19th century, when Europeans began to observe Japan firsthand) sexual behavior of the non-samurai strata. The prudish Victorian code then dominant in the West made Japanese leaders who had been abroad think that Japan had to emulate the West in sexual morality as well as in other areas. The new regime encouraged the control of sex by the family (*ie*)[17] and the governing of society by Confucian ethics.[18] After World War II, sex again became an individual matter, but this happened before relevant ethical standards could become established; in postwar Japan, a "liberated woman" also implied a sexually liberated woman, that is, one who broke away from tradition to be faithful to her true feelings and impulses.

Women who engage in extramarital affairs in Japan today seem to think of marriage as a mere institution and to feel that the bond it implies holds little importance to the two principals.[19] Many couples share living space but are far removed from each other emotionally. Their mutual autonomy has gone too far. Yet surprisingly few divorces result. The women maintain the household as far as functions and appearances are concerned, and their husbands studiously avoid knowledge of or involvement in their wife's affairs. These women are committed to the institution of marriage and the status of wife but are relatively cool about the relationship with their husband. They have made the home their territory and castle, and they have no intention of abandoning it because of an oblivious husband, who, after all, provides them with so much freedom and autonomy. The pragmatic Japanese woman knows that life has its ups and downs and that if she makes a decision too hastily or reacts too radically, she may lose out in the long run.

DIVORCE

Although the Japanese divorce rate is comparatively low, the recent increase can be attributed to the increasing number of financially independent women, their rising demand for companionship, and their desire to maintain their freedom and autonomy, as well as to the extended life expectancy and the changing attitudes toward divorce. Women are less likely to put up with a marriage they find intolerable, but divorce can also rob them of options, since they will be forced to work to support themselves.

The divorce rate per 1,000 persons in Japan rose slowly and steadily between 1963 and 1983 and then turned slightly downward; it is still the lowest among advanced nations in the world. In 1990 it stood at 1.26 percent, well below the 4.80 percent for the United States and 2.89 percent for the United Kingdom.[20] This low divorce rate in Japan reflects a variety of factors, such as the practical approach to the marriage commitment, the large number of stable relationships among couples, and the importance attached to preserving a stable home environment for children. It also reflects how women in their forties and fifties today have weighed the trade-offs between satisfying their emotional needs and maintaining their economic freedom and security.

Some may wonder whether the social sanction against divorce still functions. In fact, the situation has changed radically. In 1972 the Prime Minister's Office conducted the first of its series of studies on divorce. At that time over 70 percent of men and women polled opposed the idea of divorce, and a weakened but similar trend was still observed in 1984. In a survey conducted in 1987 the trend was reversed, signaling the recent change in attitudes, with over 60 percent indicating agreement that a divorce should be sought if a marriage was not going well. A generational difference is manifest, with more acceptance of divorce found among the younger generations, especially single women. In urban settings at least, people no longer regard divorce as shameful, and divorced men and women and their children are generally not looked down upon as they once were.

As in the United States, the majority of divorce cases in Japan involve persons 29 and younger.[21] These divorces, occurring in marriages of less than five years, have decreased in Japan as couples today tend to wed after getting to know one another better than was the case in prewar times.

Apparently well-established marriages, which have endured for as long as 15 to 20 years, meanwhile, break up more often now than in the past, the rate for this group tripled to 15 percent of all divorces during the last 20 years, although the actual number of cases is still small. These divorces among couples aged 45 and older are a new phenomenon. They reflect the pragmatic thinking of Japanese women as well as the psychological autonomy and freedom they attained as a result of the absence of the husbands who provided for them for many years. A relatively common pattern is for the wife to wait until the children are grown and her husband has retired from his company, a point at which he receives a large lump sum in severance pay; she then asks for half the sum and a separation. Another juncture at which older women ask for divorce is after the marriage of the last child, which often comes while a woman is still in her early fifties.

With women looking at an average lifespan of nearly 82, some are not anxious to endure further decades of cohabitation with a mate with whom they find difficulty communicating and sharing. The once "healthy and absent" spouse now litters the pathways of her busy life and hardly knows how to relax in the long days in his own home. Throughout most of their marriage many women felt forced by their husband's employment-imposed work schedule to carry the weight of family affairs and important decisions alone; once they became accustomed to this burden, they gained great independence, learning to function completely without a husband's help. By holding onto the purse strings and working in part-time jobs, women can save substantial amounts, often enough to maintain a modest lifestyle living alone (and divorced women are entitled to a small public pension). Having won this kind of economic and psychological autonomy, some wives are inclined to think freedom is more attractive than growing old with a husband with whom they feel they have little in common.

Some women are known to plan long in advance for divorce. One woman spent over 10 years planning her divorce, presenting her demand to her husband on the evening he retired from his job of 32 years. Two months earlier she had rented an apartment and moved most of her belongings there, spending time there during the day when her husband was at work. Their two children had married and moved elsewhere, and the husband never noticed anything that diverged from the usual routine. On the night of his retirement he arrived home carrying a gift for her. It was a present for her from his colleagues, presented to him at his farewell party. Great was his surprise to find her waiting for him with two suitcases beside her. He thought she was joking as she told him she was leaving. Even a year after she moved out, he cannot believe what happened. He painfully recalls her remark as she finished telling him of her plans: "This is the first time I've ever talked to you this long." He cannot comprehend how the woman he trusted completely, and left everything to over the years while he devoted himself to his work at the company, could have come to prepare so deliberately for a divorce. He had been so confident in his work, thinking his dedication to his job would be rewarded by the care his wife and children would lavish on him even after retirement, and then the real bill came due. This is the sort of gap that yawns between the judgment and expectations of some husbands and wives of the older generation.

Some men, shocked to their senses by a wife's request for a divorce in middle age, manage to transform themselves into more caring husbands and persuade their wives to stay. One woman had prepared for divorce for 25 years, saving money by working part-time and scrimping on such things as clothing and hairdressing. Realizing that her husband, who had totally relied on the services she provided, would be unable to survive without her, she reluctantly decided to stay, saying she changed her mind out of pity, more for what she called "humanitarian" reasons than for love.[22] Americans might find such a reason totally untenable, but it does demonstrate the stuff of which Japanese marriages are made.

The data show that it is more often the wife (55 percent) than the husband (35 percent) who initiates a divorce, the remaining cases being those in which concerned parents act on behalf of a son or daughter. The major grounds for seeking a divorce on the part of the wife are economic problems involving the husband (e.g., he does not provide sufficient economic support), incompatibility (*seikaku fuichi*), and the husband's extramarital affair. On the part of the husband, the main reasons are incompatibility and the wife's extramarital affair. Lawyers point out that incompatibility most often implies sexual incompatibility.[23] Many of the reasons cited can be assumed to be only euphemisms for a variety of real causes. Whatever they are, research shows a change in the reasons cited by women from the very tangible, like drinking and physical abuse, to the more cerebral, like differences in ways of thinking (e.g., the wife's desire for companionship vs. the husband's attachment to his job), the importance of which men have not sufficiently grasped.

Incompatibility comes in various forms. One 39-year-old wife of an insurance company vice president told how she reached her decision to seek a divorce. With two lovely children and an attractive husband her family looked picture-perfect, yet she was rarely able to talk with her husband. She began to wonder why she should live with a man to whom she could not talk. He liked to read, but if by way of chitchat she mentioned her impressions of a recent best-seller she had read, he would only deride her tastes, telling her bluntly that it was a stupid book. If she found herself overcome by emotional stress and confessed to him that she felt "unhappy, somehow dissatisfied," he never asked her why but only demanded, "What in the world are you dissatisfied with?" as if to say, "How could you be unhappy? My income is greater than the average company employee!" If, catching the hint, she would say, "No, of course it isn't money," he would declare that she was being just plain selfish (*wagamama*). There was no way to start or carry on a conversation with him. So this woman filed for and got a divorce with custody of the two children and is now working part-time to support them. Her husband still cannot understand why she asked for a divorce; his ego would never let him understand. Presumably, all he did was follow the pattern he observed between his own mother and father and didn't think there was anything wrong. Because couples like this appear so stable on the surface, the news of their divorce often comes as a complete surprise even to parents and close friends.[24]

Another trend has been observed with the first postwar generation, says Madoka Yoriko, organizer of the *Niko-niko Rikon Kōza* [Course on Divorce with a Smile] series designed to promote understanding of divorce.[25] The type of divorce has shifted toward those caused by a discrepancy between ideas of what a family should be and how it actually turns out. Marriage may begin with a glamorous wedding and overseas honeymoon, dazzling the couple with the fantasy of their dreams, but the fantasies soon dissipate in the drudgery of daily housework and childcare and in the disappointment in a husband who is either absent or exhausted. Many divorced women say they "had a living but no life (*seikatsu ga attemo jinsei ga nakatta*)."

Although Japanese marriages hold up inordinately well in the face of extramarital affairs, these do constitute another major reason for divorce. One fairly typical pattern is illustrated by a 42-year-old woman with two high school–age children. Her husband is employed by a major computer company. They met in graduate school and married. After her children were born, she was offered a full-time teaching job at a junior college, and she decided to take it. A perfectionist, she did everything to make sure she could handle both her job and her family responsibilities: moving to a home within an easy commute of work, bringing in someone to help with the housework twice a week, and hiring tutors and playmates for the children. Her job turned out to be very demanding, but she refused to slight her responsibilities in either role, inside or outside the home, often working until 2:00 A.M. Few Japanese women would push themselves this hard, trying to perform with 100 percent efficiency in two roles. Her husband, preoccupied by his job in the highly competitive computer industry, behaved as if he did not notice what she was doing, neither recognizing her financial contribution or professional achievements nor cooperating with her efforts in running the household.

This woman was earning about $32,000 (about ¥4.5 million), a sizable income but not equivalent to that of a man of her age. Her dissatisfaction with her husband's obliviousness mounted, and then she met a man at an academic conference who praised her work and criticized her husband for not giving her talents a chance to blossom. Her relationship with the man eventually became intimate, and his affection confirmed her confidence in herself. She surprised her husband by asking for a divorce. Certain she was leaving because she had found a lover, he was relatively accommodating, predicting that with such a liaison she would be back home within six months. Thinking the separation would be only temporary, he moved out. Even if she had a lover, he reasoned, she was a woman with two children and could not remarry. She became more adamant in demanding a divorce; perhaps her fervor was a sign that she hoped someone would stop her. She hoped and even expected that her parents and friends would gather and try to persuade her to change her mind. But they did not, as she was known for being stubborn and not taking advice from anyone. Though she began to regret her decision, she could not reverse it. Her belief that her husband did not understand her became all the more firm. A year after the separation the divorce was finalized. In spite of an agreement made at the time, she does not let the children see their father and has refused to accept child support from him. She seems to have been unable to resolve the conflict between the traditional sex role and her role as a progressive female academic. Her former husband has remarried.

Another phenomenon that has recently become rather common is the husband who is still tied to his mother's apron strings. The typical example is a man who is an only or eldest son of a high-income or elite family, who has been spoiled and indulged from infancy by a mother who is a full-time housewife, and who has had little companionship with a largely absent father. He turns to his mother at the slightest moment of indecision (like calling her from the hotel where he and his bride are on their honeymoon to ask what he should do). When the symbiosis between mother and son is extreme and continues even after the son's marriage, it causes great dismay and displeasure to the wife; divorces shortly after marriage often stem from this problem. (The problems of mother–son relations will be discussed later.)

Other changes have made the marriage bond quicker to crumble than it used to be. When a woman did not possess significant earning power, she had to cling at any cost to even a rocky marriage, suppressing her feelings and desires with all her might. She had no choice but to persevere despite all odds. Today, even the least-educated woman can earn enough to live modestly; she also knows that since a woman may live to be 80, the possibilities of starting over after an unfortunate marriage are quite good. Those who do not wish to face the consequences of legally breaking up a marriage can manage by maintaining what is known as "divorce within the home." The necessity of keeping up appearances was crucial until not too long ago, when the stigma of divorced parents was such that a young man might be denied a job or a young woman excluded as a marriage candidate for a man of good family. This is not generally the case anymore. Divorce is now easier because it is considered a private (i.e., between the couple themselves), rather than a family (in the sense of the extended family) matter.

Indeed, the efforts made by the go-between in the marriage (now mainly a formal fixture of marriage ritual) and the parents on either side in keeping a shaky marriage together have virtually ceased. Professional marriage counseling services are now emerging, but they are not yet widely used. With the old Confucian and samurai ethics now relics of the past (when the stigma of divorce was so great that brides were told they could never return to their own home), some parents, who had only one or two offspring instead of eight or ten, are even delighted to have their divorced son or daughter return to the parental nest, which has become lonely without them.

Nor does the presence of children seem to be a strong consideration in salvaging a marriage. In the mid-1950s the number of divorces of couples with children surpassed that for couples without children, and 70 percent of divorces today are between couples with children. In the majority of cases the mother takes custody of the children. In 71 percent of the cases (in 1989) the woman assumes the entire responsibility for child support; in only 23 percent of cases does the father provide full child support.[26]

A little over half of divorced husbands provide their ex-wives with alimony, but the amount is generally very small.[27] Recently, reflecting the growing earning power of women, there has been an increase in the number of cases in which the wife pays alimony. In 1988 of all cases involving the division of assets or payment of alimony, women were ordered to pay alimony in 10 percent of the cases, although the amounts were rather small. Two thirds of divorced women work (about one half were already working before the divorce). Since wages for women are low compared to those for men, women have a difficult time and often have to rely on public support or help from relatives.

As long as a divorced woman has a place to live, her situation is by no means destitute. If she is in a situation where she cannot work to support herself, welfare payments for single parents provide fairly adequate funds. Therefore, a woman no longer has to put up with an intolerable marriage just to assure her and her children's survival.

Since women usually put the well-being of their children before resolution of troubles in relations with their husband; they may either abandon the idea of divorce or postpone it until the children grow up. In the meantime, the absence of the spouse from the household on a daily basis makes a bad situation easier to tolerate until an advantageous time arrives.

The majority of men remarry after divorce, while the majority of women do not. Most divorced women had enough after their bad experience and harbor no desire to try again. If they have children, they are reluctant to remarry for fear that the children and the stepfather may not get along. Men, on the other hand, hope to remarry (52 percent), especially if they have custody of the children. Seventy percent of men either desire or have plans for remarriage at the time of divorce (implying, in the latter case, that the cause of divorce is relations with another woman, whom they plan to marry.[28] Americans divorced more than twice are fairly common, but this is relatively rare in Japan.

In spite of (or because of) the lack of communication between couples, divorce is still not a likely path for many Japanese women today. Many admit to having considered the option, but generally decide against it after careful and objective deliberation of relevant factors. According to the VSR Survey, Japanese men and women meet attractive persons of the opposite sex relatively often; they consider the great obstacles involved and energies required to engineer a change of partners and often decide that the other person might not be that different from their current spouse. Only if the person is so clearly preferable to their present mate that the difficulties seem well worth enduring will they seek a divorce. Women tend to harbor the apprehension that a man who is devoted to her as a lover would become domineering and distant (just like her present husband) if he were to become her husband.

The rate of divorce in Japan is not expected to rise rapidly but rather slowly and steadily as the societal obstacles against it are lifted. The factors that will propel the rate of divorce, especially among urban couples, include, on the one hand, women's demands for communication and partnership (when they cannot be met) and, on the other, their urge for autonomy and freedom. Another factor favoring divorce is the ability (supported by the wide variety of household services now available) of both sexes to take care of themselves, even in old age, if they have solid economic resources.

LATER LIFE

Even if a couple manages to navigate two or more decades of marriage without rupture, a further crisis confronts them when the husband retires. The average retirement age for men in the civil service and in large corporations is usually between 55 and 60. Many may shift to a private or smaller corporation and continue working full-time, but eventually they do enter genuine retirement, staying at home for the first time in their lives. What does this mean for the wife, who has built her life around the absence of her husband? Women, whether working or not, generally establish a variety of reliable social networks; their lives are busy and their contacts multiple.

Men, whose lives have been dedicated entirely to their employers, can cultivate few friends outside the limited sphere of their workplace. When they retire, they are severed not only from the work that occupied all their thoughts and hours but from the friendships, leisure activities, and social interactions that centered around their work. For these men, the company was family for all practical purposes—the place where they spent the majority of their waking hours and made most of their contacts with other people, the entity upon which they relied for financial support, health benefits, recreation, entertainment, and so on. When they retire, returning to the family, it is no wonder that they are sometimes received less than warmly.

The predicament of the newly retired man can be serious, for he is totally unprepared to redefine his sex role. Practically a stranger in his own home, he feels out of place. He can hardly take part in his wife's activities, about which he knows almost nothing. He has no friends to speak of in the community, and he has forgotten how to use time for anything but work. He cannot fix his own meals or otherwise take care of himself and is inept at such household chores as doing the laundry, tidying up, or taking care of the shopping. In three-generation households, he may be useful for minding grandchildren or taking them to day care or kindergarten and bringing them home (whether he likes these tasks or not). A daughter or daughter-in-law who is working may be anxious for his help with small children if she is working or active in community activities, but he may not appreciate having such responsibilities foisted upon him.

The wife of a retiree, who long ago abandoned any emotional reliance on her husband, sometimes finds his returned presence in the household more of a nuisance than a pleasure. After enjoying great freedom and autonomy over the years, she must now be more frequently at her husband's service and must give up some of her activities. If she wants to go out, she first has to see to his needs (which include three regular meals a day) in one way or another. While her daily activities thus become more intense, the retired man suffers from having too much time on his hands. After decades of early mornings and late nights, strenuous commuting, and heavy drinking with colleagues, the bliss of a quiet home with no demands imposed upon him at first seems almost worth the boredom. The newly retired man has never cultivated any hobby and may have little inclination to try one. He may make no effort to occupy his time but rest on the veranda in the sunshine with the newspaper, lounge on the couch in front of the television, or hover over a cup of tea in the dining room while his wife bustles about her chores in preparation for going out.

Wherever he sits or lies, he tends to be in the way of his busy wife, who has so much she wants and has to do. For this reason these men are often dubbed *sodai gomi* (oversize trash). This rather cruel epithet first came into use in the mid-1970s when older women were first becoming active outside the home. In this phase the wives of retirees were usually forced by unbudging menfolk to abandon their outside activities and return to the quieter life of housewifery. In the 1980s a new name came into use for the "useless" retired husband—*nure ochiba* (wet fallen leaf), an expression that evokes an image of a busy wife trying to brush her bothersome husband away, only to have him cling to her the way wet fallen leaves stick to the ground when one tries to sweep. But women in this phase continued pursuing their activities nonetheless. The most recent name for overdependent retired men is *"kyōfu no washi zoku* [the take-me-with-you terrors]." Whenever a wife prepares to go out, her husband offers, much to her horror, to go along. She does not want her husband there, spoiling the fun. It is pitiful to see these men, once proud and purposeful, with no place to go, clinging to their wives.

The changes that unfold in the household of a retiree have become the stuff of a great deal of fiction, drama, and nonfiction writing.[29] Most husbands retiring from their job think they can now enjoy freedom and the companionship of their wives. They expect that their wives will appreciate their long years of work to support the household and will revel in the retirement as they do. They are caught completely by surprise to find their spouses angry and frustrated by their constant presence in the home. Far from enjoying the husband's retirement, these women find their household work doubled. Such men are struck with dismay and disbelief when their wives declare their retirement from the role of housewife. After recovering from the initial shock, some men realize what their wives are saying, and they gradually transform themselves, learning to do housework and taking care of themselves.

Many men caught up in the workaholic tide do not take the problem of what they will do in their retirement to heart until it is almost too late. They naively believe that it will not be they who become the victims of purposelessness and loneliness in advanced age, but reality eventually catches up with them. It is far better that they consider early that if they devote themselves totally to their workplace and its world, they will have nothing left when retirement brings an end to their career. Their refusal to share responsibility in the home can be their own undoing. If the distance between husband and wife is not to become too wide to allow for the companionship desired in advanced age, a greater degree of sharing is probably needed throughout the marriage.

COOL FELLOW TRAVELERS

The crises of communication and relationships between the sexes described here, while they are definitely shaking up long-established norms and customs of married life, are unlikely to threaten the very fabric of family life in Japan. Because of the acceptability of maintaining appearances while pursuing extra-marital relationships and the availability of diverse options for women (work, hobbies, community work), the rate of marriage breakups is unlikely to reach the level now seen, for example, in the United States.

It is clear that more women will spend time outside the home and more will be exposed to the possibility of forming relation-ships with men other than their husbands. Men, who once may have been prevented from engaging in extramarital affairs by the short allowance they were kept on by wives concerned about their fidelity, may stray anyway, especially now that the women they are tempted by have ample funds to sustain themselves and such a relationship. Relationships and sexual behavior between the sexes will be freer (until the AIDS epidemic spreads further), since women have more liberty today than ever before to explore their sexuality and potential in relationships.

If Japanese wisdom has anything to offer, it is in this ability to maintain a long-term view of life and in a realistic willingness to accept human weakness. In this sense, the more impalpable the "air" of the relationship, the easier it is to maintain autonomy and freedom on the part of both spouses.

5

MOTHERHOOD AND
THE HOME

The Japanese woman's consciousness of her role in the family centers on motherhood, the principle sphere of family life. In spite of her enlarged role today, motherhood retains for her its traditional importance. After becoming a mother, a woman's life cycle markers are keyed to the phases of her children's lives rather than her own. Women pursue outside work, hobbies, and leisure activities only as long as they do not threaten the foundations and functions of the family. In prewar modern Japan, children were considered family assets (*kodakara*): Among farming families they represented manpower necessary for perpetuating the operation of the farm, and among middle-class urban families they represented the potential for climbing the social ladder.

Under the *ie* system of old, children were needed in order to assure the continuance of the family line; thus, it was literally the duty of a woman to give birth to at least one child, preferably male. Women who could not give birth were at times divorced, even if the husband was happy with her, and a new bride sought because of the importance attached to preserving the family line. That day is long gone, and the changing roles of women today affect both their attitudes and their behavior as mothers. Naturally, in the traditional context, the role of a woman as mother far exceeded her role as wife. Even in the days when the status of women was very low, the mother of a prominent man (e.g., the shogun or a powerful prelate) might have been quite powerful. Women were recognized as fully adult only after entering motherhood: "Women are weak, but mothers are strong." Under the old family system a woman's position in her husband's family remained unstable and vulnerable until she gave birth (particularly to a son). For a woman with ambition or dreams, social stature hinged on the conditions of motherhood.

Okaasan (mother) is a term that is greatly idealized. What it evokes for Japanese adults are feelings of close attachment, the bliss of security and comforting warmth, and bittersweet memories of childhood. The television commercial with a boy's cry of *"Okaasan!"* echoing across a rural landscape in the dusk capitalizes on the sense of longing and nostalgia the word evokes. While father (*Otoosan*) was the symbol of authority and discipline (if not the actual dispenser of discipline), mother was the embodiment of inexhaustible love and warmth. Even when a mother was very strict, her severity was believed to be the loving sacrifice she made of natural instincts for the sake of preparing her child for the role he or she was expected to play in society as a responsible adult.

Today, with militarist feudal traditions a thing of the past and the patriarchal family system largely overwhelmed by the nuclear family, unprecedented affluence, and child-centered households with few children, strict mothers are few and far between; they are more often loving and protective to the extreme. The contemporary father might be the supporter of the household financially, but it is the mother who watches over the health and well-being of each member of the family, runs the household, and keeps the family bonds strong. A child forms a very strong sense of trust in his or her mother, believing she is a guaranteed ally, sometimes even against the father (as Akiko's mother was when Akiko wanted to go to a four-year university rather than the junior college her father thought was suitable). The mother is the source as well as the cultivator of the strong feelings of *amae* (dependency) that Japanese carry even into adulthood. In Japanese men this emotional dependency is carried over from mother to wife after marriage. The characteristic often observed in adults—both men and women—of being unprepared to take responsibility and feeling that they ought to be understood and forgiven no matter what they do can be attributed to this dependency nurtured in childhood. The enhanced importance of the maternal role of women is the natural result of the fact that they are the target of dependence by all family members.

The protectiveness and magnanimity of the Japanese mother does not extend to nonfamily members, even daughters-in-law. A clear demarcation is drawn in Japanese culture between insiders and outsiders. Inside (*uchi*, also meaning "home") is the warm haven centering around the presence of the mother; outside is harsh, cold, and threatening, by contrast intensifying the attachment to home and mother. The most terrifying threat that can be held over the head of a naughty child is to be told to get out of the house, to be cut off from the source of warmth and security. By this means mothers develop their children's need for attachment and dependency (in contrast with American disciplining tactics, where a child may be kept indoors for bad behavior, a constraint that punishes the independence-oriented impulses that are encouraged). The Japanese mother's childrearing techniques engrave the actual and symbolic warmth and importance of the home managed by the mother in the minds of her children, forming a strong association between home and mother.

The importance of the home is noticeable everywhere. If a person's family background was solid (*shikkari shita katei*, which essentially means that the person was reared by a good, traditional mother), he or she is considered a trustworthy individual. At the same time, this belief implies that it is crucial to the sound development of children for a family to be stable (i.e., for divorce or breakup to be avoided) and for a husband to be able to perform his breadwinning role acceptably. This renders the woman's maternal and homemaking role very important, a demanding job with great responsibility.

MATERNAL BONDS

A common expression for describing a child—"*hara o itameta ko* [the child for whom I suffered the pain of childbirth]"— emphasizes the unique bond between mother and child that the father cannot share. Because of this bond, it was traditionally thought that motherhood came naturally, that a woman did not need to learn to be a mother, and that this guaranteed the mother a special place in the life of the child. Men could not intervene. (Nowadays men may wish to observe the birthing process and to participate as much as possible in assisting the birth, but since they do not suffer physical pain themselves, their involvement remains relatively detached.) Thus, it was easy to take advantage of this natural alienation, leaving the tasks and responsibilities of daily care, discipline, and education of children solely to women. Recalling their own close relationship with their mother and the warmth and comfort it gave (in contrast with the aloof, strict, and authoritarian presence of their fathers), men believe it is better to let the mother handle things.

In the traditional family the father had ultimate authority (the remaining legacy of the *ie* system) and the final say in family affairs; his power went unchallenged because he was the gate-keeper of information and the main channel of contact between the family and the real world, that is, society outside. In today's information society, the father no longer controls information or contact with society, nor does he hold ultimate authority in the home; indeed, his lack of information concerning the education of his children makes it difficult for him to maintain any sort of status save that of major wage earner. The relative status of the mother has grown stronger as paternal power has eroded—and even more so as women seek employment and bring in income that can be used to please the children.

In the traditional family a mother was regarded as the incarnation of warmth, devotion, self-sacrificing love, forgiveness, and strength protecting the child, and these qualities were especially poignant and observable when Japan was poor. Among the prewar generation, stories of maternal self-sacrifice abound, such as the one of the mother who had so many children to feed that she would pretend at mealtimes to use her chopsticks and chew her food while, in fact, her own bowl was empty.

Motherhood today remains largely the same at the core, but the image of self-sacrifice has largely faded. With affluence and the many conveniences available in a postindustrial society, there are few occasions on which a mother might be called upon to make painful material sacrifices for her children. With the growing emphasis on self-actualization for women, mothers are finding it harder to gain sufficient satisfaction only through devotion to their one or two children. Contemporary mothers have assumed other roles as well, but until children start elementary school, for many women the principle role is still that of mother.

Even today, as the roles of mothers have broadened, motherhood is still not defined in terms of the mother's identity as an individual but by the way she relates to her children. Her influence over her children, moreover, does not take the form of providing a model in terms of behavior so much as by providing all kinds of services, services upon which the child is encouraged to be totally dependent. If the father's role is to exercise authority, that of the mother is to complement his sternness and provide a haven, that is, to protect the child and serve as mediator in relations with the father. Thus, the role of mother has been greatly glorified, causing women without children to feel their lives are incomplete (there was a time when the childless mother was considered abnormal). At the same time, because of the demanding nature of the role of mother, some younger working women are postponing or refusing altogether to take on this role.

Many Japanese women used to say that watching their children grow was all they needed to make "life worth living" (their *ikigai*). Childrearing remains the pivot of the lives of most women. While clearly some women do not want their destiny to be determined by biology alone, neither men nor women in Japan think that giving birth or raising children is the source of inferior status. Since, at least for the present, only women can become pregnant and give birth, the quest for equality between the sexes is irrelevant here.

Perceptions of the role of mother have also become sharper. Women of the prewar generation regarded conception as a gift from the gods (the verb often used for "conceive" was *sazukaru*, which is used for things received from the realm of the divine),[1] and the first postwar generation regarded childbirth as a matter of course. More recently, however, contraceptives have given women greater control over their biological destiny, and their role has become far more active in planning their family. Today, the role of the divine has been shunted into the background (some couples have been known to plan their children's birthdays). Today's young women would never use the expression *"Kodomo o sazukaru* [A child is bestowed upon us]"; instead, they say *"kodomo o tsukuru* [make a child]." This has given women the feeling that having or not having children is subject to their personal choice; it also adds to the illusion that they can control their children's lives.

THE DECLINING BIRTHRATE

In repeated polls, half of Japanese women (and men) say that ideally they would like to have three children; in reality, 40 percent of these women do not have a third child. In 1947 the average number of children was 4.5. In 1957 this figure dropped by more than half to 2.0, where it remained fairly stable until the early 1970s, when it started to go down again. The average number of children per family fell to 1.57 in 1989 and then to 1.53 in 1990. To women, the figure was no surprise; to men, it came as quite a shock. The reaction in the world of men, especially those in government, was actually rather comical; the lowest birthrate in Japan's history shook them for perhaps the first time into considering women's problems seriously. The comments and reports presented in the media, however, made it clear that they still did not understand women's thinking.

Realizing the implications that this low birthrate will have for the labor force and for the care and support of the elder generations, the authorities expressed deep concern: What were the causes that made women "refuse" to have children? Committees of male politicians put their heads together to try to come up with policies that would induce women to bear more children. What they came up with was a new policy for providing a modest stipend for each new child and a proposal for a child care leave law (see the section Working Mothers later in this chapter). What effect these measures will have remains to be seen, but many women feel that the issue of family size is not a subject for government policy but entirely a private matter. What is most repugnant to women today about these measures is the suggestion that they bear children for the sake of the country.

The birthrate is not expected to rise as long as a large number of women are enjoying extended single lives and pursuing challenging careers; women of "double income–no kids" couples (DINKs) are leading glamorous lives, which causes them to postpone having children (as observed in the United States also). The high cost of education and adequate housing has also made Japanese hesitate to have more children. The average cost of supporting a child through four years at a university is roughly equivalent to the entire annual income of a male company employee (the 1990 average was ¥4.25 million, or $32,700).[2]

The lower birthrate has greatly affected women's behavior in the maternal role in several ways: First of all, when a woman has only one or two children instead of five or six, the number of years she spends raising children is drastically shortened, promising her in some cases as many as 35 years of life after her children become independent adults, years that can be spent in a variety of purposeful and self-fulfilling ways. Clearly, women need more than childrearing to occupy them throughout life, and this need has led many women to join the work force.

Second, with fewer children, mothers become more intensely involved with their children, even to the point of overinvolvement. The situation is especially acute for full-time mothers; ironically, today's mothers exhaust themselves psychologically in their maternal role with two children even more than their grandmothers did in the prewar period with six or eight. The women of the older generations were relatively relaxed and philosophical about their broods; there were plenty of children, and, though every life was precious, they were inured to the price exacted by fate and felt it couldn't be helped if one or two were lost. They were content if their children were healthy and not delinquent, and they concentrated their energies mainly on making sure the children were fed properly. The rest was left up to nature and the community.

Today, when the average number of children is (statistically) less than two, children are raised with exceeding care, and parents devote great energy to guiding them down the royal road to success in society. The majority of women come to hold very high expectations of themselves for finding "self-actualization in motherhood," but the effort required is quite stressful, which in turn infuses the relationship with their children with stress.

Third, contemporary young women remain inexperienced mothers from beginning to end. In the days when a woman had four or five children, she had accumulated enough experience by the third child to make her a calm, wise parent. Today, most mothers don't have a chance to accumulate such experience, so the majority of children are raised by uncertain, barely trained mothers (and, to a certain extent, fathers). Such parents often overreact to quite normal childish behavior, vacillate over disciplining procedures, and misunderstand their own offspring. Inexperienced parents often try to compensate for their lack of confidence by doing too much for their children and by giving them too many material goods. The nuclear family structure makes it all the harder for these novice parents to rear their children effectively, since access to the older generation is no longer an inevitable part of family life. To offer help to isolated parents, hotlines like "Baby 110" and "Angel 110" (copying the number called for emergency police assistance) have been established to provide toll-free advice and moral support.

The majority of urban women overcome these handicaps and disadvantages, of course, by taking the mothering role very seriously and by availing themselves of help from the community. Nonworking mothers cultivate friendships with other mothers to exchange information, join circles that enable them to give their children wider contacts and experiences, and hook into networks that provide a wealth of information via television, books, municipal programs, and so forth. Working mothers' efforts are supported and greatly aided by the staff members of day care centers and nurseries, who are instrumental in children's upbringing (in toilet training and in teaching children to dress and undress, brush teeth, use chopsticks, sing songs, play games, etc.). In this way, the community and community services offer supports to today's nuclear families that make up for the absence of grandparents and the extended family of traditional society.

MOTHERHOOD RECONSIDERED

The three most common reasons Japanese women today give for having and raising children are "to grow as a person through raising children," "to strengthen family ties," and "to build a new generation to carry on society."[3] Although how much childrearing really makes them grow as a person may be a matter of debate, women choose that reason more often than men, who do not participate enough in childrearing for this to be a major motive for them. The first two reasons are supported more by the younger generation, while the latter is more popular among members of the prewar generation, who still feel the vestigial influence of the old family system with its emphasis on producing an heir and maintaining the family name. Older people's thinking is also affected by the desire, widespread among the generation who reached their prime before the establishment of social security and old-age benefits, for children who would take care of them in old age. A surprisingly small percentage of men and women cite as their reason for having children "because it is enjoyable."

Japanese love and treasure their children, but childrearing is widely associated with hardship, not pleasure (as will be explained in the following paragraphs); thus, there is little encouragement to have more than one or two children if it can be helped. In fact, there is a tendency among both mothers and fathers to demand from their children the kind of performance that will compensate them for the difficulties they feel they have undergone. Far from preparing their children for independence, they try to maintain a measure of control over their children's lives. By making their children dependent, women justify the demands of their role as mother, the result being that the more dependent the child, the more indispensable the mother is, the more "meaningful" her existence becomes, and the greater the gratification she receives. And, by extension, a child is expected to be grateful and to feel obligated to the mother.

Perhaps if raising children were more enjoyable, the Japanese mother could more easily wean herself from them and let them go out on their own. But why is it such a hardship? Regarding their offspring as *jibun no ichibu* (part of themselves), mothers find it difficult to treat them objectively or maintain the detachment that will allow them to enjoy their children. If their children are criticized, they feel it is directed at them personally and react accordingly. If their children are praised, they bask in the reflected glow. If their children fail, they take it as their own failure. Japanese women driven to suicide sometimes kill their children before ending their own lives (*oyako shinjū*), convinced that the hardship the children would face after losing their protection would be unbearable. Since a mother considers herself responsible for her children throughout their lives, she considers killing them a necessary act of maternal mercy.

When the "good wife, wise mother" was the ideal image of them, women were excluded from the opportunity to actualize themselves through work or outside activities and therefore found vicarious fulfillment through their husbands and children. Evaluating themselves in terms of the achievements of their children and husband, they soon realized there was no point in cheering on husbands (whose positions in their companies were far beyond their control), so they threw themselves into the role of head cheerleader for their children, urging them through the game of life with all their might. Fortunately, the mother role has been redefined and many mothers are no longer full-time cheerleaders, having themselves entered one race or another through work or community activities.

If a son or daughter receives an honor, the cheerleader mother may enter the limelight, but the same thing may happen if a child does something awful, such as committing a crime. This was illustrated in an incident that happened some years ago: In the city of Osaka a middle-aged man broke into a major bank and held a number of people hostage while making many demands and terrifying his captives. The technique used by the police to persuade him to give up was to ferret out the whereabouts of his aged mother and bring her all the way to Osaka from a small village on the island of Shikoku, where she lived alone. As a mother, it was infuriating for me to watch the police bring forth a tiny gray-haired woman who was awed and frightened by the row of television cameras and microphones pointed at her and who could only bow deeply and apologize profusely to society watching on six channels. It was a cruel way to treat an innocent old woman, yet the whole idea of involving the mother in the incident and placing her in the public eye demonstrates what is expected of a mother in Japan. No wonder raising children is not associated with enjoyment! Because a mother is expected to be answerable for the behavior and achievements of her children, usually without much input or burden sharing from the father, her role compels her to keep a close eye on them, and ensuring that they are dependent rather than independent is the best way to monitor their behavior. In turn, children develop an exceedingly strong attachment to their mothers. It tends to be even stronger if the father is absent a great deal and no other adult is present to offer an alternative companionship or viewpoint.

THE CHILD-CENTERED HOME

Once children are born, the couple cease to call each other by first names, relying more as time goes by on the family-centered names, either the traditional *"Otoosan"* and *"Okaasan"* or the Western-style "Papa" and "Mama." This practice reflects the dominance of the parental role over their identity as individuals or as husband and wife. Parents cease to show overt affection to one another (husbands and wives never kiss or hug in the presence of their children), and the precedence of their parental identity over their husband–wife relationship strengthens, causing them to shift to increasingly neutral, asexual behavior toward each other.

The majority of Japanese, women more than men, consider the family to pivot around the children, not the adults, and women regard their role as mother to be more important than that as wife. Topics of parental discussion, as observed earlier, tend to concentrate on the children, and their welfare is always upper- most in the wife's mind. Taking care of the children and involvement with child-related matters (such as day care and school affairs) ultimately supersede tasks performed on behalf of the husband until the children grow up and leave the home. (Not infrequently, this priority is revealed in daily life by the more elaborately prepared dishes or extra snacks that the children receive.)

If the American family can be described by the letter T, with the father and mother at both ends of the bar at the top and the children along the vertical line joining the bar in the middle, the Japanese family is more like the letter L, with the father at the top of the vertical line, the mother at the bottom corner, and the children along the horizontal line that starts from the mother's corner. The mother is the hinge between father and child, and the mother–child line contributes more to the stability of the family than the husband–wife line. Under these circumstances, an absent husband merely encourages the wife to devote her energies to the mother role and neglect her wife role. A mother regards her bond with the children as stronger than the bond with her husband while the husband regards his bond with his wife as stronger than that with his children.[4] This discrepancy is one of the weak points of the Japanese family.

INDULGENCE AND EDUCATION

As in many societies, disciplining (punishment) of the children in the Japanese family was traditionally more the role of the father than the mother, but this is no longer the rule among contemporary Japanese, largely because of the absence of the father from the home. Surveys show that in 49 percent of cases studied, the mother plays a greater role in disciplining the children than the father, while another 43 percent think it is a role played by both parents equally. Only 4 percent think discipline is to be left to fathers.[5] In short, all facets of childrearing become part of the mother's role.

Unlike their mothers, who had a very clear set of guidelines, aptly expressed in an array of old proverbs designed to prevent disgrace of the family name and dishonor to the ancestors,[6] Japanese mothers today have less to guide them and a tendency to be very permissive. Without the support or cooperation of the fathers, the mothers' tendency to spoil their children becomes all the stronger; mothers often do little to control their children, giving them much freedom to do as they like (sons always have the greater freedom).

Mothers have infinite love for their sons, especially when they are small. No matter what a young son does, his mother quickly forgives him. A common sight is that of a toddler traveling with his mother on the train; bored and restless, perhaps also hungry and tired, he begins to hit his mother hard with his tiny fist. His mother does not try to stop him, merely enduring his blows. Rather than scolding him, she gently asks him to be patient. She appears to think that this is part of her role as mother, and she tends to be even more lenient and indulgent because he is a boy.

The popular comic strip artist Saimon Fumi describes this common pattern in an essay that describes how a mother will give her seven-year-old daughter a bitter scolding, resulting in a quarrel between them, but is immediately forgiving no matter what her three-year-old son does.[7] Occasionally, the mother in this essay realizes that she should try harder to keep her son in line, but her severity is transparent and the little boy knows it; as she glowers at him, he runs circles around her, grinning. The mother tries to be stern, but the insincerity of her scolding delights the boy, and the testing and tension between them provide a certain kind of closeness. Such situations, the essay concludes, may provide "moments of perfect happiness." As Saimon's title for this essay ("Now I Know How the Woman Feels Who Will Lend Her Life's Savings to a Hopelessly Untrustworthy Man") illustrates, Japanese women's willingness to accept any misbehavior on the part of their small sons extends to older males as well. No matter how bungling, miscreant, or foolish he is, if the man in question is one a woman loves, she is willing to forgive virtually anything. The obverse of the mother–son relationship can be observed in father–daughter relations, although the latter tend to be much weaker when the father is away from home a great deal.

Why are some mothers attached so intensely to their sons? Part of the reason is that physical expressions of affection or closeness are tightly restrained among Japanese, especially toward the opposite sex. When the son is small, he can be the object of much of a woman's need for physical contact, a need that is not satisfied by her husband. When a son is older, he may become a surrogate husband of sorts (close, communicative, and affectionate, although not in an incestuous way), a development that helps to fulfill the older woman's emotional needs. This closeness is also a remnant of the *ie* system, under which sons reared to carry on the family name were lavished with greater care than were daughters, who married out of the family. Eldest sons were expected to look after their parents in old age, and with that in mind mothers invariably invested more in sons than in daughters, both emotionally and financially.

The improved status of women (resulting from the abolition of the *ie* system and the relative lowering of the status of men in the family) has noticeably affected mothers' attitudes toward their daughters. Younger mothers have a special closeness with their daughters, often finding in the activities of their daughters some satisfaction of their own dreams or a vicarious enjoyment of pleasures they themselves were denied. And in today's aging society, the role of daughters in the care of aging parents has become greater than ever before. Daughters-in-law are no longer duty-bound to care for their husband's parents, but daughters can be counted on (or are reared in the hopes that they can be counted on) to care for their own parents, another example of Japanese pragmatism in human relationships. The changes in the social environment and in women's status and roles that we are witnessing in Japanese society today are behind mother's efforts to rear their daughters to be independent.

In the United States children are taught the difference between right and wrong, lying and telling the truth, good and bad, and so on from a very young age. Parents apparently turn to models of honesty, nobility, and integrity, like George Washington or Abraham Lincoln, to inspire small children, but this is not done in Japan. The main reason for this may be that proper behavior in Japan is not necessarily principled action but situation-appropriate behavior, and no one model can suffice for all situations. The job of teaching children morals and values, of developing the superego (a process that begins very late in Japan, generally in the upper grades of elementary school), is something most Japanese mothers and fathers leave to society—the schools, in particular. The mother's job is thought to be not so much to teach right and wrong as to console the children when society forces them to behave. If she suffers because the child's behavior has been bad, she feels the pain contributes even more to her strong identity as a mother. In Japanese culture, as intimated earlier in the discussion of the *"hara o itameta ko* [the child I suffered the pain of childbirth for]," we can see the positive value of pain and suffering in the building of emotional ties. Traditionally, motherly devotion and self-sacrifice (whereby the mother would put up with anything the child did or demanded) may have acted to implant in children a sense of obligation to return that care by tending to parents in their old age. The implicit message of old-style childrearing was "We'll do everything for you as a child, so as an adult it is your duty to repay us by taking care of us in our old age." Not always altruistic, the self-sacrifice and devotion of the Japanese mother was unconsciously tied to egocentric motives.

Even today, what it means to be a good mother in Japan is measured by how much a mother does for the sake of the child. Society (the schools, in particular) demands that mothers work closely with their children, especially in the early years of primary school, preparing some of the supplies needed for attending school, monitoring the child's homework and preparations for school, and otherwise keeping a close eye on what the child is doing. Such close involvement by mothers has been a source of great success in assuring that small children acquire solid basic knowledge and skills (such as writing and arithmetic skills), and this involvement is not supposed to be given short shift even if a mother is working (which can impose considerable stress).

Most mothers today are well educated and, unless they are working outside the home, have quite a bit of free time. They are eager to get their children into the best and most prestigious schools, and thus they are more closely involved in their children's studies than the fathers. Surveys show that only 8 percent of fathers take the principal role in helping with children's studies, while 47 percent of mothers serve as the principal family tutor.[8]

The competitive educational system and the academic achievement-oriented society have created, especially in urban areas and among the well-to-do, a particularly extreme example of the devoted mother, the *"kyōiku mama* [education mama],"* sometimes likened to the Jewish mother. These women are mainly the mothers of the children taking junior high school entrance examinations. These children make up only about one third of their age group even in the most competitive city, Tokyo, since the majority of sixth graders enter public junior high schools that do not require entrance examinations. The mothers of these children provide them with full support, taking them to special study classes if necessary, helping them drill in math or language late into the night, playing them with snacks and treats to urge them on, and collecting any and all information useful for and necessary to a child's successful negotiation of the tricky waters of what is known as "examination hell." For children of this young age, success or failure in entrance examinations is thought to be attributable as much to the mother's efforts as to those of the child. Such maternal efforts also apply to children taking senior high school exams; it was what made Kazuo think he was entitled to blame Akiko for their son's failure to pass the entrance examination to private high school. These mothers become fully involved whether they like it or not, and the child's dependency on them is that much more advanced, further strengthening the sense of oneness between mother and child. If the father is absent, as when posted to another city for a two- or three-year stint, the mother–child symbiosis may develop even further, sometimes making it very difficult for the father ever to join or participate in the parent–child relationship. For older children preparing for university entrance examinations, the parents cannot be as involved with their actual studies, but mothers devote great attention and effort to providing the optimal study environment for the children (a room of their own, quiet in the house, favorite meals and snacks, etc.). Supporting her children's education can occupy a large part of a Japanese woman's role as mother.

The dangers of overprotection and too much parental involvement in a child's development have often been pointed out, but a mother feels that everything she does is done for the sake of the child and in this she has utter confidence. Many parents, especially mothers, have a strong desire to give their children what they themselves were deprived of, both materially and in terms of opportunities. They rarely question whether what they are doing is really good for the child as an independent person; they concentrate on protection and coddling.

Some mothers fear that if they do not make sure a child is following the straight-and-narrow as far as social expectations are concerned, they will be considered a failure as a mother and their children will suffer as well. At the same time, feeling that the harsh rules of society are really too hard on young children, they tend to be very permissive and lenient. The effects of their overprotectiveness and overrestrictiveness, however, can be devastating, sometimes developing into violence in the home. This violence is not parental abuse of children, which is often reported in the United States, but acts of extreme violence by children (especially boys) directed at their parents, usually mothers. It is believed that such violence is the result of mothers' inability to clearly judge what is right and wrong at critical points in a child's development and establish firm discipline, thereby leaving the children without any clear referents for guidance.

This overly permissive modern approach to childrearing has been called to task for producing adults who are unprepared to take responsibility. Many Japanese in their early twenties do appear immature due to a lack of training for independence. As more mothers enter the labor force and devote long hours to work outside the home, however, many children are being left somewhat more to their own devices. Surveys show that the greater the income of the mother, the more responsibility children take in the home; thus, the increase in the number of working mothers can be expected to lead to the rearing of more independent children. Women who work tend to be more objective than full-time mothers in their relations with their children, expecting the children to look after their own needs and solve as many of their own problems as possible without constant parental intervention.[9] Conditions that have drawn more of the overinvolved full-time mothers out of the home and into the work force have had the positive effect of alleviating stress between mothers and children. In another culture, such as that of the United States, where mother–child relations are oriented toward independent development of children from the outset, the impact of daily daytime absence from the home of a working mother could be very different.

WORKING MOTHERS

As long as a man or woman considers work the ultimate priority, placed ahead of other activities like housework, community activity, or hobbies, ceasing work temporarily to raise small children will be viewed as a handicap. When the culture of work is accorded higher value in society than the culture of the home, the minimum of five or six years required to raise a child from infancy to first grade is apt to be considered "wasted," a time during which women (to whom the main job of parenting continues to fall today) may feel hobbled in their lives and careers. Considering that a certain balance is desirable in the various activities we engage in throughout life, perhaps this obsession with work needs to be reevaluated. Indeed, the five or six years spent in childrearing can be a time of tremendous satisfaction and growth for the parents as well, and the loving, careful rearing of the next generation is an important investment in social stability and growth. Even in an individual-centered society, people have a responsibility to themselves and their posterity to contribute to and foster social stability.

Still, for Japanese women, simply being a full-time mother/housewife no longer offers sufficient challenge. Especially for urban or suburban women, homes are too small to offer space for hobbies or an enjoyment of the domestic arts, gardening, or other pleasures, and the lure of organized activities, such as those offered by local culture centers or civic clubs, is strong. Because being without adequate means of disposing of idle time in a cramped home can be intolerable, many women seek outside employment. In 1990, 35.8 percent of Japanese mothers with preschool-age children (compared to 58.4 percent in the United States in 1989) and 65.0 percent of those with elementary school–age children (compared to 72.6 percent in the United States) were working.[10] The rate was even higher for junior and senior high school children.

At one time a theory arguing that the children of working mothers were apt to suffer behavioral problems and were prone to be troublemakers or delinquents was advanced and became the focus of considerable controversy. Today, this theory has been virtually dismissed. A consensus has formed that the effects of maternal employment on children depend on various factors including the age of the child and the work schedule of the mother.

As in many other societies made up primarily of nuclear families without domestic help, the most serious problem for working mothers is finding proper child care. In Japan, where the role of the mother is considered very important and where a mother's income is often not an absolute necessity, the justification for work must be very explicit. As mentioned earlier, women try to work only on the condition that it does not impose a burden on other family members. This is particularly true for women born before the war. The cases in which mothers absolutely have to work out of economic necessity are, of course, a different matter.

Japanese women do not feel that childrearing or taking maternity leave are handicaps that infringe on equality between the sexes. Rather, like British women,[11] they believe that good maternity and paternity leave is a precondition for achieving sexual equality in the workplace. The 1991 child care law allows either mothers or fathers to take a child care leave of up to 12 months. The remarkable passage of this law in the male-dominated Japanese Diet is believed to have occurred because of widespread unease among male legislators about the future of Japan's population, given the current birthrate. Existing laws provide for women to receive, upon request, six weeks maternity leave before childbirth and eight weeks child care leave after birth, of which six weeks are compulsory, sometimes with pay (but if not, health insurance pays 60 percent of salary), and employers are forbidden to fire women within 30 days after maternity leave is over. Working mothers with infants under one year old are supposed to be permitted two nursing breaks (on the assumption that infants could be cared for close to the job) of at least 30 minutes each day.

Employers who already have maternity-leave-with-pay policies are subsidized by the government at $50 per eligible female employee per month in addition to child care support funds when they start the system, but today they make up only 15 percent of employers. How many parents will take advantage of the new child care leave law remains to be seen. Since the law does not stipulate that the leave be with pay, observers are doubtful of its real effectiveness. At a time when Japanese businesses are competing for workers from a limited labor pool, companies may utilize the law to make their working conditions look attractive to women, and a large number of young married men and women may hope to take advantage of the law. But if there are insufficient replacement resources, the law may prove unworkable.

For a working mother of a nuclear family with small children, finding adequate child care can be difficult, especially if she has to commute an hour or more to her job. Help from grandparents is often solicited; they are relied on as frequently today as are private and public day care facilities.

Japan has the largest number of day care facilities of any industrialized nation, currently (as of 1991) utilized at only 87 percent capacity because of the decline in the birthrate. The facilities cater mainly to children over one year old, and a shortage in qualified day care for newborns and infants remains a major problem. Public care for infants under one year is used by only 2 percent of all children in this age group, for children between one and two years by only 5 percent, and for children between two and four years by nearly 13 percent.[12] These figures reflect the tendency among many mothers with infants to either drop out or temporarily leave the work force to care for their children. The hours of these facilities—even including the extra hours in the morning (starting at 8:00) and evening (mostly ending at 6:00) through the hiring of nonprofessional attendants

—may be too few for mothers commuting from the suburbs to inner-city jobs. Some companies do provide child care facilities on their premises for their employees, but they are still not very common. It is thought that the current labor shortage may prompt the increase or improvement of child care facilities. Women who wish to keep their jobs in the national civil service, in hospitals, and in other professions where working hours often begin early in the morning or extend into the evening must contrive to find adequate back-up care (called "double day care") in an individual or private day care center that cooperates by taking children early, ferrying them to the public daytime facility, picking them up in the evening, and keeping them until the mothers return. Babysitters who will come to watch children in their own homes are not widely available, and trustworthy live-in domestic help is very expensive and hard to find today, a result of the higher standard of women's education and their preference for office (nondomestic) jobs.

Mothers who quit their jobs to raise small children most often return to work, many to part-time jobs, after the youngest child starts school. A mother who returns to work at this stage cannot take a full-time commuting job if she does not have someone (husband, grandmother, or friend) who can cooperate with early morning and evening care of the child. In Japanese elementary schools, classes usually start at 8:30 in the morning, but first graders' classes end at noon for the first three months and at 1:30, after lunch (which is usually provided by the school), the rest of the year. Classes for grades two through six end at around 2:30. After-school day care (*gakudō hoiku*) for first through third graders is available on site or at nearby facilities in most urban areas, but is still far from sufficient. Mothers have to plan their work or other aspects of their schedule according to the child care conditions available to them.

After her children enter third or fourth grade, a mother may feel that they are old enough to be responsible for themselves until she comes home from work. The low crime rate in Japan allows mothers to accept this arrangement, even though it is not the ideal. Many children's after-school hours are often filled, at least some days of the week, with piano, abacus, calligraphy, or swimming lessons or (in the higher grades) with extracurricular sports and club activities; and as long as the children are thus constructively occupied, mothers can rest easy that they are safe and appropriately entertained.

Many mothers who are dissatisfied with the maternal role alone still wait patiently until their children can start school before they go back to work, believing that a mother's presence is crucial for the development of preschool children and that she is therefore doing what is best for the welfare of the child. These good intentions may cause unexpected problems, however, if the mothers indulge and spoil their children in the usual pattern instead of training them to be independent. For a child accustomed to leaning on a very protective mother for everything, it can be hard to make a transition if the mother suddenly starts working and is absent from the home. Children of mothers who continued working after their birth are accustomed to the separation and better prepared to cope.

A group set up to study the lives of families in which both parents work found that working mothers push themselves especially hard to fulfill all expectations for child care, housework, and service to their husband, as well as for performance on their job.[13] Over 80 percent of mothers do dishes and laundry (including hanging up clothes to dry; dryers are seldom used) before leaving for work in the morning. Most manage jobs, marriage, and children virtually without help from their husbands. When asked in the VSR Survey, "Which gets slighted the most where the woman is a working woman, wife, and a mother?" 24 percent of Japanese women chose the response "none get slighted," and those who felt their children were slighted made up only 17 percent of the sample. The largest proportion of American women in the survey (44 percent), on the other hand, felt their children were slighted; 29 percent indicated that their marriages were neglected but their jobs did not suffer. These figures may reflect the comparatively greater weight children carry in the minds of Japanese working mothers and the strong desire among American mothers to prove themselves as committed professionals. This may also reflect the differing economic and employment conditions in the United States and Japan; for example, it is less likely for Japanese women to lose their jobs as a result of less than 100 percent performance and their income is often not a must for their families to survive.

Women trying to balance all their roles must do a great deal of juggling, adjusting, and compromising as well as learn to cope with the inevitable stresses and frustration. Japanese women working full-time with preschool children "feel guilty for not spending more time with the family" and admit that the "conflicting demands of family and job put [them] under a lot of stress." The demand imposed on working people to socialize with colleagues and stay late to complete important projects (both of which are important adjunctive activities of the Japanese workplace) presents particular difficulties for women with families. There are, nevertheless, a whole range of services and systems available to support the endeavors of working mothers.

In Japan's big cities, such as Tokyo, Yokohama, Nagoya, Osaka, and Kobe, where the population is densely concentrated, many time-conserving services are available. Grocers, druggists, and convenience stores stocking essential foods, dry goods, and household necessities are open until very late (and sometimes 24 hours a day). Supermarkets and other stores specialize in ready-made meals that can be heated in the microwave and in miscellaneous prepared foods that satisfy the needs of busy people who barely have time to eat. If one is tired out from work or other commitments, an instant meal can easily be purchased from an amazing variety of Japanese, Chinese, or Western-style prepared foods. Department stores include among their services grocery delivery systems. A catalog is mailed weekly to customers, who can place orders by telephone any time of the day or night to have a weekly stock of supplies delivered to their doorstep and placed in a locker while they are away at work during the day. Payment is easy: An account can be set up to automatically pay the department store bill by electronic bank transfer once a month. Consumer cooperatives, now used widely in Japan, work in much the same way, offering economical and increasingly healthful and environment-conserving products. Bills—not only for department store and cooperative shopping but for newspaper delivery, utilities, and other regular charges—can be paid automatically through the bank. Housewives are thus spared even the trouble of making out checks or standing in line at the bank. Working mothers have access to public or private day care services for tots as young as three months. The cost is comparatively high and the quality of care is not guaranteed in many privately run, unlicensed facilities, but in a society where continuous employment can be crucial to one's career, relying on full-time day care is sometimes necessary for a woman who plans a lifetime career.

Has the quality of children's elementary education deteriorated as a result of the increase in the number of women who work? In Japan this does not seem to be a visible problem. The reason may be that working mothers make very determined efforts to keep their work from detracting from their obligations to their children. The stress on mothers, of course, is considerable. If a mother feels that her work schedule is the cause of the poor academic performance of her children, she is very likely to cease working until the problem can be remedied. But some mothers feel the best way to get their children to improve their grades is to send them to remedial study classes (often in the neighborhood), and because of the additional educational expenses this involves, they often have to continue working.

What children think of their mother's working and what effect it has on them has a great impact on working trends among mothers in Japan. Children's reactions differ, and depend on their age and sex, as well as on the mother's working schedule. According to a 1984 study of the effects of mothers' employment upon children (grades four to eight), effects are more visible in the younger children.[14] Younger children of working mothers, compared to those with full-time mothers, spend less time in home study and more time watching television. However, by the time they reach the sixth grade, these differences between the two groups of children disappear. According to teachers' evaluations of children's behavior at school (uninformed of the mothers' working status), the younger children of working mothers have a greater tendency to forget things they ought to bring to school and their school performance tends to be poorer, but, again, by sixth grade such differences disappear. Mothers are very concerned and feel guilty about any loneliness their children suffer, and fourth grade (age 10) girls feel the loneliness the most. By the time they reach the eighth grade (age 14), however, more children are aware of how working outside the home invigorates their mothers.

In the aforementioned study, we asked children to write essays about their mothers to see how they evaluated the effects of her working; these revealed loneliness among fourth and sixth graders and complaints about the difficulty of preparing meals and handling other housework. We found that as they get older, the children acquire more household skills, learn to help, and develop a feeling of concern for their mother's health. Once they reach 8th grade, the majority develop a respect for their mothers and their work, as the following quote indicates: "What I like about my mother is that since she started working she is more energetic. She seems to have gained a sense of accomplishment that I think has made her a better mother." According to another student: "When mother was at home all the time, she got fat and read cartoons all the time. Since she started working, she is more concerned about her appearance and lost weight. She has much more bounce and variety in her life and has started reading the newspaper." Needless to say, the absence of the mother gives children a freedom that is often greatly welcomed, especially if the family is very education-conscious ("I'm happy that mother is away at work and is not always here telling me to study," one student admitted), but of course this is also a source of concern for mothers.

When children of full-time mothers were asked to write about what they thought it would be like if their mothers worked, the worries and concerns they expressed were quite different from those of children of currently working mothers. The former thought they would have to prepare their own meals and complained about how taking care of themselves could take time away from their studies. This self-centeredness continues even after they reach junior high school age, making them critical if their mothers are not there to prepare their meals regularly. (For example, one student said, "If she wants to work, I cannot stop her, but I won't say anything as long as she takes care of all the housework and doesn't cause me any trouble.") In tone and phraseology, it appeared to analysts of the essays that some students were imitating what their fathers say to discourage their wives from working. One remedy for the tendency among Japanese children to be self-centered is for mothers to work outside the home, although they have to take special care to explain to their children why they are working and what they are doing. A mother's absence from the home can be a good stimulus to verbal communication with her children and can eventually change the mother–child relationship—the prototype for all interpersonal relations and for communications in society as a whole—for the better.

GROWN-UP CHILDREN AND THEIR MOTHERS

The close and intense care both working and nonworking mothers provide their children continues through high school. The educational system forbids high school students to work in part-time jobs (and their studies are too intense to permit it, anyway). Parents provide them allowances and as much as possible help them purchase whatever they want. As long as the child's academic performance is good, the parents' generosity is bounded only by financial circumstances. Supervision is also intense, especially of girls' activities (who are expected to acquire a certain degree of cultivation and good manners and who are considered particularly vulnerable sexually). Yet interaction between parents and children is information-centered; they rarely share hobbies or activities in the home or even outside. Mothers may share shopping with their daughters and chat a lot about trivial matters of common interest, but they do not discuss feelings or what they consider to be important in life. The home and family have become the venue of consumption rather than production, and mothers no longer make much effort to teach their daughters skills such as cooking or sewing. Sharing activities with sons comes even less naturally for mothers.

Japanese children take the love of their mothers for granted; the unquestioned bond between mother and child assures them that their mother is genuinely concerned about them. The scene in Ingrid Bergman's film *Autumn Sonata* showing a pianist mother and her daughter in a violent argument over whether the mother really loves the daughter is quite alien to many Japanese viewers since a Japanese child rarely feels called upon to question maternal love. Mothers and daughters seldom confront each other on serious issues, and daughters' behavior today is just as apt to be influenced by women in the media, their friends, and other women as it is to be molded by their own mothers. Role models are diffused, for female roles today are rapidly changing. Although girls may not make role models of their mothers, a strong mother may present a model of positive competition for her daughters. The father as a role model is problematic. Ideally, they inspire their sons, but since fathers are often absent, many sons find it difficult to graduate from overattachment to their mothers.

The mother–son relationship is much less relaxed than the mother–daughter relationship. Especially with an only son, it can be quite tense because of the mother's desire to control the son by making him dependent and a faithful ally in the family. A Japanese mother has a tendency to think of a daughter-in-law as a rival, as a woman trying to usurp her son. In the absence of husbands to fulfill their needs and desires as wives, mothers who essentially play the role of a single parent often develop very strong attachments to their sons, and an only son sometimes becomes the focus of treatment usually reserved for a husband. In extreme cases, incest sometimes occurs. Certain isolated cases have been much sensationalized in the media; it is perhaps more likely for such a relationship to develop in a small family, but no reliable statistics or information is available. In the United States cases of incest usually result from the father's sexual advances toward a daughter, but in Japan they more commonly involve a mother and son, perhaps resulting from the desire of the mother to ease her son's stress, her mothering instincts spilling over to sexuality; but we can only speculate.

An adolescent son's dependence upon and close cooperation with his mother are generally cultivated particularly in the process of preparing him for the entrance examinations to high school and, later, university. Boys remain tied to their mother's apron strings inordinately long and have little incentive to become psychologically independent.[15] The father is forced to accept this mother–son closeness, since he wants his son to study hard and get into good schools, and there is little he can do except leave childrearing and education-related matters to his wife. Fathers are often too busy with work to take time to read and digest the massive amount of literature providing guidance on how to navigate the high school entrance exam situation,[16] and their co-workers and friends are likewise less informed than mothers who both study the situation carefully and network among themselves.

Sons may become incapable of making decisions on their own because of the way they are raised. So psychologically dependent have they become on their mothers that they often turn to them for advice even after they are married, much to their wife's consternation. A relatively recent phenomenon, especially among the sons of wealthy families who have gained entrance to the academic elite of Japan, this dependent behavior has been attributed to men who have what is described as a "mother complex" (*mazakon*). In some cases, these men are so severely fixated on their mothers that they are unable to have a normal sexual relationship with a girlfriend or wife.[17] The father's absence accentuates the problem; he is often the target of a mother's bitter complaints (she may openly criticize the father and warn her son not to be like him) and has hardly any opportunity to serve as a sex role model for his son. Some of these young men find themselves divorced by wives who cannot compete with their mothers-in-law.

Such extreme cases are, of course, rare, but Japanese men show a strong desire to have an indulgent mother in their life. When they marry, many of them expect their wives to take over their mother's role. In the workplace their bosses are also cast in the mother's role. They retain a strong need for indulgence, seeking out the soothing, comforting treatment of surrogate mother figures like the "mama-sans," the local bar owners who serve as confidantes, and sometimes lovers, for regular clientele.

Many of the distortions and problems inherent in these patterns of parenting are a product of recent social and institutional changes. If women are to have happier marriages and healthier relationships with their children, they need to establish a strong self-identity as individuals and to gain a better perspective on their own lives. Being a "part-time mother" is one way to achieve this goal. Fathers, too, need to extricate themselves from their jobs long enough to assure the healthy development of their marriages and their children, reestablishing their role and presence in the home.

While the number of mother-fixated men in the generation now in their twenties is considerable,[18] the number of men of an opposite type—those who make a conscious effort to free themselves of such dependence—is increasing. These young men are likely to be the sons of mothers who have successfully engineered for themselves a redefinition of the traditional female roles. The redefinition of female roles is rapidly progressing, although the roles still revolve mainly around motherhood. This process, however, has been facilitated by the shift in viewing children's development more as the responsibility of the children themselves and less as a sign of the success or failure of the mother. Another factor is the relatively decreased weight of the maternal role in female identity as a result of women's pursuit of fulfillment in other roles.

A major task in Japanese families today is to build and sustain a warm and nurturing home with close family ties but without overreliance on the mother. The information society, working mothers, absent fathers, and excessive academic demands have put inordinate pressures on the family today, leading to much-weakened family bonds. As the mother ceases to function as the pivot in the fan of the family, some fear that family members will quickly develop such independence that the household will become little more than a convenient hotel and that women will increasingly seek the pleasures to be found outside the family and the closeness to be forged with other women. While still anxious to maintain the warm household, they will increasingly seek part-time work, and their close support of their children's activities may fade (even to the point of mobilizing the children to help with household chores, a phenomenon that has been rare in postwar Japan). Their reliance on purchasable household services will increase, and this, in turn, will add to their incentive and need for wage-earning employment. This trend is expected to grow stronger in the coming years.

The changes occurring in women's roles in Japan today are having significant impact on motherhood and mothering. Women want children as much as ever, but they also want other forms of gratification and fulfillment. What is now being tested is how far the autonomy and freedom of women to determine the course of their own lives can go before children and childrearing are marginalized to a dangerous degree.

6

WORK AS OPTION

At a time when women all over the world are entering the workplace, taking their places beside men or even replacing them, many wonder whether Japanese women today remain tied to the home, subservient to husbands and children. Statistics indicate that this is far from the case. Women make up 38 percent of the total employed labor force (as of 1991), and this does not include the self-employed and farmers. Actually, a considerable proportion of Japanese women have worked for a long time; what *has* changed, and quite drastically, is which women work and why. Also, the types of work they do have greatly diversified, and the way they go about work has changed. Less a means of survival, work for the vast majority of women is now an option, a means by which they can gain and enjoy freedom and economic autonomy. At the same time, they have become virtually indispensable to the Japanese labor market, which suffers from a shortage of labor, although it must be said that workplaces are still overwhelmingly staffed by men.

TRADITIONAL ROLES AND WORK

We can gain a more accurate perception of the contemporary situation by first looking briefly at the role and conditions of working women in the past. A surprisingly large number of women have worked in nondomestic jobs since the beginning of the modern period (late 19th century). In prewar times (1920s and 1930s), it was quite common for women to be engaged in farm work, sales, domestic service, factory work (such as weaving), and cottage industries (e.g., sewing, embroidery, toy assembly).

Whatever type of work married women did, however, it was of a kind that could be done even while keeping an eye on children and attending to regular household tasks. It was also work done out of necessity. Both single and married women worked not only to improve their own lives but also (and more importantly) to make things better for their families. In prewar periods of famine, very poor farming families were often forced to sell their daughters into prostitution (the number of cases increased sharply around 1934). The prettier ones might be snapped up by the geisha houses, but the less lucky ended up in ordinary brothels. Most Japanese were very poor before World War II, incredibly so by today's standards, and the only alternative to indigence was hard work. As a farming people accustomed to the unpredictable and sometimes destructive forces of nature, Japanese accepted their hardship as fate, comforting themselves with the refrain "It cannot be helped [shikata ga nai]." Perseverance and obedience became virtues along with diligence and self-sacrifice.

The passivity and diligence that characterized Japanese before World War II have not changed much even today, but life has become much easier for both men and women as a result of economic growth and the affluence that made possible technological advancement both in the home and the workplace. Today, Japan has become sufficiently affluent that the number of women who have to work out of absolute economic necessity has dwindled. A totally new type of woman is joining the labor force: those who do not have to earn money to support their families but who choose to work for other reasons. The fact that they no longer work only for economic survival has been a factor in the slowly rising status of working women.

After World War II, and until 1965, the proportion of working women in the total female population was one of the highest among developed nations throughout the world owing to the large farming population. But while in other countries women joined the labor force in growing numbers, in Japan the trend was actually in the other direction, with fewer women working as economic growth gained momentum and the farming population entered the cities, where men became salaried workers and women became full-time housewives.

Japan reconstructed its virtually annihilated economy during the 1940s and 1950s and rode smoothly on the wave of economic growth with an approximately 10 percent annual growth rate during the 1960s and up to the mid-1970s. While men devoted themselves to the expansion of the gross national product, women enjoyed the fruits of economic growth, many becoming nonworking housewives. Then, in 1975, the trend again reversed, and the increase in the number of women in the work force continues today. As the economy developed and society grew affluent, women who had seen themselves only in terms of their family's and their children's goals began to ask themselves, "What do *I* want out of life?" And they have begun to seek concrete answers to that question. One answer has been to work and earn an income to spend as they wish.

THE FEMALE WORK FORCE IN THE 1960s AND 1970s

Industrialization and urbanization in the 1960s and 1970s set the stage for the first transformation in the female work force. In 1960 the largest percentage (43 percent) of working women were employed in the primary sector, mainly agriculture; 20 percent, in secondary industry (manufacturing); and nearly 37 percent, in the tertiary sector (schools and offices). Those employed in the secondary sector were mostly young junior high school graduates (having completed compulsory education) who worked in factories, large and small.

In the tertiary sector, women worked as teachers (53 percent of working women who were college graduates worked as teachers in 1965) and in clerical positions (21 percent of female college graduates who were working in 1965 were "OLs" or "office ladies"). Full-time employed women with high school or college diplomas were called "*sararī gāru* [salary girls]" or "BGs" (business girls). As suggested by the use of the word *girl*, these women were almost all single and young, and they uniformly quit their jobs upon marriage. Some companies routinely set the retirement age for women separate from that for men, sometimes as early as age 35. It was not surprising that women were known as the "flowers of the office [*shokuba no hana*]"—pretty to look at and decorative but insubstantial and transient.

Duration of continuous service is a particularly important factor in the lifelong employment systems of large corporations in Japan. In order to achieve high status in a large organization in the business sector, women have to stay on the job long enough to compete with men for promotion (at least until employment practices shift toward greater job mobility in Japan). Men find it hard enough to gain promotion in the first four years after joining a company, but for women, the vast majority of whom stay employed for only four years, the hurdles are even greater. Recent surveys show, in fact, that it takes some 20 years for the average woman in the business sector to be promoted to a managerial post.[1]

Social images of work outside the home discouraged women from pursuing careers or long-term employment. Working was considered to be secondary since a woman's place was "naturally" in the home. Marriage was known as "*eikyū shūshoku* [lifetime employment]" and considered to offer the greatest possible security and fulfillment for a woman. Jobs outside the home were referred to as *koshikake* (temporary seat) and were valued primarily as a chance for a woman to observe and learn about the world outside the home (*shakai kengaku*) while not incurring a long-term job commitment.

In the world of business, women were temporary pinch hitters, or supporters, not regular players in the game. In terms of salary, promotions, and type of work assigned, the worlds of men and women in the corporation were clearly and distinctly separate. Women seemed to affirm (and many still do affirm) the separation, considering themselves to be short-term, noncareer workers who therefore do not need to take equal responsibility with male employees. Their lower wages and the less responsible tasks they were expected to perform did not (and still do not) generate tension in the workplace. They contented themselves with simple clerical tasks and services for their male supervisors (such as answering telephones, serving tea, and emptying ash trays). Essentially, they were performing the housekeeping chores of the office, applying traditional womanly skills.

In the early 1960s the Japanese economy began to shift toward the service sector—finance, information, commerce—a develop-

ment signaling the advent of the postindustrial age, and the
number of women working in the tertiary sector increased along
with that of men. By 1970 those in the primary sector decreased
sharply (to 26 percent from 43 percent in 1960, see Fig. 6–1).
Women in the secondary sector increased slightly, with the
tertiary sector accounting for the majority (at 48 percent of all
working women).

Although it is seldom noted or acknowledged, working wom-
en can claim, through their contribution to the work force, at
least one third of the credit for Japan's miraculous economic
growth—and perhaps even more since they also provided home
environments that supported and sustained the overworked,
embattled men caught up in the cogs of Japan, Inc. (as the
political/industrial complex of postwar Japan is often described).
There is no question that Japanese industry surged ahead in the
postwar period partly because the role of women was such that it
allowed men to put work above everything else. Yet women are
all but invisible as far as anyone outside Japan can see; men seem
to be the only moving forces in the country's history, society, and
economic growth.

Figure 6-1 Industry Distribution of Women Workers (in percent)

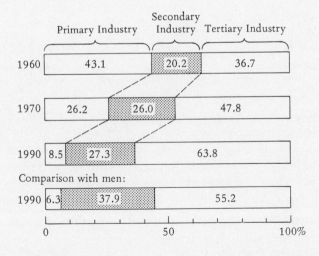

Source: Bureau of Statistics, Management and Coordination Agency. *Labor Force Survey* and data from the national
censuses.

By 1965, reflecting the zeal and respect for education in Japan, nearly 70 percent of the women who completed junior high school (compulsory education) went on to senior high school. The concomitant decrease in the number of nimble-fingered young women entering the work force for whom manual labor was the only option forced the secondary sector to look elsewhere to fill its demands. The economy was growing rapidly, and the labor shortage in the secondary sector was acute.

Industry's needs were partly fulfilled by part-time workers (persons working 35 hours or less per week by choice, a classification borrowed from American management practice), mostly housewives under the age of 35 with children of primary school age or older and with time to work outside the home. However, day care, for the entire day or for after-school hours, had yet to become widespread, and many of the children of these women had to fend for themselves, letting themselves into their homes after school and waiting until their mothers returned in the evening. The problems of "latchkey children" became a key social issue and the concern of many adults starting around 1965. Some factories, determined to attract and keep cheap female labor (primarily part-time blue-collar workers with small children), started up on-site day care facilities. The general trend was for mothers with infants and small children to remain at home, however, so the number of working mothers did not substantially increase. In the 1960s part-time female workers came mostly from lower-income families and were primarily engaged in blue-collar jobs; socially, therefore, they continued to be looked down upon.

There were other notable changes among working women during the decade of the 1960s. The percentage of single women among those who worked as a whole decreased drastically and that of married women increased, to 51 percent by 1970 (from 38 percent in 1960). The expanding economy produced considerable demand for female part-time labor, and by 1970 the number had increased to 12 percent of employed women (from 9 percent in 1960). Nevertheless, mothers with infants and small children working outside the home in full-time, white-collar jobs were still a rarity, except in the professional careers in which women have long played an important role, such as nursing and teaching. One reason was that domestic help was rapidly becoming a

luxury, partly due to high wages and partly to the greater attractions of regular office or factory work over live-in domestic
service. In addition, as a result of urbanization, nuclear families
had proliferated and grandparents who could take care of
children were not available.

Another reason inhibiting women from joining the work force
were the beliefs, widespread in the sixties, that improper maternal care was the cause of juvenile delinquency among children
and that children of working mothers were quick to get into
trouble.[2] This myth was exploited in the media and served for a
long time to discourage many mothers from seeking outside
employment. Even today, when a child becomes delinquent, it is
the mother who takes the brunt of the blame, not only from
society and the schools but from the father, who is not expected
to play a role in molding the behavior of his children. Working
mothers, nevertheless, gradually multiplied.[3]

Although the number of working women increased, their lives
remained hemmed in by many discriminatory practices and customs. For a long time women did not make a big issue of such
practices, working around them and despite them. While American society was going through a traumatic women's liberation
movement, Japanese women as a whole had yet to voice their
complaints publicly or seek legal redress for the disadvantages
they suffered.

It was not until the United Nations Decade for Women that the
issue of equal opportunity and status for women came to the fore.
Existing laws for working women tended to be protective rather
than concerned with equality, as evidenced by the Labor Standards Law (discussed later in this chapter).

WORKING WOMEN TODAY

Several characteristics of the Japanese workplace affect the
circumstances of working women. First, nearly 90 percent of
companies are either small- or medium-sized enterprises with
less than 300 workers; these companies employ over 80 percent
of working women and 70 percent of men. Many women, especially part-timers, are absorbed by this stratum of industry.
Second, compared to that in the United States, there is less job

mobility in the Japanese job market, especially in the case of the larger corporations. Third, promotion and accompanying pay raises are connected more closely to seniority than to achievement. The latter two characteristics make the hope for equal treatment unrealistic for women who want to (and have to) stay at home while their children are small and return to work when the children are older. Therefore, women are eager to obtain qualifications (or certification) of some sort on the basis of which they can break through the barriers of seniority.

By 1985, reflecting structural changes in the Japanese economy, the proportion of women working in the tertiary sector further increased, leaving only a small portion in the primary sector. In the 15 years between 1970 and 1985 the number of employed women increased by 50 percent, totaling nearly 15.5 million. By 1990 the largest number of women workers were in clerical positions, with the next largest category being that of crafts and production process workers; together, these represent the profession of more than half of all working women (see Table 6–1). Figures show that the number of women working in traditional occupations such as nursing, typing, nutrition, telephone operating, and garment making have decreased, while those venturing into the jobs previously monopolized by men— such as medicine, law, and the civil service, as well as the newer occupations like engineering, marketing, merchandising, sports instruction, journalism, and business consulting—are increasing. Highly motivated and capable women looking for equal employment opportunities are especially attracted to the latter, newer, occupations, where men have not necessarily been dominant. According to International Labor Organization statistics, 46 percent of women workers in Japan were employed in professional and technical jobs (the majority of these are in teaching and nursing).[4] This figure for Japanese women was not much lower than the 48 percent for American women and the 55 percent for Swedish women. However, about 10 percent more Japanese women were engaged in factory work than elsewhere and only 6 percent of managerial jobs were held by women, as compared with 34 percent in the United States and 21 percent in Sweden.

With more women continuing to work even after they marry, the females in offices today in Japan are no longer insubstantial, transient "flowers." The percentage of women who work for the

Table 6-1
Female Employees by Profession

PROFESSION	PERCENTAGE OF FEMALE EMPLOYEES —AS PART OF TOTAL FEMALE WORKING POPULATION (%)			PERCENTAGE OF FEMALE EMPLOYEES —AS PART OF TOTAL MALE AND FEMALE WORKING POPULATION (%)		
	1975	1980	1990	1975	1980	1990
Professional and technical workers	11.6	13.0	13.8	44.4	48.4	42.6
Managers and officials	0.9	0.8	1.0	5.4	5.1	7.7
Clerical and related workers	32.2	32.7	34.4	48.5	51.1	58.0
Sales workers	11.1	11.6	12.5	30.2	31.6	33.8
Farmers, lumbermen, and fisherman	0.8	0.7	0.6	22.0	25.0	28.2
Mining workers	—	—	—	—	—	—
Cummunications and transport workers	1.5	1.0	0.5	7.7	6.1	4.2
Craft and productions process workers	24.6	23.2	20.6	23.6	24.9	28.2
Laborers	3.7	4.0	5.6	32.6	36.5	41.6
Protective service workers and service workers	13.7	12.9	10.7	50.8	50.9	51.3
Total	100.0	100.0	100.0	32.0	34.1	37.9

Source: Bureau of Statistics, Management and Coordination Agency, *Labor Force Survey.*

same company for 10 years or more has increased over the past 10 years from 9 percent in 1980 to 26 percent in 1990. The average age of working women in 1990 was 36 years, ten years older than the average for 1960. Married women make up the bulk of working women, and the percentage of part-time workers rose to 28 percent (as of 1990) of all employed women. Many of these women are returnees—those who left full-time jobs to raise families and came back to the work force once their children were grown—in the middle and older age groups.

An interesting anecdote that chronicled this change comes from 1984, when a noontime television series called the "Pola TV Novel," sponsored by a prestigious cosmetics company modeled after America's Avon, had to be terminated after 16 successful years on the air because the target audience—married women—was no longer at home to watch the program.

Today, women are beginning to demand that their menfolk spend more time with them and their families, and if they have their way, the male-dominated pattern of employment with its long working hours that is behind the powerful Japanese economy (and the global economy in which it plays a major role) will have to change. It seems clear that women will become a driving force of change in the Japanese economy. The net result will undoubtedly be that the economy will cease expanding at its present rate. Perhaps this would be a good thing for the world economy, making Japan's competitiveness less threatening to other countries than it is today.

THE M CURVE

The overall distribution of employed Japanese women by age forms a skewed M-shaped curve, as shown in Figure 6–2, with the first peak at ages 20 to 24 and the second somewhat lower peak at ages 45 to 49. Participation in the labor force by American women formed an M curve until 1970, but today, it is a mesa-shaped curve, as is true of the distribution by age of working women in France, Canada, and the Scandinavian countries. The very sharp drop in the middle of the M is a notable feature of the curve depicting the nature of labor force participation by Japanese women. Fifteen years ago, the age curve for Japanese employed women looked like a skewed bell curve with only one peak at ages 20 to 24; the present second peak represents a new phenomenon, the result of the shifting roles of women. The dip in the curve for the 30 to 34 age bracket represents women who drop out of the labor force when their children are small and their gradual return as their children enter primary school. This trend seems to represent the preferred work pattern for the majority of women, and reflects male expectations as well (which clearly do affect women's work patterns), as indicated repeatedly in various public opinion surveys.

A 1987 survey of both men's and women's attitudes toward women working found the following five possible patterns:[5] (1) It is better for women not to work. (2) Women should quit working when they marry and stay in the home thereafter. (3) Women should quit working when they bear children and remain in the home thereafter. (4) Women should quit working when children are born but return to work when they are old enough to need less care. (5) Women should continue working even after giving birth. The fourth option, the quit-and-return pattern, received the largest support among men and women (43 percent and 52 percent, respectively), and this is, in fact, the pattern portrayed by the M-shaped curve (see Fig. 6-2). Clearly, many women

Figure 6-2 Labor Force Participation Rates for Japanese Women

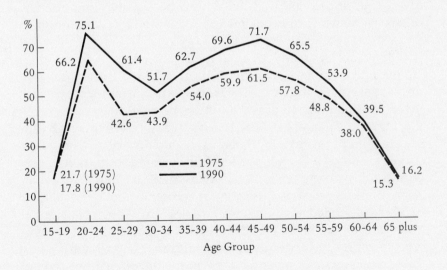

Source: Bureau of Statistics, Management and Coordination Agency. *Labor Force Survey.*

recognize the need to put work aside when their children are small. Dropping out of the labor force is, for many, the desired choice when all factors are considered. Many women who initially launch into careers are forced to abandon the idea because they cannot manage the difficulties of balancing work and family. Whether a man has small children or not generally does not affect his working life at all unless he becomes widowed or divorced with child custody. The fifth option, of continuing to work even while rearing small children, was selected by a much smaller number of men and women, 12 and 16 percent, respectively. Because men do not count on women's income, women have the option to quit working if they so desire.

In 1982 a similar survey was conducted among women in Japan and several other countries.[6] Forty-four percent of Japanese, 53 percent of German, and 62 percent of British female respondents chose the quit-and-return work pattern, while 43 percent of American and 55 percent of Swedish women selected the continuous-work pattern, showing that Japanese women are closer to British and German women than to Americans and Swedes in their attitudes toward work. The difference between these two groups stems from differences in women's role expectations as well as from the relative importance of the woman's income in maintaining the family's economic level.

If they are so ready to quit their jobs, does it mean that Japanese women are dissatisfied with their work? Survey data do not suggest that is the case.[7] The work environment for women in Japan is apparently improving, for 58 percent of women think the current situation makes it easy for women to work, an increase of approximately 10 percentage points over the previous survey conducted 7 years earlier. Still, women tend to be more critical of working conditions than men. In terms of what they think makes it difficult to continue working, child care was identified as the greatest problem (by 64 percent), along with care of the elderly and the sick (45 percent); housework (28 percent) and education of children (27 percent) were lesser problems. Men tend to be more uncomplaining about their jobs because they are exempt from the many household chores.

THE FIRST PEAK OF THE M:
WHY YOUNG WOMEN WORK

For men, working outside the home is taken for granted; it is when they *do not* want to work in regular jobs that they encounter problems. There is still no stigma for women who do not work, although it is taken for granted that most will take a job upon graduation and work at least until they marry or have a child, even if not out of financial necessity. In 1990, the percentage of both men and women graduates of four-year universities entering employment was 81 percent, the first time the percentage for women rose to a level equal to that for men.

While there are self-supporting independent women, many women who work remain living at home with their parents as long as they are single. They use their income primarily for clothing, hobbies, and pleasure, such as vacations abroad. The self-supporting independent women are not very different from those in the United States in terms of their financial responsibilities and lifestyles, but they are a minority. The lack of real financial responsibility of these young working women who live with their parents surely makes it easier for them to take an easygoing attitude toward work. If the work is intrinsically uninteresting, if opportunities for promotion are lacking, and if they intend to quit and stay home upon marriage, they tend to leave their jobs without a second thought. The attitudes their parents take do not encourage them to take their jobs more seriously. Parents do not hesitate to pressure their daughters to quit working if the work seems too stressful or demanding, and, in general, Japanese women do not consider work so important to them that they are willing to sacrifice their health to continue. Mothers are more concerned with protecting their daughters from the harsh winds of society than in seeing them develop a career or obtain equal employment treatment. By contrast, they expect their sons to put their work first, even if their health suffers.

As noted, many women do not have to work full-time. Some really enjoy working, but for others it is just better than being bored at home while most of their friends are working. As long as affluent and overprotective parents will indulge them, they can get by with a weak motivation for work, yet they eagerly seek income that they can use freely.[8] A survey conducted by the Prime Minister's Office (1989) on reasons for working found that the primary reason (57 percent) for women in their twenties to work is "to make money to use freely." (Such freedom and affluence contrasts poignantly with their unfortunate forebears two generations ago who might have been sold to geisha houses to pay their parents' debts.) Today, these affluent women are making a substantial contribution to the Japanese economy. The second most common reason (54 percent) was "to save money for the future" (which we may interpret to mean the immediate future, e.g., when they decide to marry or travel abroad), and the third (38 percent) was "to broaden [their] perspective and make friends."

Two particular attractions of the workplace to women in Japan are the glimpse it gives them of the "real world" and the opportunity it offers them to make a wider circle of friends than they would find staying at home. For those who are not fully independent, there is great allure in being able to set out each day into this real world from the safe refuge of their parents' home. They seek the company of women who are comrades and friends rather than sexual rivals. After work and on weekends and holidays, they go out together. The Japanese workplace offers many after-work activities, such as choral singing, volleyball, flower arrangement, and English conversation. The worlds of men and women remain clearly separated in Japan, so friends of the same sex are especially important.

This social context makes the reasons Japanese women work completely different from those of American women. The latter usually choose one job over another because it offers better pay or better professional experience that they can build on in obtaining their next job. Japanese women of all ages lack this kind of goal orientation. They are more concerned with a pleasant or friendly work atmosphere.

If Japanese women suffer discriminatory treatment, they become annoyed and voice complaints, but as long as other women are subject to the same discriminatory treatment, they are likely to accept the situation and be unlikely to move to combat it, having little desire to disrupt the harmony of the workplace. This goes for women of all ages. In this case, they are more concerned with equality among themselves than with equality with men. Given the major motives for working that we find among women in their twenties, it is unlikely that they will contribute much to fighting sexual discrimination in the workplace. If the sexual discrimination they face in a particular job is intolerable, they simply leave that job and find another, for as we have seen, there is much more job mobility among women than men. Japanese women seldom evaluate their workplace in terms of only one criterion, such as sexual discrimination. Other factors, such as enjoyable after-five activities or good fringe benefits, are taken into account in evaluating a workplace. In other words, sexual discrimination may be something that can be tolerated if the other factors make it worthwhile.

YOUNG JOB HUNTERS

The common pattern among both career-minded and non-career-minded young women upon completing their education, be it high school or college, is to look for an attractive job either through placement offices in their schools or through connections provided by parents, relatives, or acquaintances. The overall trend is to enter a job that may have no connection to their interests or training. The reason for this is that people are usually not hired for a specific job but for the company as a whole and are then assigned to a particular job according to management discretion. Most young women looking for jobs dream of a position with one of the large and prestigious companies with attractive offices located in the major business districts of central Tokyo or other big cities.

The company name and location are a greater concern for many non–career-minded women than equal status with men, opportunity for promotion, career development, or type of business. Small and medium-sized corporations, which find it difficult to attract enough males from the cream of the university crop, actually offer more opportunities for women to develop and utilize their abilities, but young female graduates of leading universities rarely consider them. The fields most popular among young women seeking jobs are banking, insurance, sales (for example, in a large department store), advertising, journalism, and broadcasting. Many of these jobs are in the information industry, in which individual ability counts most and sexual discrimination is not much of a problem. Those with talent, be they men or women, can blossom in these fields. Once hired by a firm, however, employees are customarily rotated once every two or three years, so they tend to establish identification with the firm as a whole rather than with a certain position or branch of the firm. As long as the company is strong and reliable, employees feel they will eventually receive a post that they will find really interesting and challenging. (In the United States, people who want to work in a different kind of job have to quit one job and search for another; in Japan, companies shift employees from one department to another, fostering versatility and broad experience among their own employees.)

Furthering one's professional worth by job hopping is less common in Japan, for workplace values are based on trust. It is most advantageous to be working for a prestigious company that holds a stable reputation (i.e., no danger of bankruptcy and assurance of a good working environment). Such companies, moreover, tend to provide better recreational facilities, more congenial colleagues, and—for husband-hunters—a better batch of eligible bachelors. Another factor influencing a woman's choice of employer in recent years, reflecting the recent phenomenon of young women who want to continue to work after they marry and have children, is a company's policy on maternity leave. In interviews with potential employers, even leading corporations, young women can freely ask questions irrelevant to the work itself, such as what kind of conditions are offered for maternity leave, day care facilities, and so on. In Japanese women's own minds, their role as the bearer of children does not appear as a factor of inequality between men and women in the workplace.

One of my former students at Keio University, Tomoko, majored in social psychology and graduated with the class of 1990. She took up employment with the Japan Long-Term Credit Bank for the following reasons:

> First of all, I am interested in the general area of financial dealings and project financing. Second, I was attracted by the bank's understanding of women as reflected in their maternity leave policy, the comparatively long average length of service of their women employees, and their practice of hiring back former employees who had quit within five years.

She is guessing that the bank is "woman friendly." Notably, she makes no mention of job and pay, potential for promotion, equal opportunity, or the possibilities of developing a career. Her

concerns are fairly average for graduating women of elite universities.

According to a survey of young women's career plans, Japanese women were found to map out their career plans rather later
in life than American or British women. Of 22-year-old women,
60 percent of American and British women already had made
fairly clear career plans, whereas less than 40 percent of Japanese
women had done so. Japanese women's approach to life (in
contrast to that of men, who have a fairly clear career plan by the
time they are 22) is not set by mapping out clear goals and
working toward them but by making decisions at each point in
time on a situational basis, depending on the various factors
involved, and leaving open as many options as possible.[9]

"WOMAN-FRIENDLY" EMPLOYERS

There are a number of foreign companies that have been
operating very successfully in Japan for some time. Many of them
have attracted bright young women with career ambitions and
some foreign language proficiency. Ninety percent of these
foreign companies are small or medium-sized corporations, but
they also offer challenging jobs and good pay on a more equal
level with men than most Japanese companies and are therefore
famous for being "woman friendly." One reason they do offer
such good conditions for women is that they have trouble
drawing from the pool of the most talented male employees.
Their handicap in recruiting outstanding male employees, due to
their not providing the security and benefits offered by large
Japanese corporations and to their lower ranking in terms of
prestige than that of Japanese companies, paid off unexpectedly
in the windfall of bright, elite young women.

It is not at all an anomaly to find Japanese women on the
management staff of foreign companies. They had difficulty
finding interesting jobs in Japanese companies, and because
working women are not part of the mainstream of the Japanese
work force, they are freer to take the risks involved in working
with foreign companies. Compared to men, they have less to lose
in terms of social standing by not being employed by the
companies at the top of the hierarchy of employment prestige in
contemporary Japan.

Foreign firms hire workers for what they are able to do at the time they are hired, not for their potential abilities to be developed through on-the-job training. Japanese firms give new recruits several months of intensive on-the-job training, thereby molding them to their specific needs and purposes. Because of foreign firms' different managerial and procedural practices, women whose first jobs were with such firms usually have to remain within the circle of foreign businesses in Japan. The capabilities they develop there may be quite different from their sisters trained to work in Japanese companies. If Japanese companies begin to hire highly qualified women in greater numbers, foreign-owned companies may find it harder to draw as many from this talented female labor pool as they have in the past. At the same time, the allure of international business continues to grow, and the possibility of travel and the opportunity to work with people from other countries are strong attractions to ambitious, capable Japanese women.

Although the majority of working women would like to stay in a secure job with a well-reputed big company, they are often dissatisfied by the lack of challenge in the work. Many leave the security of such jobs after a few years to do free-lance work or take jobs with foreign firms and find the switch relatively easy. Temporary staff agencies proliferated when large numbers of women began to enter or reenter the work force, and they have recently begun to attract many of those women who left their first job for various reasons and who have particular skills to offer such as word-processing proficiency or computer accounting. Working through such agencies offers women greater freedom: They can accept or reject requests to go to this or that company, and as transient workers, they do not have to perform menial tasks like tea service and tidying up. They can determine how long they will work in any one job, allowing them to reject work when they have other plans (travel, care of small children or sick family members, etc.). The income, moreover, is comparatively good, although there are problems: Such jobs lack the security that Japanese so greatly prize. Temporary staff members are "outsiders" in the places where they work and tend to feel alienated from more permanent staff members, and they may be summarily dismissed at the convenience of the employer.

Among men, temporary work is considered socially disgraceful; a man with good social standing is expected to have a regular, permanent job and to stay with it for many years. Women's jobs are not taken as seriously, so working on a temporary basis does not carry negative connotations. It is ironic that the marginal status women hold in society—at least as far as the world of business is concerned—gives them greater mobility and freedom. The majority of working women, especially the non-career-minded, exist outside of the hierarchy of seniority and status based on the vertical structure of Japanese society. Their existence as well as their pattern of job mobility can be a force for changing Japanese society from a tight vertical one in the direction of a qualification-based horizontal one.

Most women who free-lance are working in what are known as *katakana* jobs—*katakana* comprise the phonetic syllabary used for loanwords, such as *furōa redi* ("floor ladies," who assist bank customers in dealing with their business), *kopi raitā* (copywriter), *ripōtā* (reporter)—as well as in the many new jobs that have emerged from changes in the economy, developments in high technology, and the introduction of professions from other countries for which there may be no Japanese equivalent (like counseling, graphic design, or head-hunting).

THE SECOND PEAK OF THE M CURVE: RETURNEES

Women returning to the work force after their children have grown from a second peak in the M curve of Figure 6–2, and the women of the first postwar generation are part of this large peak. More are engaged in part-time than full-time work. Why are these women, these "returnees," reentering the work force? What sort of work patterns do they display? What kind of impact are they having on workplaces? Women entering or reentering the work force in mid-life are very different from the young women whose numbers form the first peak of the M curve of Figure 6–2 in terms of job-hunting behavior, motivation for working, and the kinds of jobs they take. Many find their jobs through employment magazines, newspaper classifieds, or other advertising. These advertisements offer a great variety of positions (both full-time and part-time, for example, advertising, cleaning, bank customer service, and sales). While it may be difficult for women to work on an equal basis with men during the ten years or so that they are raising young children, it is perfectly possible for them to begin working around age 35 and continue for 25 years or longer—and on an equal basis with men if they are willing and if companies provide them with such opportunities.

The valuable experience these women have gained while raising children and participating in various community activities can be utilized to great advantage. They have gained the know-how for dealing appropriately and quickly with all manner of situations, and they bring new energy into workplaces where male employees may be overburdened and jaded. Returnees are a gold mine for the labor market if the appropriate opportunities are provided, but their abilities and experience are still not being fully utilized.

A convenient location and flexible working conditions are more important to returnees than a prestigious or exciting place of work; the years they have remained at home bringing up small children have made them into very practical people.

Some returnees discover with regret the consequences of not having acquired any specific skills during their early work experience. They learn the lesson that middle-aged women without special skills have to settle for jobs without any promotion potential or the possibility of developing into a career. Observing what happens to returnees without qualifications, many younger women are now eager to acquire skills and special know-how.

Unlike those in some other countries, employers in Japan are free to stipulate sex and age qualifications in help-wanted ads. For example, sales personnel are usually required to be under 50 years old, although some companies put the limit at age 35 in order to promote sales to younger customers. Maintenance or cleaning jobs are generally open to older people, up to age 65, because younger people would not consider such work unless they had no other option. Some ads, in an effort to attract middle-aged women, advertise fringe benefits like discount travel packages, after-work sports activities such as volleyball, or on-site day care. Actual job descriptions are rarely given in recruiting ads. Some advertisements emphasize the "cheerful and comfortable atmosphere" and "short and flexible working hours," features expressly designed to appeal to part-time working mothers.

On the whole, these women have a clearer idea of why and what they are working for than the young women in the first peak of the employment curve. According to a Prime Minister's

Office survey (1989), one of the main reasons is economic;[10] although returnees can often live fairly comfortably on their husband's income alone, the extra money allows them to spend more generously on their children or on luxuries and to indulge in personal hobbies or diversions. Some want to put away savings of their own for old age, separate from household accounts. Others work to fill their extra free time or simply because they enjoy working or to satisfy a need to attain self-actualization outside of the home and pursue a meaning in life that traditional sex roles may not adequately accommodate. The reason employers offer such features as sports or other hobby clubs is that women also seek jobs as a way of making friends and broadening their social circle. This desire is especially strong with some who have been tied down by small children for a number of years.

At first it might seem that returnees end up taking part-time jobs because they cannot find full-time positions, but polls show that the vast majority (78 percent) of women part-timers do not want to become full-time workers. Only 14 percent of part-time workers work on that schedule because full-time jobs were not available. In Japan, in contrast to the United States, part-time work is not considered a preliminary step to full-time work but is typically a deliberate choice of women who want to work only part-time because of family obligations or other activities. With the increased need for family care of the aged, the number of such part-time working women is now increasing.[11]

Obviously, part-time employment has a special appeal in spite of low wages, but what is responsible for the recent sharp increase in part-time workers? Paid holidays, pension plans, and other benefits to which regular employees are entitled are not provided. The work often spreads over six days a week, although working hours may vary (57 percent of part-time working women work six days a week). Over 70 percent are employed in small companies with less than 100 employees. In manufacturing, the majority are engaged in production line work, while in the retail and wholesale business they are evenly divided between sales and clerical or cashier jobs.

What makes such jobs so popular among women and employers are the advantages they offer for both sides. From the employer's standpoint, part-time jobs are a way of obtaining additional workers without having to spend more on employee benefits or worry about more people vying for promotion.

Generally speaking, returnees are hired on a contract basis, with a limit on the number of hours they may work per week; their pay raises are irregular; their twice-annual bonuses equal one half or one third that of regular employees; and they may be laid off at any time at the company's discretion. Regular pay scales are based on seniority, a basic feature of the long-term employment system; since women who return to work do not fit into this scale, the part-time category eases the adjustment of salaries employers must pay. Part-time jobs are, as sometimes described, the safety valve of the Japanese economy, protecting both the jobs of full-time employees and the growth of industry. In this respect, part-time workers are exploited by industry.

From the employee standpoint, the appeal of part-time work was described in the results of the 1989 Prime Minister's Office survey: Such work is "more compatible with household chores and child care" (68 percent in agreement), "allows for flexible and convenient working hours" (68 percent), and "involves less responsibility" (23 percent). We may also presume that many women prefer jobs they can quit with ease if family considerations so require. The necessity of preserving part-time status is a reflection of the culture of the small and medium-sized Japanese business, which resembles a kind of large family. The members of such organizations are related not on a contract basis but by mutual trust. If a person becomes a full member of the family, it is difficult to drop out without hurting the feelings of other members. Full-time employment in Japan involves quite a heavy commitment to the employer, and women want to be able to leave a job if they find a more attractive job or an appealing hobby, if their husband is transferred to a different post, if elderly parents are in need of intensive care, or if some other such contingency develops. Valuing freedom over a close sense of belonging, these women content themselves with part-time status in order to avoid deeper obligations to the organization.[12]

Returnees clearly do not think of full-time work, either for men or women, as something to be envied, preferring a situation where they can maintain work, family, and personal interests all at the same time. As a result, unless the working conditions are really poor, part-time jobs suit the returnee's lifestyle very well, and this type of worker will no doubt increase. Some full-time working women, meanwhile, criticize the burgeoning numbers of part-time working women and their lower wages as a force that inhibits the improved status of working women, and it is true that part-time jobs separate working women into different camps.[13]

Corporations today are beginning to use part-time workers in a completely different way from the past. Once part-timers were taken on as supplementary labor to assist tasks already being performed; more and more, they are being used to handle specialized tasks or to act as partners and assistants of regular staff members. The results of a survey conducted in 1990 show that 16 percent of corporations already have part-timers in managerial posts and another 28 percent are planning to do so.[14] This may be a sign that corporations are increasing their dependency on returnees rather than on younger women whose job commitment may be unpredictable. This trend can be expected to lead, in the long run, to a shortening of working hours for men and women and, by extension, some improvement in the quality of family life and relations between husbands and wives. The problems of inadequate companionship, which wives often mention in a description of their marriages, and of alienation of fathers in the home may be somewhat relieved. The other side of the coin will no doubt be less freedom of activity for married women as their husbands become more involved in family life and closer witness to their wives' activities.

Reflecting the relationship between husbands and wives described in Chapter 3, many women are concerned that their husbands not object to their working and that their jobs not infringe on the time needed to fulfill household duties. As long as the job is not socially questionable or disgraceful (such as working in bars or in lowbrow entertainment establishments in which they may be sexually exploited), husbands usually do not mind what their wives do. Men tend to think that their superior position in the home is unquestioned and that whatever salary the wife might bring in would never be substantial enough to threaten their authority as head of the household. Women make the most of men's one-sided understanding. When men are asked why they are working, 93 percent select the response "in order to support the family," but only 33 percent of women select the same answer. Married women tend to cite "to add to household income" as their reason for working, although it may not be an absolute necessity.[15] Many women work relatively close to home, the ideal being within bicycling distance. The parameters of their freedom to work outside the home may be defined by what they can do without altering the household status quo as far as their husbands are concerned.

With more women working outside the home there has been an expansion of the branch of the service industry catering to household needs and providing support in many of the jobs central to managing the home, such as cooking, cleaning, care of the elderly, catering, and security. Some women of entrepreneurial spirit have met this trend by starting up new businesses in these areas. For example, a group of housewives who loved to cook, led by a former writer for the long-established women's magazine *Shufu no tomo* [The Housewife's Friend], started a catering service featuring reasonably priced homemade foods with no chemical additives. They have made their lack of professional status—their status as ordinary housewives—their selling point. The increase of working women with families is producing a new kind of entrepreneur as well as stimulating consumption.

THE LEGAL FRAMEWORK:
PROTECTION VERSUS EQUALITY

For nearly 40 years, protection of women was a more important priority than guaranteeing them equality with men in labor practice and law. It was believed that women needed protection to prevent their exploitation. The Japanese Labor Standards Law, enacted in 1947, contains a protective clause created especially for working women; it stipulates special treatment for women such as menstruation leave and restrictions on overtime work, night shifts, and dangerous jobs. These protections were won through years of effort by labor unions at a time when working conditions were bad and factories were far less mechanized than they are today. The law became a symbol of the victory of the Japanese labor movement.

Beginning in the 1980s, however, some working women felt that the protective clause of the labor standards law was working against the interests of women who wanted careers on an equal footing with men. Protection ought to be extended to all workers, men and women, and it is absurd to think that women should try to participate in hazardous jobs along with men in an attempt to prove they are equal.

In 1986 the Equal Employment Opportunity Law (EEOL) went into effect, and it helped to relax the overly restrictive (if well-intentioned) clauses of the Labor Standards Law in recognition of the large number of women who are as highly educated, motivated, and talented as men participating in the labor force. This law was passed after years of heated discussion among women, with some for and others against it, and is still controversial. Although the EEOL encourages employers to provide equal opportunities in recruiting and hiring, job assignments and advancement, vocational training, and dismissal procedures, it does not contain any stipulations for enforcement. It was meant to combat situations in which women are deprived of opportunities simply because they happen to be female and, therefore, does pave the way for highly motivated women to succeed professionally by providing them opportunities to advance alongside their male colleagues. Opponents of the law charged that it left the way open for women to be forced to work long and arduous hours and perform hazardous tasks and that it would mean categorizing women as strong or weak, that is, as powerful and career oriented or as vulnerable, unskilled, and not career oriented. And since the law has no teeth, it offers no guarantee of equal treatment.

The most glaring fault of the law (in contrast to American equal opportunity laws) is that it addresses equality only as far as women are concerned. It does not have anything to do with equality for men. It is not possible for Japanese men, for example, to evoke this law to achieve better treatment in employment.

At the time the EEOL was passed, many were skeptical about its effectiveness. There does appear to have been some visible improvement in employment practices, particularly as far as job opportunities are concerned, although it is not at all extensive enough to satisfy many women.

Japanese behavior, which tends to be shaped by situational demands rather than clear-cut principles, has been criticized by many,[16] and a similar lack of principle can be detected with regard to the EEOL. One deep-rooted problem is that companies appear to be making changes not because their management believes discrimination on the basis of sex is wrong but in order to preserve a good corporate image in the eyes of women and the public in general. One suspects that the changes made are less a matter of conscience than a result of efforts among the leading corporations to keep pace with one another (*yokonarabi*) in their employment practices in order to maintain their reputations with the public. In Japan fear of the perils of falling behind the times can affect corporate behavior as significantly as can any law. Since companies do not utilize the law out of agreement with the principle of equality of the sexes, they might quickly ignore its guidelines if business should take a downturn. Current conditions, under which the labor market is tight, offer women a valuable opportunity to impress upon management that they are capable, committed workers and an asset to business.

According to a survey conducted by the Ministry of Labor ten months after the law went into effect, from 3 to 15 percent (depending on the different aspects of employment policy treated in the law) of companies surveyed reported "some changes" in their employment policies in favor of treating women as more equal to men.[17] For example, a great number of companies had previously not even considered women for certain jobs in their regular recruiting of university graduates; after enactment of the law, many adjusted their policies and began to accord women equal opportunities with men. The results are reflected in a survey conducted by the Japan Institute of Women's Employment, which reported that in recruiting from the class of 1986 (before enactment), nearly 23 percent of the opportunities for university graduates were reserved for men only. That proportion decreased to less than 3 percent in the spring of 1987. On the other hand, job opportunities with no gender distinction more than doubled, from 32 percent of all job opportunities in 1986 to 72 percent in 1987.[18]

For a law that does not include measures for enforcement, the EEOL has so far been relatively effective. The main reason stems from Japanese attitudes toward laws in general. The most effective law, as far as Japanese thinking is concerned, is one that is flexible and adaptable to the diverse situations of real life. Japanese believe that no matter how noble a principle, the way it is put into practice and applied must fit the way people actually live and think; otherwise, it is useless. The EEOL has many loopholes and areas it does not adequately cover, but it has nevertheless had considerable impact. In part, the very fact that it was loosely structured and left much up to the corporations themselves turned out to be effective in the context of Japanese corporate society.

NEW PATHS FOR FEMALE WORKERS

Japanese corporations are faced with the very practical tasks of providing equal opportunity for women, securing talented female employees, and absorbing the business risks of workers who leave after only a few years on the job. After the Equal Employment Opportunity Law went into effect, many large-scale companies openly began to offer women employees with university degrees one of two different employment tracks: general and integrated. The general track is offered to women who prefer to be treated separately. Their jobs are usually less demanding, being the kinds of girl-Friday routine jobs traditionally carried out by women; promotion is slower and more limited, and the jobs do not involve potential transfers to branch offices in other cities. The integrated track treats women the same as men, expecting them to accept transfers as well as promotions and to put in overtime. This is a typically Japanese way of adapting the ideal to reality: Companies can demonstrate their faithfulness to the ideal of treating capable and motivated women equally with men while assuring themselves of an ample pool of female employees who will fulfill the support functions to which they have become accustomed. One wonders if this sort of adeptness in compromising with reality may, in the long run, work unfavorably for women because it permits the postponement of fundamental changes that can only be achieved by squarely confronting the problems. Nevertheless, it is a clever and realistic way of taking into account the very diverse needs of working women today.

So far, only 3 percent of all corporations are offering these two sorts of options to women employees, but among the bigger companies with more than 5,000 employees, 42 percent (as of 1989) offer these two courses. This practice is spreading especially in financial and insurance-related firms. Some offer only one of the two tracks; others offer both and give every female recruit the opportunity to choose. Others limit choice of the integrated track to women who have majored in certain subjects such as

economics, commerce, or political science. Some companies offer
women the chance to switch from the general to the integrated
track under certain conditions. Tomoko, who works at the Japan
Long-Term Credit Bank, for example, is eligible to switch from
the general to the integrated track (but not the reverse) by taking
an examination after three years. Still other companies, after
three or four years of experience using the new system, have
created a third alternative to better suit women's working needs:
an integrated course but without the obligation to accept transfer
to a branch office in another city. Here again is the pragmatic
approach to applying principles flexibly, in accordance with real
circumstances.

Men, of course, are not given two tracks to choose from. They
are expected to take the integrated track; they may earn the
lowest score on the entrance examination but are on this track by
virtue of being male. On the other hand, only the brightest, most
dedicated career-oriented superwomen are admitted to the integrated track. Thus, this process seems intended only to integrate
the most competent minority of women into the existing male
track while the majority of female employees are confined to the
old supportive track.

In the spring of 1991, Tokyo Marine Insurance, a very prestigious firm, hired 424 men and 24 women in the integrated track
and 553 women in the general track. Isetan Department Store
hired 80 men and all of their 65 women in the integrated track.
When another company very popular with women, Japan Air
Lines, recently hired 150 persons in the integrated track, only 3
were women (in addition to 52 in the general track). Asahi Beer,
on the other hand, which only instituted its integrated track for
women in 1989, hired 103 women and 111 men in that track and
none in the general track in 1991, foreseeing that business
increasingly has to depend on the female work force as the
number of younger workers starts to decline around the year
2005. Major insurance companies already make it a practice to
send women to serve stints in their branch offices in Paris and
New York, assignments formerly limited to the most promising
male employees. The content of their work in these cases is
the same as that for men, involving them in both general administrative tasks and investment planning. In fact, women employees—who tend to be coddled and overprotected—often get the

choicest assignments to "safe, sophisticated" cities abroad, while men may end up in the more risky, less attractive locations.

Observations suggest that women may hesitate to apply for the integrated track. Some companies claim that the reason they hire only a small number in this track is that few women apply for it. This may be because women who may want to work on an equal basis with men also know that the number of openings for the integrated track is small, and this may prompt them to apply for the general track where the chances of securing a job are much greater. Some applicants decide not to try for the integrated track after meeting women already working in that capacity, because the latter seem so exceptionally able. Even after shorter working hours for everyone are assured, as they must be, it is unlikely that sexual equality will become established in the Japanese workplace until all men and women are offered the same employment options to choose between and a much larger number of women (in numbers on a par with men) enter the integrated tracks.

How do women end up in one employment track rather than the other? Two rather typical cases can illustrate the actual process of choice. Makiko, a 1990 graduate, originally wanted to find a job in which she could work on an equal basis with men, and she applied to three completely different types of corporations, all big concerns: Toshiba Electric (a manufacturer of computers, televisions, and refrigerators), Isetan Department Store, and Tokyo Marine Insurance. The first two are known for their policy of fostering female talent by offering many posts in the integrated track. Makiko had graduated from the faculty of letters (humanities) of her university, and Tokyo Marine had a policy of not accepting female faculty of letters graduates for their integrated track posts, although they did offer her a general track position. She was offered a job by all three companies but ultimately decided to work for Tokyo Marine. Her reason: "I simply could not turn them down because I applied through connections provided by my parents. Besides, they offered the highest pay." Clearly, neither promotion nor career opportunities were as important to her as honoring the interpersonal relations network maintained by her parents. The importance of connections in finding a job is related to the practice in Japanese companies of hiring workers on the basis of their reliability and potential rather than particular abilities or skills. Companies are

therefore more apt to hire an individual with a family background they know is solid and dependable than someone whose
background is unknown to them.

On the other hand, there is Keiko, who lives alone in Tokyo,
apart from her parents in Shikoku. Eager to accept an offer to hire
her at the prestigious Hitachi Electric Company, she chose a job
on the integrated track, since according to the company's policy
only women living with their parents could be hired to work in
the general track (the assumption is that the parents would
therefore supervise the women's conduct, specifically with men
—according to the paternalistic ethos that still reigns in these
large companies). She did not know what sort of work she would
be doing. She expected, she said, that a company of Hitachi's size
and prestige would be "above average" in all respects.

Either way, as these examples show, regardless of whether
they choose an integrated or a general track option and regardless of the fact that they are very capable, women make their
decisions in a rather passive manner. Rather than establishing
goals and searching actively for a position that fulfills them, they
settle for the best they can get under the conditions that surround
them at the time. Even in a general post, Makiko foresees the
difficulties of working after marriage. Faced with the choice
between the two tracks, her first concern is whether she can
eventually get married and have a family and the second is what
the toll of the heavy work load of an integrated post would be for
her health; ultimately, these considerations lead many women to
choose the general track. For them, work is only a part of what
they consider important in life, and so the general track does not
necessarily seem inferior. They may have to work but prefer to
save their energies for other pursuits as well. In the general track,
moreover, they have the comfort of numbers, and in this
collectivist society, it is most secure to be a member of the
majority. Women challenging the man's world are no longer a
novelty, but it takes more courage and self-confidence to stand
out among one's peers in Japan than in an individual-based
society.

Women in integrated positions encounter many problems.
Because male superiors of a woman on the career track hesitate to
ask her to do the supportive jobs (such as making copies of
documents or attending to simple errands dealing with customers) that they might request of the men whom they are training,

it is possible that day-to-day relations may be strained. The personnel office of a company may assign a woman to a certain post only to have the department in question request a male instead because this kind of strain is too great. Then there are the women in integrated track positions who are so determined to live up to the expectations placed on them (aware that their salaries are higher than those of their age-mates in the general track or the junior college graduates who started two years earlier) that they work overtime every night and eventually burn out. Women in the integrated track, especially when they are few in numbers, find relations with general track women particularly delicate. This is especially true in Japan because the workplace is more than simply a place where one makes one's living but may be the central arena of one's social life, learning, and pursuit of hobbies. Women in the integrated course have to work overtime, like their male colleagues, and often cannot join general track women for after-work meals or shopping. It is not long before they are virtually excluded from the women's groups when they go out to lunch.

One 27-year-old female television producer on the integrated track tells how she vacillated every day over whether she was one of the "girls" (the clerical staff) or could consider herself included among the permanent employees who happened to all be men. At lunchtime, one of the men would stand up and mutter something about going to lunch, prompting all the other men to follow him. She was apparently torn every day over whether she should consider herself included among the men as a colleague or should stick with the other women in the office who were not on the career track. Her anguish over this decision was considerable and ended only when one of her male colleagues assured her that she was welcome among them and told her to just decide on her own which group to eat lunch with.

Integrated track women have to put up with the same grind as the men but still have to act like women; if they refuse to do tasks like serving tea or making copies, the women in the general track may become critical and resentful. If they eat lunch with the men, they may find it difficult to establish closeness with the other women in the office and may even be the target of gossip and hostile barbs.

Problems like these are not as common in companies that have a large number of women in their integrated track. Hiring a

greater number of women, providing opportunities for employees to switch between tracks, and making the general track an
option for men as well as women are ways companies can help to
alleviate the pressures the women in integrated positions struggle with today. Still, many questions remain about the merits and
flaws of the new system as far as women are concerned: Hasn't
the introduction of the two tracks for women created conflicts
among women by dividing them into two different groups? Will
women in the integrated track be able to stand up for women's
interests, or will they be masculinized and end up siding with
men? Does the introduction of a two-track system that leaves the
corporate culture as far as men are concerned unchanged really
benefit women at large? Doesn't the introduction of the two-track
system simply obscure employers' continuing discrimination
against women? Is it possible to eliminate the mounting dissatisfaction of middle-aged women who have been working continuously since before the EEOL was passed and who are now facing
the possibility of seeing younger women in the integrated track
emerge as their superiors (a situation hard to take in hierarchy-
prone Japan)?

Much more time is needed before we can make fair evaluations. In terms of aspirations, women in the integrated track are
not much different from young career-oriented women in the
United States. But the women in general track jobs are quite
different from college-educated working women in the United
States. Although they may be graduates of very prestigious
universities, they do not regard themselves, nor are they regarded, as professionals when they first start working. The
reason may be that job descriptions in Japan are not clearly
defined and the number of years of work may be of greater
importance than amount of schooling. Interviews with white-
collar American women in 1990 indicated that, by contrast, most
considered themselves professionals from the time they graduated from college.

These general track women generally wear uniforms provided
by the company. They receive training in etiquette, personal care,
and company expectations. Their work consists of being in the
office early, making tea for the management staff and whatever
guests come, clearing away and washing the tea utensils, wiping
desks and washing ashtrays, and being at the male staff's beck
and call to do such chores as copying, running errands, deliver-

ing packages and messages and taking telephone calls. They may
have keyboard skills and spend long hours at a computer
terminal, but they are not given tasks of a more responsible
nature. They do not participate in business discussions and are
free to take regular lunch hours and to leave the office at 5:00
unless expressly requested to help men working until late into
the night. (According to a male manager of a bank I have
interviewed, these women's conversations center around pleas-
urable activities, such as shopping or travel, whereas conversations among women in the integrated track center around their
jobs and their desire to undertake interesting projects.) The
disparity among women themselves is clearly increasing.

LIABILITIES OF FEMALE LABOR

Women in both the integrated and general tracks present employers with an investment risk. Japanese employment practices
are such that large enterprises invest a great deal of money and
energy in the new employees they recruit annually from colleges
and universities. Men, in particular, receive extended and extensive on-the-job training with the expectation that they will
remain with the company for a long time, often until they retire
around age 60 (although, increasingly, men are changing jobs
mid-career rather than staying permanently in one). Such companies naturally expect their female recruits in the integrated
course to remain as long as the men, yet some have been
disappointed to see their women quit after only a few years of
service. When this happens, their investment is wasted. A
Ministry of Labor report published in 1990 showed that 15
percent of women in the integrated track had left their jobs
during the last 18 months.[19] This tendency makes employers
wary of putting women in responsible posts. Eventually, employers may test female employees after a few years of work with
a view to then redistributing them to the general or integrated
tracks, rather than ask them to decide when they are first hired
which track they prefer. This approach would probably be less
risky.

Keiko, Hitachi's recruit for the integrated track, recounted the
questions she faced in job interviews related to her career plans,
inquiries a potential female American employee would probably

never hear: How many years did she plan to work? What would she do if she married? How would she handle child care? Keiko could only answer hypothetically, that is, that she would expect her future husband to cooperate and would try to avail herself of day care services. What else could she have said at that stage? Yet that was all the personnel officer expected, Keiko believed.

In reality, many women in both the general and the integrated tracks do quit upon marriage or birth of children, which accounts for the dip in the M curve for women's labor force participation rates (see Fig. 6–2).[20] The vast majority who quit (42 percent) cite marriage as their reason for quitting and a large portion (29 percent) cite "child care."

It should be kept in mind, however, that there are at least two groups among those women who give up their jobs: those who leave of their own choice and those who are reluctant to do so but find the odds in continuing too great. Some observers say that since so many women do, in fact, leave their jobs upon marriage and childbirth, corporations cannot expect sufficient return on the investment they make in training female employees. In other words, the loss incurred when women trained at considerable cost decide to quit when family duties intervene is too great.

The tendency of women ultimately to quit upon marriage or childbirth has naturally caused employers to be more cautious when recruiting women for integrated track positions. The shortage of labor (partly due to industrial restructuring and continuing growth of the economy) and the difficulty of finding enough male recruits has forced corporations to depend increasingly on women and to grapple with the realities involved, whether they like it or not. Some employers have a system for rehiring former employees who left within the previous five or so years. Integrated track employment is still quite new, and employers often appear uncertain as to how to treat these women employees. There are too few precedents to provide what Japanese companies could consider safe guidelines.

Meanwhile, women's career consciousness and commitment to the organization they work for remains poorly developed.[21] In Japan's affluent society, single young women have other attractive options besides work, including going abroad to study or undertaking graduate study. Married women, as long as their situations are secure, may quit work if they desire (if their marriage is unstable, they may not be free to quit). They consider a life that is pleasant and enjoyable more attractive than the possibility of gaining power and prestige in a profession or job. This also means that since they know they cannot expect to attain a well-paying, prestigious post, they may feel there is no point in trying hard and that they might as well content themselves with the easy life. Behind their lack of commitment to career work is their skepticism about the kind of lives led by working men. In interviews with women who have left jobs on the integrated track after only a year or two of service, it is somewhat disappointing to learn that they feel no concern or sense of responsibility for how their decisions are likely to affect their employer's treatment of the women who come after them. Perhaps they do not appreciate the significance of actions that further or reverse the status of women because they were not involved in the fight to get the EEOL enacted.

While many women quit upon childbirth or marriage, an increasing number of women, although still a minority in both tracks, are opting to work and raise children at the same time. Some companies, like Seiko (manufacturer of wristwatches, calculators, and word processors), hire so many such women that they regularly issue special maternity uniforms for expectant workers. When looking for jobs, young female university graduates take into consideration how far an employer is willing to go beyond the compulsory child care leave (six weeks before birth and eight weeks after) as symbolized by the availability of maternity uniforms, willingness to agree to nursing breaks, and allowing vacation time to care for sick infants.

A woman employed in a large advertising firm who recently had a child offers some valuable advice to women who hope to have both career and family. Citing the long-term relationships that women in particular rely on, she advises young working women to go out of their way to help their male and female co-workers and colleagues while they are free and unencumbered, thus accumulating a substantial stock of favors that they can then expect to be returned in kind at some subsequent date. Then, when they bear children and have to request extra leave from their jobs or other special treatment, their co-workers will gladly support and encourage them. Here again we can see an example of Japanese women's wisdom.

As described in Chapter 5, a new child care law was passed in 1991 allowing either the father or mother to take leave to care for a newborn infant. This is evidence of the desire of corporations to keep women employees, but if both men and women begin to take advantage of this law, the already tight labor market may become even tighter. How corporations will deal with this problem remains to be seen, but they are likely to find ways to make it possible for families to care for small children without either the mother or father taking prolonged leave, such as by shortening working hours and providing better child care facilities.

The effect of the EEOL can be expected to diversify the motivations, status, and lifestyles of women over the years, making it increasingly difficult to deal with women as one homogeneous category. More and more, women will come to be treated on an individual basis, while men may remain as one homogenous category. Male working habits are not yet affected by the few women who have entered integrated track positions. However, younger men seem not only to readily accept able women as colleagues but, quite naturally, to depend upon them. In time, men will be more and more influenced by women in the workplace, and their own attitudes and behavior will grow more diverse. Eventually, as the disparities that have separated men and women lessen, there will be members of both sexes among the able and ambitious workers as well as among those who are less motivated and satisfied with more modest goals.

7

WORK AS PROFESSION

In contrast to the great number of women who work as an option
and for whom employment is subordinate to their main roles as
wife and mother, a smaller but increasing number work full-time
in lifetime careers. In Japan, as in other countries, for decades
women have been staunch and important members of professions such as teaching, law, medicine, nursing, pharmacology,
and the civil service, where they earn the same amount as men
and are accorded equal respect and status in their workplaces.
While they may suffer certain disadvantages in terms of influence
and recognition in their fields, where decision making may be
dominated by men, on the whole the formal certification and
qualification procedures for these professions are as open to
women as to men, and some women have taken full advantage of
the opportunities available.

In business and industry the doors are ostensibly just as open
in terms of the law and the qualifications required, but the
hurdles to be overcome are greater. The first hurdle is a woman's
own perception of her role in society; she must decide whether
she wants to break away from, or marginalize, traditional female
roles or whether she can work alongside men while handling
traditional household responsibilities. The second hurdle is the
lack of role models that might provide inspiration or guidance to
those brave enough to move into male-dominated occupations;
those few women who have made successful careers for themselves in business or industry have many problems and struggle
with many dilemmas. The third, of course, is the chauvinism and

189

tradition-bound thinking of men. All things considered, it will be some time before the ranks of business women appreciably increase. In business much depends upon how successfully the Equal Employment Opportunity Law (EEOL) is implemented and on how well integrated track management turns out to be.

EQUAL PAY FOR EQUAL WORK?

Equal pay for equal work is theoretically and legally guaranteed, and it does seem to be realized in Japan among men and women in the professions and in the career track in business and industry. A comparison of monthly salaries of workers in general, however, shows there is a large gap: Japanese women make only 61 yen to 100 yen for men (as of 1990).

What is responsible for the discrepancy? First of all, men tend to occupy higher-level jobs and therefore hold higher-paying positions than women (the proportion of working women who are in managerial posts is only 5 percent whereas the portion of working men in managerial positions is 29 percent). Second, women (except those of the younger generation) may, in fact, have less education than men and therefore do not qualify as often for higher-paying jobs. Third, men do much more overtime work. Fourth, many women (especially of the first postwar generation) are part-time employees, a category that is rapidly growing; the greater the increase in such workers, the greater the disparity in average income between men and women will become. Lastly, although special benefits, such as allowances for dependents or housing allowances, can be claimed by either the husband or the wife, it is usually the husband who claims these benefits. Benefits make up over 5 percent of scheduled earnings and are usually paid to the husband even if the wife is a full-time regular employee, thus widening all the more the statistical gap in average wages between men and women. The shorter duration of service of most women, and their failure to gain seniority and promotion and the accompanying salary increases, also contribute to the discrepancy in wages. If age, education, and years of service are controlled in a comparison of average monthly salaries between men and women, the difference for those under 25 years of age is quite small: 90 yen for women to 100 for men. The disparity widens with age: At around age 40 women make only 70 percent what men earn. The widening gap for older age groups can be attributed to their lower job status and their status as dependents of their husbands, as well as to their part-time employment.

The issue of comparable work of different types of jobs has not been discussed in Japan. One reason is that Japanese women feel that the disparity between jobs is hard to pin down and define. Job descriptions are not the basis for hiring in Japan, and it is difficult to define the "comparable worth" of different types of jobs. In order to evaluate current performance accurately, it is thought, previous experience and performance must be taken into account (again the long-term perspective comes into play), and this makes comparison all the harder. Many women, in fact, do not want to shoulder the heavy responsibilities that men are carrying; they refuse to work like men. This attitude, of course, is based on the belief that the husband's salary will go to sustain the household while that of the wife can be used for incidental or nonessential purposes. Gain and loss (advantage and disadvantage) of salary differentials are considered in the total context of the family situation. Furthermore, the disparity in income of women resulting from their level of education is much greater than for men. More highly educated women are paid similarly to men, but the wages of less educated women are definitely lower. The former feel no responsibility or sympathy for the latter, and this is a factor that has inhibited solidarity among women in voicing dissatisfaction with perceived unfair wage practices.

PROMOTION: HOW WOMEN WORKERS SEE IT

For women who work continuously, promotion is a matter of concern, but because of the close relationship between promotion and continuous service in Japanese corporations, most of those women who drop out of the work force temporarily and return in middle age (of whom many today are members of the first postwar generation) know from the start that there is little likelihood of attaining promotion and do not expect it. In the past, most corporations, especially the larger ones, did not expect or even allow women to work long enough to earn promotion, and they seldom had any sort of explicit policy on female promotion. There were so few cases in which women served continuously for their entire working life that corporations simply dealt with each case as it came up. More recently, with more women staying on the job long enough to be eligible for promotion, some corporations have begun to revise their rules.

For younger women, the situation is rather different. When I ask former students how they feel about promotion, the usual reply is that they are not so much interested in promotion as in the kind of work they will be doing. In other words, as long as the work is interesting, they are satisfied. Even younger men appear to be less preoccupied with promotion than was once the case. Part of the reason is that the qualifications of the employment pool have changed in that now there are so many people with a college education that there are not enough managerial posts to go around. Apparently, the disinterest in promotion exhibited by younger workers is their way of avoiding disappointment. In Japan's rapid growth period, promotion was the goal of every salaried worker, and organizations capitalized on their employee's optimism and loyalty. Today, with promotion at work a less realistic goal to strive for, men as well as women seek self-fulfillment through other channels (hobbies, study, travel, etc.) that are little exploited by the middle-aged and older generations of men.

CAREER WOMEN

Although the number of women in managerial jobs is still very low, the opportunities are steadily growing. In 1970 the number of women in managerial posts was 8,400 (0.25 percent of working women), but in 1985 the figure had risen 5.2 times to 44,000 (1 percent of the total). The figure for men, 16.3 percent, is of course much higher, but it is important to view the situation in the context of Japanese employment practices.

As noted, promotion is based not only on merit but also on educational background and length of service to the company. In the case of service industry occupations such as retail sales, where a large number of women are employed, only 0.3 percent of women with service records of four years or less are in managerial posts but the figure is 4.5 percent for men. Among women who have served for more than 30 years, the proportion jumps to 24 percent (but is 46 percent for men).[1] Of working women with four-year university degrees who have served for more than 30 years, the percentage occupying managerial posts (of chief clerk [kakari-chō] and higher) is 27 percent (55 percent for men). Fifteen percent of men who have worked for 10 to 14 consecutive years reach at least the post of chief clerk, if not higher, but for women employed the same number of years the figure is only 1.6 percent. Under present circumstances, unless a much larger number of men start changing jobs more often (thereby accelerating the practice of promotion based on merit rather than seniority), women will have to continue working more years than men in order to get ahead in management.

Another reason for women's reduced chances of attaining promotion to managerial posts is undeniably the tendency of their male colleagues to lock them into traditional female roles. Just as they expect their own wives to have dinner and a hot bath waiting for them, so too do they expect their married female cohorts to perform a similar supporting role for their own husbands. With all good intentions, therefore, they urge the women in the office to leave early but remain late themselves to clear up unfinished work. Naturally, this gives them the upper hand in the office.

The Japanese career women working with men who continue to see them as housewives first rather than as colleagues rarely react strongly, interpreting such gestures not as belittling but as rather old-fashioned consideration. But when Japanese executives working with American staffs in the United States extend the same offer to female American subordinates, sparks are quick to fly. American women become livid at the suggestion that they should go home early to do housework while men need not do so. Japanese women recognize the time lag in male thinking, but they are loath to launch attacks on individual men, considering the matter a major social problem that will take time to solve.

In addition, the Labor Standards Law stipulates, ostensibly to protect them, that women may not work from 10:00 P.M. to 5:00 A.M., although exceptions are made for certain jobs (e.g., TV announcers and nurses). It goes without saying that men, too, should be protected from having to work such hours; the rising figures for deaths attributable to overwork (karōshi) are proof enough of that. One of the major flaws in Japanese employment practices today is the tendency to think that equality between men and women can be attained by protecting women from the harsh conditions that men are still expected to endure.

A further reason for the scant number of women in managerial positions is lack of motivation on the part of women themselves. As things stand today, the majority of women (79 percent in 1990) do not particularly desire managerial status, while 81 percent of men anxiously await it (although this trend is changing among younger men).[2]

MANAGERIAL WOMEN IN BIG CORPORATIONS

A 1989 study of female managers in major corporations reported that one in every four companies has women managers in positions higher than division chief (*kachō*), but there are great differences from industry to industry.[3] Finance and insurance companies have the highest percentage (58 percent have women managers) and construction the lowest (16 percent). On average, there are eight female managers per company; 52 percent are in charge of administrative/accounting positions, 34 percent in sales, and 23 percent in personnel relations (duties do overlap). Almost none have reached the position of board member in a major corporation, except in distribution (department stores, supermarkets), fashion, and cosmetics. It should also be noted that 59 percent of these women are unmarried and another 36 percent have no children.

These figures reflect clearly the actual or assumed difficulties of managing both family and work in the still very recent past, when women now in managerial positions were young. The reasons these women attained a managerial post may be because male managerial staff considered the fact that they had given up marriage and family as proof of their commitment to their job. The factors that militate against women's ambitions to attain managerial status are clear enough. Managerial women put in long hours; 25 percent of them claim to work an average of more than 10 hours per day. Still, the number of women in managerial posts is so small that they are under considerable pressure to prove themselves and to perform at least as much as expected, usually to the sacrifice of their private lives. They are forced to put work before family, and if they happen to have children, they can spend little time with them, relying on double day care services, mother, or mother-in-law, if they are lucky, or on the children's own independence. Male management staff can work long hours but only if they have a wife who will do all the housework and take care of the children; women managers rarely have husbands who will play such a supportive role. Yet among Japanese professional women, few of the first postwar generation make an issue of the principle of sexual equality as far as housework and child care are concerned, as do women in the United States, according to the book *The Second Shift*.[4] The trade-off for Japanese professional women for the inevitably greater physical labor they accept is a certain peace of mind (they do not have to barter with their husbands over every detail of daily life). Younger women, however, do seek more substantial cooperation from their husbands, and younger husbands are more accustomed to and accepting of the idea. Shorter, more humane working hours are an absolute necessity for both men and women if families and households are to be kept together.

As far as their ability to fulfill the demands of managerial posts, surveys show that Japanese managerial women consider themselves to have good judgment (78 percent of women in managerial posts), leadership ability (51 percent), and health and physical strength (33 percent).[5] Women managers differ from nonmanagerial women in terms of motivation; 54 percent report that they are working for the purpose of supporting a family,[6] and this helps them to withstand the pressures against their working.

Under the circumstances, women tend to be satisfied with lower-level managerial posts. A fuss will be made over a woman who attains section chief status while a man who ends up there and remains in the same post for many years may be derided for not having the talent to go higher.

There are no specifically *female* traits of female managers except their tendency to give greater attention to detail and more personal consideration to others.[7]

OTHER MANAGERIAL WOMEN

Few of the small and medium-sized enterprises with less than 300 employees that make up the overwhelming majority of

Japan's corporations faithfully observe those management practices (lifetime employment and seniority-based pay scales) that
have been cited as characteristically Japanese. These corporations
do not necessarily give women formal managerial posts, but they
nevertheless rely on them substantially as managers. Seven
percent of corporations with fewer than 99 employees have
women in posts of department chief (*buchō*) and above, while
12.2 percent of corporations with 5,000 or more employees have
women in equivalent managerial and executive posts.[8]

Small businesses tend to operate more on the basis of merit
than larger corporations and to be less concerned with gender
because of the difficulty of attracting men of outstanding ability.
Organizationally, too, they are less elaborately structured because of their small size and tend to delegate more responsibility
to employees, a factor that offers motivation to women in
particular. Work in a small or medium-sized enterprise resembles
the jack-of-all-trades character of the housewife. Jobs there often
require a worker to handle all kinds of tasks and to give personal
and sometimes instantaneous attention to situations, a work
pattern women know best. Smaller businesses, moreover, are
more flexible and able to adjust to employees' individual needs,
such as emergency leave to care for a sick child.

It will be some time before more women enter the ranks of
management in large corporations, but small and medium enterprises can offer breakthroughs for women seeking advancement.
A survey of such managers conducted in summer 1991 indicates
that a major problem involves misunderstandings not so much
by male coworkers as by older women workers.[9] A company's
reluctance to promote women to managerial posts may often
stem from the desire to prevent jealousy and dissatisfaction
among workers.

No reliable statistics are available giving the number of women
presidents of corporations in Japan, although a report by the
Teikoku Data Bank in 1990 estimates that 4.5 percent of all
corporations have a female president and gives a figure of 39,058
for women chief executive officers, which is double its estimates
for 1980. If women owners of individually run shops and small
businesses are added, the figure would increase considerably.
The largest number of women presidents is in ladies' and
children's garment retail sales, and the second largest number is
in real estate. For the largest 100 companies, in terms of sales

volume, the average age of women presidents is 56 years, and over half of them are women who have inherited their business from husbands or parents.

A study led by cultural anthropologist Hara Hiroko examined, among other topics, how male presidents of small and medium enterprises evaluate female presidents of similar firms.[10] Among the compliments male presidents pay their female counterparts are "attention to minute details" (23 percent), "cheerfulness" (20 percent), and "wise management" (15 percent). One woman president of a pharmaceutical company I interviewed for the study was impressive for her attentiveness to minutiae that men often overlook. Since seasonal gifts are exchanged in Japan in mid-summer and at year's end and the majority of individuals and companies send off their gifts in July and December at the height of the gift-giving season, this woman deliberately waits till the end of the season, in August and February, respectively, to send remembrances to those to whom her company is indebted, because by then earlier gifts have been consumed (gifts of food are common) and the late arrivals are appreciated and remembered twice as much. This kind of thoughtfulness is a forte of Japanese women.

On the negative side, male presidents see women presidents as "narrow-minded" (46 percent), "emotional" (42 percent), and "indecisive" (22 percent). These criticisms may derive equally from actual experience with female presidents and from their stereotyped images of women. Among the conditions these men list as requisite for a top executive are "health" (66 percent), "foresightedness" (53 percent), and "decisiveness" (48 percent). Health is given high priority because so much responsibility rests on the shoulders of the executives of small and medium-sized corporations that an illness can deal a heavy blow to the firm, leading even to bankruptcy. If foresightedness (more or less the opposite of narrow-mindedness) and decisiveness are requisites for company presidents, the possibility that more women will enter the ranks of top management in Japan does not seem particularly good, at least in the eyes of these male presidents.

There is great variety among female presidents. The Hara, Muramatsu, and Minami (eds.) study examined 66 entrepreneurial women grouped into three categories: continuous workers, returnees, and late starters. The continuous workers were further divided into two types: The first type had worked continuously because of personal situations, such as the need for economic independence following the death of their father while the women were still young. Women in this group tended to be single, although they regarded marriage as the natural path of life for a woman and therefore considered themselves deviant. The second type formed plans to pursue a career quite early in life, rather unusual in Japan's cultural climate, where women tend to let fate take its course and passively follow what comes their way instead of setting goals first and actively pursuing them. These women were goal-oriented and knew both what they wanted to do and what they could do career-wise. (The father of one of them had lived abroad and had encouraged his daughter to be economically independent, the opposite of the Japanese norm.) These women took it for granted that they would work, and they enjoyed working. Most were married.

Many of the returnees had resumed work upon the death of their husband (and a few upon divorce). The third category, late starters, had married young, before gaining any work experience. They stayed at home as full-time housewives but acquired broad personal networks and skills through such activities as PTA or free-lance translation, which later became valuable assets when they contemplated returning to work or decided to set up businesses of their own. Many of the late starters were also women who went into business for themselves upon the death of their husband.

Whatever way women in the Hara et al. study entered the business world, it was found that they tend to display the following traits: They avoid taking major risks and are reluctant to expand their business (men tended to be much more expansion oriented), placing greater weight on sound management and quality work. Their enterprises therefore tend to be small in scale. It is possible that success means something different for men and women. For men it may be expansion whereas for women it might be a stable income and solid credibility with a steady clientele maintained through reliable and high-quality service.

In the United States there was a time when women had to start up their own banks because they could not borrow money from male-dominated banks. In Japan such visible discrimination was never a problem because the banks know that businesswomen tend to be more reliable and follow sounder management procedures than men, who are more apt to take greater risks in order to gain larger profits. I once asked a male Japanese bank executive whether sex discrimination existed in the banking business, and he told me, "Bank notes have no gender. As long as the deal is profitable and sound, it makes no difference what the gender of the bank note's owner is."

WOMEN MANAGING MEN

In academia, title and seniority rather than gender tend to be the major determinants of how an individual is treated, but in business work performance evaluation tends to be much more subjective and women are often the target of unreasonable criticism as well as resentment and jealousy. To find themselves outshone by a brighter or more able female colleague, to see a choicer assignment given to a woman, or to have a superior favor a female employee over them, for example, can cause Japanese men to become overly emotional, jealous, and even hysterical— characteristics, ironically, that are usually associated with women. Does this also happen to men in other cultures when they feel threatened by women? Or is it a reaction of Japanese men in particular, who are aroused because any perceived threat from women, who have traditionally been considered to be inferior in status to men, poses a serious loss of face?

Having a woman as superior or colleague in an office elicits a variety of responses from men and women. According to a survey conducted in 1986 by *Asahi Shimbun*, 60 percent of men and 40 percent of women said that they would not want to work under a woman.[11] Obviously, the situation would vary depending on the age and other personal attributes of the woman (as well as on the type of workplace), but for the majority of men, the image of a female manager is not positive. Problems often arise when a female manager scolds or finds fault with a male subordinate. Save for young men who have been reared in households where mother and child are inordinately close, few have had the experience as adults of being scolded by women. When they find themselves being taken to task by a female superior close in age to their own wife, they find it difficult to suppress feelings of anger.

For women seeking to work on the promotional track, therefore, dealing with men as subordinates in a work situation takes special attention and skill. A question frequently posed by companies in interviewing female applicants for integrated track positions concerns how they would deal with having men working under them. Women in jobs that can only be acquired by passing difficult qualifying examinations, such as those in the civil service and the medical and legal professions, seem to have fewer problems gaining respect and recognition in the workplace and in handling managerial responsibilities. Partly owing to the fact that such women are formally proven to be smart and able, men both under and over them depend on them, and the number of women in these professions is large enough so that they are treated as relatively equal to men and can interact with their male colleagues as equals.

Perhaps unconsciously avoiding male resentment, many managerial women take care to present a very feminine appearance, wearing makeup and dressing attractively, partly in deference to male expectations. Few adopt the masculine look that was popular for a time among some American businesswomen. Japanese women do not think that the path to equality with men has anything to do with emulating them in outward appearance or behavior. Perhaps they feel the obstacles they face as female managers are great enough without giving the impression of hardness and aggressiveness that men find so threatening and distasteful in women. Women can cleverly avoid that danger with a facade that reassures men and smooths the transition. If men will not let down their guard unless they see women acting inferior and in need of their help, Japanese women are not above living the charade. Indeed, there was a time when only two types of women could hope for promotion: those with very special talents or professional skills and those who cleverly used their feminine charms to influence and manage men. (Today, it is not necessary to be beautiful or charming to gain promotion.)

Female managers and entrepreneurs in Japan have been successful by making full use of their so-called feminine and mothering instincts in the treatment of employees. As long as their enterprises are small and medium-sized, they can actually get ahead by exploiting traditional-style femininity. If, on the other hand, they hope to attain the status of president of a large corporation, they have to graduate from family-style management and motherly attitudes toward employees and assume their expected role using more standardized, impersonal, and androgynous leadership behavior. Once they have come that far, they can delegate responsibility, and put women as well as men in support positions to assume some of the heretofore female roles, while they devote themselves to larger concerns of management and decision making. So far, there are very few Japanese women who have been able to accumulate the requisite training, self-confidence, business acumen, professional experience, and information-gathering skills to compete adequately with men for such positions.

WOMEN AND JAPANESE-STYLE MANAGEMENT

Many of the characteristics of so-called Japanese-style management are also traits widely attributed to women, especially in Japan but also in the United States: for example, consideration for the feelings and ideas of subordinates and colleagues, attention to details, greater concern for quality than quantity, a nonaggressive manner in handling problems, the extension of interpersonal relations beyond strictly business concerns, and the tendency to postpone decisions if better results can be attained by doing so.[12] There is today and will be from now on, as the service sector of industry continues to expand, increasing demand for skill in handling interpersonal relations and for sensitivity to detail and the fine points of service. In the United States, corporate culture in general is more masculine than feminine and more aggressive, decisive, and profit-oriented than interpersonal and harmony-oriented. Business planning stresses short-range ventures rather than long-range commitments, and the female attributes mentioned earlier, which are culturally (rather than biologically) determined, are sometimes considered a valuable antidote and addition in the workplace. In Japan, on the other hand, where corporate culture is already "feminine" in this sense in many ways, these female attributes do not add much that is new to corporate culture. Women can, however, make the best of their strong points in the context of the prevailing management style. If women can capitalize on their so-called mothering instincts to meet the needs of Japanese business with its emphasis on family-like management practices, they may be successful without having to actually either overturn the established system or discard female traits that they think are worth preserving. If

Japanese management shifts more toward the aggressive, merit-oriented methods widespread in the United States, it remains to be seen how such a change would affect the advancement of women in the Japanese workplace.

ON SERVING TEA

Working women in Japan put up with much discriminatory treatment, such as being expected to serve tea to male colleagues and not being given jobs or positions of responsibility in the office, treatment that many American women would feel to be blatantly sexist and unacceptable. How do Japanese women feel about such treatment?

Many women employees are openly called *ochakumi* (tea fetchers), and it is their job to serve tea to other workers and to guests in the office, keep the office tidy, and otherwise fetch and serve for other employees. More recently in many companies, each employee as a rule helps himself or herself to tea or coffee, except for executives or management staff with secretaries. It is also not uncommon for younger men in an office, laboratory, or other workplace to be the ones expected to serve the tea. When visitors come into an office, it is still customary to serve them tea or other refreshment, and women are tacitly expected to perform this job. In some offices women employees take turns serving tea and are expected to arrive at the office early to tidy up before the day begins, by wiping off everybody's desk and telephone and emptying ashtrays (tasks not expected of the maintenance staff but designed to be carried out by office workers in order to promote a close, familial atmosphere in the office). This practice began in an era when women unquestioningly accepted decisions made by men, and it became a custom among people working in offices.

Asked what they think of the fact that serving tea in the office is considered part of their job, former female students of mine seem little troubled by the issue. Chieko, who is in the integrated career track in a computer software company, says that although her employers told her and her female colleagues that no distinction would be made according to sex, she feels that, in fact, they would like the women to serve tea (her "feeling" is typical of the guessing game that is part of Japanese interpersonal communications). Chieko said she herself is not bothered by the idea; she does not think that it is something to fuss over. She does not seem to feel that having to serve tea is a critical symbol of sexual inequality. For her it is not an issue that requires a clear settlement but one that can be left to individual discretion. Other responses revealed similar thinking and show clearly how Japanese women's own attitudes either prevent or deliberately sabotage the realization of sexual equality. As explained in Chapter 1, Japanese women have a tendency not to make an issue of equality when they do not feel that their individual situation is impaired. Equality as a noble principle to be championed is one thing, but the task of pouring tea is another and not an issue upon which they are willing to disrupt office harmony.

At Tokyo Marine Insurance, Makiko writes: "When I want to have a cup of coffee, it just seems the natural and considerate thing to do to ask others around me if they would also like one. But I don't think a company that believes tea serving is a woman's job can be a leading company." In other words, if she serves others on her own volition, without being asked, a company's personnel policy cannot be called into question. If she *has* to serve them, that's a different matter. Makiko's attitude becomes firm if the act in question is not just tea but drinks. She recalled with anger an experience at a company dinner party when the man in charge asked the newly recruited women to sit evenly distributed among the men, like hostesses in a bar, as if he were expecting these young women to serve their male colleagues drinks. Interestingly, she told me that none of the young women, who clearly objected to the idea, openly expressed their disapproval; instead, as a sign of resistance, they deliberately talked with each other rather than to the men sitting next to them. This response reflects the common practice in Japan of avoiding confrontation or forthright expression of feelings. Women believe that if men are sensitive enough, they will understand women's point of view.

Serving tea, incidentally, is not just a symbol of service. In Japanese society, tea (or other refreshments) can be an important lubricant in daily activity and human relations and a medium for removing tension from certain situations. A 27-year-old woman producer of the national broadcasting company recounted how in creating a program one day she and her (predominantly male) colleagues found themselves in a very tense argument over how to proceed. Then one of the men got up and made coffee for everyone, and as he passed it around, the tension abated and the discussion began to progress more constructively. This woman explained how defeated she had felt not to have been the one to think of that way of defusing the situation and how frustrated that her male colleague had gotten the better of her. In general, she said that she thought there was no point in making an issue of equality over tasks that anyone can perform without much training; equality has to be pursued, she thinks, only when obstacles are put in the way of acquiring the training for specific jobs. She pities women who are so narrow in their thinking that they have to oppose serving tea as a way of seeking equality.

Gender obviously plays an important part in determining roles in Japanese society, but so does seniority. When both gender and seniority are salient factors in human interaction, which takes precedence? The answer depends upon the situation, but seniority and status seem to be more important than gender when it comes to serving tea in the workplace or drinks at work-related parties. At meetings, therefore, we frequently observe that the youngest man or man of the lowest rank serves the others, including women who are of higher rank and age. This certainly is a change from the days when gender automatically put women in the lowest rank and only the rare woman occupied a higher status than men.

Especially for nonprofessional women, the Japanese workplace still abounds with forms of discrimination, other than those related to wages, that are practiced and maintained by both men and women. Obviously, discriminatory policies, such as earlier retirement ages for women, have been disappearing as lawsuits (although rarely brought to court) have been brought by women and, more often than not, been settled in favor of female employees' rights.

SEXUAL HARASSMENT

In 1989 a new term appeared in the Japanese media: *sekuhara* (short for sexual harassment), one of many Japanized abbreviations of difficult-to-pronounce English phrases. For all the use the term has received, there does seem to be some confusion about what it really means.

When the Tokyo Metropolitan Government set up a program to advise citizens on problems related to the workplace, about 10,000 women came for consultation during the year 1989 alone. Of those cases, 373 were concerned with so-called sexual harassment problems. In most of the cases the women reported being forced into sexual relationships against their will. Gutek reported that Asian-Americans in the United States tended to report fewer cases of sexual harassment, interpreting this finding as reflecting a cultural tendency to keep such incidents secret as personally embarrassing and not to consider them a matter for legal attention.[13]

The summer of 1989 saw the filing of Japan's first lawsuit by a woman against her superior at work, a man whom she charged had forced her to have sexual relations at the risk of losing her job. After she refused, the man spread the rumor around the office that she was drunk and constantly having affairs with different men. It took unusual courage for the woman to file the suit, but she won and obtained ¥1.65 million (approximately $12,000) in compensation in a decision made in April 1992. The incident took place in a company in a medium-sized city in Japan, an environment in which rumor can effectively ostracize a person and cause great personal injury. The woman had to stand up and file the lawsuit in order to protect herself and her family. If a woman in a large metropolis like Tokyo encounters such difficulties in a job, she can quit and find another job or move to a different part of the city to protect herself and her family, but that would not be so easy in a smaller town or city.

When questioned about sexual harassment, young women's responses vary widely. One woman employed in a bank found the issue amusing, remarking that "if a man commits anything close to sexual harassment, he will be the laughing stock of the office and no one would associate with him or take him seriously." Apparently, the traditional Japanese culture of shame is working effectively in the environment she describes. A woman employee at a broadcasting station reported that when she was young and working as a producer in the entertainment program department she often had to endure pats on the behind and lewd remarks and innuendos but that she had no such trouble when transferred to the educational programming department. Even within the same organization, therefore, male attitudes and behavior vary widely. Some men never think of sexual harassment; others are completely unrepentant, such as the man who declared, "It just shows that a woman is in the prime of life. If nobody wants to touch you, that's the end." Generally not brought up to understand women or expected to pay attention to their feelings, Japanese men can be amazingly insensitive toward their female coworkers and even their own spouses.

Since the work environment has been dominated by men for so long, the very decor of workplaces can also be distasteful to women, and calendars and posters of female nudes are commonplace. Generally speaking, it is women in small and medium-sized enterprises who tend to suffer from sexual harassment, for men in larger companies are much more conscious of protecting their reputations and status. They are also better educated. Very slowly Japanese men are recognizing the kind of behavior women consider to be sexual harassment, but it may take a few more highly embarrassing lawsuits to make them cease and desist. Young women, too, are slowly but surely gaining the confidence in themselves to say no to unwanted offers when they can still be declined. In reality, however, many middle-aged and older men know firsthand only three kinds of women: their wives, the women who do supportive jobs and errands at the office, and bar hostesses and other women in the entertainment business. For many men, the encounter with a woman who is an equal and respected colleague is rare. It is clear, however, that from now on such opportunities will increase.

THE CONSEQUENCES OF CHANGE

How has the economy and the workplace in Japan changed as a result of the growing participation of women, whose time perspective tends to be much shorter than that of men? How will both change from now on? It is clear that more Japanese women, save for those with small children, will be joining the work force and that they will be finding, as well as creating, job opportunities of much greater variety. Their skills will be in ever greater demand as the labor shortage deepens and the graying of society advances. Some elite superwomen, although a minority, will aspire to managerial posts by juggling both work and family, while the majority will aim to balance family, work, and leisure.

Clearly, they are not taking job opportunities away from men nor desirous of following in their husband's footsteps in terms of employment. They have refused to make men their role model in the workplace, preferring a more diversified, individualistic way of life. In this respect women have moved ahead of men by taking advantage of consumerism made possible through recently attained affluence. And women are less interested in following male norms of groupism in the corporate context. Some younger men resist groupism and try to assert greater freedom of individual action in the same way as women, but overall quite a large gap continues to yawn between the worlds of men and women in Japan.

The differences in the long-range employment and life goals of men and women are at the root of the gap in their attitudes toward work. Women tend to make full use of the benefits to which they are entitled, such as systems like flextime, recreational facilities owned by the company, and paid holidays. In one company that introduced flextime, for example, as long as most of the employees were males, they continued to come in at the regular starting hour and stay until well after the regular working day was over. But when the number of female employees increased and women began to take full advantage of the system, the men slowly began to follow suit. Many people believe the Japanese do not take paid vacations, but this isn't quite the case anymore. At one big department store in Tokyo, for instance, men began to take time off when they saw that their female coworkers were using up all of their paid holidays.

Since many women in the general track hold much shorter-term views of their jobs than men, their performance is influenced not so much by the prospects for promotion later on as by how matters stand at present. If they enjoy the work, these women work very hard; if it is unpleasant, they have no hesitation in quitting. Their work can be heavily affected by the way their boss treats them. If properly encouraged, women will hustle and do more than they are expected to, but if not they will simply perform at minimal level. Indeed, while bosses in bygone days were often surrounded by young women who anticipated and attended to their every need, they now have to devote much more time and energy to showing extra consideration for their female subordinates. While a boss can give a male subordinate a tongue-lashing for some shortcoming and then buck him up again over drinks after work, the same techniques do not work with women; thus, bosses inevitably find women harder to handle in actual work situations.[14]

Some men in their twenties, watching the way women quickly quit jobs they find uninteresting, threaten to quit themselves when they find themselves in intolerable situations, and today more do, in fact, leave their jobs than in the past. Partly for this reason, young men have begun to work for temporary manpower agencies once used only by women. With younger men beginning to adopt the freer working patterns heretofore typical of women, the lines dividing the worlds of men and women have begun to break down among the younger generation.[15]

The majority of men still tend to keep their opinions about management or company policy to themselves, however, because they expect to remain at the same company for many years and self-assertiveness may not be conducive to one's prospects for long-term success in a Japanese firm. Women, who know they have the option of leaving, are much more likely to say exactly what is on their minds. Often, the top managers find the ideas of these women fresh and useful, but their immediate superiors, who feel called upon to maintain office harmony, are not necessarily pleased. The harmonious work environment at Japanese companies has been made possible by the willingness of individuals to suppress their feelings and cooperate with others for the sake of the organization as a whole, but the winds of change are bound to overtake Japanese firms as working women grow in number.

After-five gatherings used to be an integral part of company life; they played a key role in bonding and in enhancing group harmony. But they were a source of frustration for career-minded women with families, who were torn between the desire not to miss out on the information exchanged during these sessions and the urge to return home to their children. In recent years meetings on important work-related matters have increasingly been scheduled during regular work hours in the face of the growing aversion among young people to intrusions on their after-work hours by their supervisors or associates. Women managers with families are the happiest about this trend.

The influx of married women into the workplace may have a significant impact on management practices. In the past, employees used to work late into the night to get an assignment done, but signs of change are also in the making here. Unlike male office workers who tend to work at a rather languid pace and end up putting in overtime, women have a tendency to approach their work briskly, planning deliberately to complete what they have to do by five o'clock so they can leave on time. In sections of offices where women are in management positions, there is a marked decrease in overtime work, and this is welcomed by the men as well as the women.

A certain department store has a policy of changing its displays frequently to attract customers, and for many years it had its employees do the arranging after closing time, which often meant they had to stay very late. But it recently began allowing them to come in earlier in the morning instead as a way of accommodating the schedules of its female employees. One result was that women became able to move into positions of responsibility, and another was the realization among the men at the top that employees could work with undivided attention and get through in a shorter span of time a task they once had taken hours to complete. In such ways as this, women's entry into the work force will likely trigger an evaluation of the deplorable custom of having men remain in the office until all hours of the night. And if employees show they can work more intently and get assignments done in less time, it may encourage a decline in Japan's long working hours.

The appearance on the scene of an elite minority of female professionals in the integrated track has had an unmistakable impact on Japanese companies. The members of this group are veritable superwomen, extremely bright and filled with ambition. They present a striking contrast to the large number of mollycoddled young men of their age, who were raised by strong mothers and absentee fathers and tend to be quite pleasant but lacking in verve. Situations in which younger men come to female co-workers to ask their advice or counsel about tasks they are performing, as they might seek a mother's support and help, are observable in offices today as they never were in years past.[16] These women are starting, in effect, to climb an uncharted mountain, and nobody yet knows how their ascent will change them and others or what effect their success will have on, for example, their husband's aspirations or their marital relationship. These women firmly believe that they can marry, have children, and work, without being dragged down by the uncooperativeness of men. One such woman, Meiko (age 26), revealing an easy confidence in her ability to accomplish these goals, says, "I want to make every day shine, to be energetic, but without overextending myself; to take things naturally without showing off. I don't want to be one of those super career-woman types who wear sharp suits with shoulder pads and go about looking tense and businesslike all the time."

These trailblazers are filled with confidence and hope, but at the same time they are under a great deal of pressure, as indicated by rising rates of alcoholism and smoking among women. They work long hours, achieve impressive results, and win coveted posts. They tend to outperform their male peers even when the latter are also working furiously. Many companies are pinning high hopes on these women, and their male coworkers seem to be accepting their success, reasoning that people deserve to be recognized on the basis of their achievements, regardless of their gender.

Companies also know there is an added benefit to hiring women, since they bring a new perspective to an operation formerly run with an all-male mind-set. In today's society, companies know that women can be great assets to their business. Now a variety of firms are seeking to give play to the female sensibility in product development, and women— including those not on a career track—have come up with a range of novel ideas, some of which have been turned into successful products, like petite stationery items. Other products have not turned out so well, since they were conceived only from the standpoint of the consumer and failed to take into account the overall production process. For example, one women's group opened a shop selling homemade-style box lunches using quality ingredients and taking consumer tastes into consideration, but their calculations for turning a profit were weak. Sales were brisk and the shop was well patronized, but the women found they were always busy and making little profit. In this regard the proposals of the elite minority of career women are more worthwhile, since they are grounded in an understanding of the entire commercial process in addition to incorporating female sensibilities. The Nissan Figaro, a model designed by a team of women, is one case in point. It sold out its full limited production line of 21,000 and brought in 218,000 orders for more.

The work ethic of many professional women and the strength

of their commitment to their jobs seem to be akin to those of the middle-aged male workers. Deep down these women also feel it is impossible to produce quality work if they do not practically live at their office. They are an invaluable resource for the firm, but are still too few in number to have any major impact on the organization as a whole. In five or ten years, however, as their numbers grow, they will likely become a force that cannot be ignored, and the battle of the sexes for the limited number of top posts may begin.

There have been many cases in which companies no longer able to attract the top male workers started hiring women out of necessity. When they discovered that women were often even more able than male workers below the highest rank, they began to hire women much more aggressively. The big trading firms and banks that draw the cream of the crop of male recruits for employment, on the other hand, do not use female employees to full advantage.

Women in the construction business working on dam construction sites have taken their jobs because they really like the work and are therefore performing with energy and good results. Some are known to drive bulldozers and other big equipment in place of men. Hiring more women in construction work has led some employers to be more conscious of safety, and workplaces tend to be kept cleaner and neater. The men are more careful of the way they dress, and clothing has become less drab. In many cases the men are actually stimulated to try harder so as not to be outdone by female coworkers. Another advantage is that by hiring more women in place of young men, some companies have found they thereby become more attractive to young male job hunters. With attention from the mass media and the good press it provides, some of these corporations have become even more aggressive in hiring women, and the impact of this trend has been very favorable, prompting mothers to encourage their sons to apply for jobs in workplaces where many young women are working.

Small and medium-sized advertising agencies, which now use women in large numbers for sales, found at first that their male employees felt threatened by female recruits. Men and women in this industry, too, have learned to work together, divvying up jobs on the basis of aptitude to quite good advantage, rather than competing as members of opposite sexes. Here, women have proven their value not by replacing men but by doing tasks the men undervalued or did not know existed.

The move among corporations to prefer able women to mediocre men has led to fears among some men that the general and integrated track categories may be expanded to include men. Corporations that once fostered loyalty among their male employees by eschewing discrimination among them on the basis of ability and drive are therefore beginning to change their management principles. Men themselves have responded by becoming cooler in their attachment to the company, with fewer willing to make just any sacrifice for the sake of their employer.

As a result of the increased numbers of women in the workplace, some executives have been known to declare that a male manager who cannot use female employees effectively is not qualified as a manager. However, some men who do not want to be in a position to have to take responsibility for the work of female employees who may quit at their own convenience try to avoid having women working under them.

In Japanese companies it is the norm for job descriptions to be quite ambiguous, with employees assigned to, and quick to take up, posts on a flexible as-needed basis, a big difference from the United States where an employee may refuse to undertake an assignment because it is not in his or her job description. On the other hand, when the content of work is left unclear, there is a tendency for women to be used as assistants of male employees; thus, some corporations have begun to define job descriptions in more detail. This could lead to the erosion of the flexible approach to work, which has been one of the great strengths of Japanese corporations in the past.

Since passage of the EEOL and as companies have begun to realize that they may be at a disadvantage if they do not use women to the full, some women complain that the atmosphere of the workplace has become stricter, that human warmth and mutual consideration have become harder to find in the workplace. Some women find the stresses and the pace too much for them, causing them to withdraw to the freer life of a full-time housewife or part-time worker. This situation is, in fact, behind a conservative trend observable among younger women.

All that has been accomplished thus far in terms of policy, as exemplified by the EEOL, is to begin to integrate women into the existing male-created corporate culture. What has to be discussed and debated from now on is how men and their behavior in the workplace can change so as to make it easier for women and men to work together. One such change would be to shorten working hours; this would have immense impact on the lifestyle of both men and women, both in the workplace and in the home. Already as a result of the increase in number of female workers, some companies have been forced to decrease their working hours. The introduction of flextime has brought a reappraisal of the merits of the teamwork that is a feature of Japanese business as well as the development of more professional specialization.

While women once worked mainly to supplement the income of the family "ricewinner" (which meant working women were mainly from lower-income families), recently wives of middle- and upper-income families (like Noda Akiko and many others of the first postwar generation) have begun to enter the work force, a phenomenon that has ultimately worked to enlarge income disparity among Japanese households. From now on, men may not only come to count on their wives' income but to even demand that they work in order to share the earning of the household income. As this happens, the lifestyles women have adopted based on their freedom to work or not to work will cease to be as free and independent as they are today. Eventually, we will witness a conspicuous clash between those women who are unwilling to work at the expense of their much-prized freedom and men who will demand that women take a more responsible role in income earning in order to grant them (men) a greater modicum of freedom. How this clash will be resolved remains to be seen, but it is sure to lead, in any case, to much greater diversity in working patterns for both men as well as women and in household and family lifestyles and values.

8

POLITICS AND NO POWER

National politics in Japan, as in many other advanced societies, remains one of the firmest bastions of male dominance. The norms that govern it seem the most impervious to the transforming power that women have brought to the family, the marketplace, the corporation, and even to politics on the grass-roots level, as we shall see in Chapter 9. Although women are guaranteed equal political rights under the postwar Constitution, women rarely participate on the national level other than as voters. In this role they do hold considerable sway, but as members of the national House of Representatives, House of Councilors, or Cabinet their presence is faint and their role still marginal.

Japanese men see the arena of national politics as one of the most important territories for action and self-actualization (i.e., for access to and custodianship of power, prestige, and success). It is therefore a territory they zealously preserve for themselves, firmly resisting the threat posed by women to entrenched values, customs, and organizations built up within their fraternal society over the centuries. Most men would like to think that those women who have entered politics are capable of performing only in areas related to what is known as women's *daidokoro kankaku* (housekeeper's instinct)—that is, household affairs, child care, education, health and welfare, environment—and that they are unfit for positions involving political policy, economic affairs, security, or diplomacy. By confining the scope of female involvement in politics to such conventional assumptions, male politicians try to preserve the world of national and international politics for themselves.

Japanese women, on the other hand, whose sex roles have not included involvement in national politics since ancient times, do not appear to expect much help to come from that realm of endeavor. Given that the democratic political process in Japan does not function effectively and that the national government is run largely through systems and practices antedating the institutions of democracy ostensibly adopted after the end of World War II, elective politics does not incite the expectations or trust that it might, say, in the United States. The majority of Japanese, women more so than men, see politics as a remote, alien realm, a world of power mongering, influence peddling, and corruption —in short, a filthy occupation that has no relation to their lives and values.[1] Women do not see their sex roles as embracing the world of politics, and they do not feel that politics is an important instrument for improving the status of women. Thus far, Japanese women have exercised influence and power mainly in their personal or local spheres, through providing services that assure them a measure of control of economic resources and community or emotional attachments, totally outside of the formal apparatuses of national politics. It does not, therefore, occur to them that the best spokesperson for their concerns would be a member of the national Diet. Obviously, a huge gap yawns between male and female expectations of politics and politicians in Japan.

As noted in earlier chapters, the Japanese woman's approach to problem solving and pursuit of goals tends to be thoroughly pragmatic rather than guided by adherence to well-defined principles. The course of the careers of those women who have succeeded in politics, like former chairperson of the Japan Socialist Democratic Party (SDPJ) Doi Takako (to be introduced in detail later), tends to lack any fundamental principle of action. Their support base, moreover, seldom consists of constituents who are devoted to specific principles of political policy but of those who merely identify with a politician as a member of the same sex. It must also be said that in the political realm, women's behavior has not achieved substantive gains because it tends to be reactive (situation-oriented) rather than aggressive (goal-oriented). Female politicians on the national level so far have been ineffective and helpless against the scandal-ridden collusion between big business and government or in the reform of organizational structures that are still essentially premodern in nature.

There is a strong proclivity in Japanese politics to place the jockeying of factional interests ahead of rational, reasonable discussion and to treat lightly verbal communication in political forums. This means that at election time as well, discussion of policy is minimal. Voters tend to make their choices among candidates not so much on the content of their policy speeches as on the basis of personal image—their credentials and their perceived personal character, generosity, or trustworthiness. Although relatively indifferent to politics per se, many women are quite curious about individual politicians as public personalities. They are keenly aware of politicians' looks—their faces and apparel—and quick to equate physical traits with performance. They may not know which politician backed what bills in the Diet, but they are keen critics of the design of a prime minister's ties or the way a female politician dresses or uses makeup.

A typical female appraisal of Doi, for example, focuses not on the nature of her politics but on a personal impression of apparel, looks, or other superficial qualities. What interest women have in politicians is not linked to an interest in the nature of political policy, and this tendency is not limited to, although it is more prevalent among, women. In surveys of what voters base their decisions on, both men and women say they rely on the television broadcasts of candidates' political opinions, but many also confess they do not understand what the candidates are trying to say (the language they use is deliberately rhetorical, abstruse, and otherwise designed to be general enough to appeal to the largest possible number of voters). In short, pragmatic considerations, rather than matters of principle, are clearly a major factor in female voting behavior in Japan.

Few women (even if they are close to the political world) actively seek to become career politicians. While politics is ostensibly open to them, a political career is considered to be in conflict with their other roles and with many of the so-called desirable female qualities (modesty, restraint, thriftiness, gentleness, flexibility, nonaggressiveness). The women who are elected to office, meanwhile, do not cling to power as tenaciously as men, and this violates the requirements and expectations of a politician. They do not—though it is more accurate to say they *cannot*—form factions and assiduously cultivate a power base with their sights set on the post of prime minister. So, with the exception of Doi Takako, there have been virtually no women politicians in powerful positions in Japan. There are no effective organizations that support the advance of women in politics, so citizens in general—both men and women—simply tend to think of politics as a man's world, further discouraging women from seeking political office.

A PARTIAL PARTICIPATION

The history of female participation in Japanese politics goes back less than half a century. Although Japan celebrated the centennial of its national Diet in 1990, women only gained a voice in politics in 1945. During more than half of the century the Japanese legislative system has functioned, its doors were firmly closed to women.

In 1890 the first general elections were held to select representatives for the newly formed Diet, but the electorate was limited only to men and, even further, to those adult males who paid direct national taxes of more than ¥15 annually (this group made up only about 1 percent of the population). For Japanese women that year, far from being something to celebrate, marked the beginning of decades of struggle to gain the right to vote and hold political office.

Few Japanese women today realize how short is the history of female enfranchisement, and this is a factor behind their tendency to underestimate the importance of politics and their lack of a sense of responsibility for political affairs. A vigorous women's suffrage movement came into being well before the war, and although temporarily silenced by the all-out war mobilization effort, it was not snuffed out. In 1930 a bill for female suffrage passed in the House of Representatives, but the House of Peers session ended before it could be brought under consideration, and with the Manchurian Incident (1931), it remained pending. In October 1945, only months after the end of World War II, the Shidehara Kijūrō cabinet decided to establish women's right to political participation in law; in December a bill was passed extending voting rights to women on the national and local level. Because so many democratic reforms were legislated under the direction of the Allied Occupation at the time, many people, especially women born after the war, think women's suffrage was something received from the Americans. Quite recently, however, newly discovered documents have revealed that the bill was not initiated by the Occupation forces but was drafted on the independent initiative of the Japanese government.[2] It represented the fulfillment of the struggle carried on by the women's movement for decades, but the victory was muted by the tumult of Occupation-led reforms. Convinced that the vote was something not fought for but received, many women have tended to political apathy when, in fact, women's suffrage was indeed won partly as a result of years of patient activism by a small group of women's movement leaders.

When universal suffrage was adopted, some men warned that the step was premature. Prior to the general elections held in April 1946, a member of the upper house expressed the fear that "the civic consciousness of the populace is still undeveloped, and since women have no idea of the responsibilities of participating in politics, the proportion of non-voters may be over 50 percent." The paternalistic fears went unfounded. Sixty-seven percent of women went to the polls, and though somewhat less than the 79 percent of men who voted, it represented the meaningful voice of women. Not only that, of 79 female candidates fielded in the election, 39 were victorious (8.4 percent of lower house representatives), bringing a sudden influx of women into the national Diet. Of these, seven were members of the prewar women's political rights movement. As of today, there has never been a larger number of women candidates elected to office in a national election.[3] But although women have consistently exercised their right to vote, their active participation in national politics has been minimal, and the proportion of women in the national Diet remained around 3 percent for many years after that first election.

The number of women Diet members has recently increased somewhat, but the proportion as of March 1990 was only 5.9 percent, giving Japan a rank of 108 among democratic countries of the world. There are 12 women members of the House of Representatives (2.3 percent of the entire membership; the U.S. House of Representatives has 25 women or 6 percent) and 33 of the House of Councilors (13 percent; the U.S. Senate has 2 women or 2 percent). The number of female legislators on the national level has clearly not kept pace with the quite considerable advances women have made in business, academia, the professions, and the service industries.

In the 1989 House of Councilors elections, the number of women Diet members sharply increased (from the previous 3 percent to 13 percent), but the increase does not so much reflect a fundamental redefinition of the role of women in politics as other, more transient, factors, including the upsurge in the consumer movement and the impact of the appointment of a woman as chairperson of a leading political party. The male-dominated mass media made much of the new visibility of women, declaring the "advent of the era of women" and highlighting the achievements of newcomer Dietwomen. In terms of numbers, women still represent only a small fraction of the membership of the Diet, and the day when a woman might become prime minister of Japan is still far from being in sight. Nevertheless, on the level of grass-roots politics, the number of women working actively to get their representatives elected to legislative office is steadily growing. Women are gradually accumulating the expertise and experience needed to make them a viable force in politics. The number of women in local assemblies is also steadily increasing, even if only a tiny bit at a time (1.0 percent in 1976, 1.2 percent in 1980, 1.6 percent in 1985, 1.7 percent in 1986, and 2.2 percent in 1987), and 1991 saw the election of the first mayor of a major city (Ashiya, Hyogo prefecture) and the appointment of the first female vice-governor (Tokyo).

ELECTIVE OFFICE AND MONEY POLITICS

The main reasons women have been slow to enter political life are related to the practices and patterns that have gripped the male-dominated political ethos of Japan since the end of the war (and actually go back to the Meiji Restoration). The system itself is not male specific, but it is controlled by males. Except for the House of Councilors, in which the proportional representation system is partially used, a would-be politician's first tasks are to obtain party support, set up a campaign office in his constituency, form a supporters' organization, and then do everything possible to obtain the support of loyal voters. In order to cultivate a supporters' organization that will ensure reelection, candidates use massive amounts of money in presenting gifts (of money) at the weddings and funerals or other ceremonial occasions of their constituents, gestures they hope will build close ties and thereby assure support at election time. After election, the law forbids such practices (although they do continue in other forms). The larger the supporters' organization and the stronger a candidate tries to make it, the greater the amount of money required and the more a candidate cannot afford to lose.

Given the present norms and patterns of political life, becoming a politician means aiming for a cabinet position, which is the symbol of recognition and power for a veteran politician. The crowning achievement of a career in politics is the post of prime minister. According to political custom, appointment to a ministerial post is based on the number of times a politician has been returned to office. In elections, therefore, it is not so much the stand the candidate takes on specific policies or issues as the strength of the candidate's support base that assures victory.[4]

Japan's Diet is a bicameral institution with greater powers exercised by its lower House of Representatives than by its upper House of Councilors. In general, it is the lower house that is the nucleus of party politics, with the upper house being thought of mainly as a check against the excessive power of the lower. The majority of ministers are chosen from the House of Representatives, and politicians who are not members of the lower house have little chance of gaining access to the inner circles of power. This difference in the roles of the two houses of the Diet helps explain why there are more women who have been able to gain election to seats in the upper than in the lower house. Less successful at maneuvering funds and influence in order to win seats in the lower house, women face nearly insurmountable hurdles in gaining access to the cabinet, the inner sanctum of Japanese politics. When they are appointed, and the first case was as late as 1960, it is often more for political effect or—even in the case of men—on the basis of seniority and is rarely genuine recognition of their talents or accomplishments as a politician (as discussed further in the following section).

As long as such practices persist in Japanese politics, women face tremendous handicaps in their attempt to win in election races against men. The fact that it takes so much money to get elected has put political office far beyond the reach of most politically ambitious women. Women's distaste for abuse of money in cultivating influence has served only to strengthen money politics in Japan. In a sense, women's nonparticipation is also an abdication of responsibility. If politics has to be such a dirty business, women are extremely reluctant to participate. Rather than involve themselves in the questionable mechanisms set up by men in order to be part of political life, they have sought to distance themselves from the entire political process.

Some women gain access to politics indirectly (as do some not necessarily politically ambitious men), such as when a member of the Diet dies while in office and his supporters' organization drafts his widow to take his place, mobilizing the electorate in the name of her deceased husband. Usually, women elected in this capacity are not supported for their political policies or their own personal merits but are merely figureheads to tide the organization over until a real successor (often a son) emerges. The number of cases in which a politician passes on his political and financial power base to a son or son-in-law has sharply increased, but there are hardly any in which the successor is a daughter or daughter-in-law. Here again, women are not even given a chance at the training in political life that the men benefit from under successful fathers or fathers-in-law.

Another indirect route to politics in which women can exercise their talents is as wives of candidates and elected representatives. These women are expected to head the election campaigns for their husbands as well as manage all private affairs skillfully. With the candidate himself occupied by Diet sessions and committees in Tokyo, often it is the wives who do the most to maintain the electoral following and collect votes in the home constituency. The obligations these women must fulfill are immense: They must learn how to dress and speak in ways that will not provoke criticism or alienate any potential voter; they must be careful to use the proper etiquette—bowing at the appropriately deep angle for each occasion—so as not to be thought arrogant or snobbish; and they must devote themselves to the details that court the support and favor of the voters, such as hospital visits, wedding presents for the daughters of important local citizens, and appearances at sports events. Because support for politicians is not based on policy or political performance but on human relations, these activities are crucial. In everything politicians' wives do, they must suppress their own desires and individual preferences in order to assure victory for their husbands. If they are successful, they enjoy a large measure of the power and prestige accorded to their husbands. Their role is an extension of the traditional good wife and wise mother, a role in which a woman is supposed to achieve self-actualization through the success of her husband.

A recent visible example of the politician's wife was Kaifu Sachiyo (Kaifu was prime minister from 1989 to 1991), who skillfully backed her husband through his 27-year-long career. Following a supporter's advice, she made it a rule when walking down a street to bow her head in greeting to everyone she met, whether she knew them or not. She has described the discipline she had to practice constantly in preparation for the time when the way she herself behaved might mean the difference between her husband's winning and losing. The real challenge lies in the fact that while there is no one to replace the candidate, there are plenty of people who can take the place of the candidate's wife.[5]

The wives of politicians have many opportunities to enjoy the limelight in their husband's constituency, and this may provide some satisfaction and fulfillment. Since a political wife cannot interfere with her husband's political assertions and can only contribute by supporting her husband's position, it is a role hardly linked to self-actualization. Some compensation may be found, nevertheless, in the knowledge that her husband is in great need of her support for a successful political career and in the fact that the immense contribution made by a wife is verbally recognized by others.

A less admirable example of how women have been "successful" in Japanese politics was demonstrated by the 1989 elections. The majority of the women candidates of the SDPJ who won in that election were actually never expected to. Believing that its candidates were sure to lose in the election anyway, the party made the thoroughly pragmatic decision that they would run women instead of subjecting male candidates to the beating at the polls that seemed to be in the cards. This strategy reveals, of course, the tendency among all the parties to treat women as expendable figures or stand-ins, as opposed to serious candidates for political office. The reasoning goes that if a woman loses an election, she can always be supported by her husband; if a man fails, there is no consensus that the reverse is acceptable. No wonder few women voluntarily seek careers in politics.

OBJECTS RATHER THAN SUBJECTS

The changes occurring in the attitudes and behavior of women in recent years have not, as observed earlier, been sufficiently grasped by men as a whole, and the perception gap is especially severe in the ruling Liberal Democratic Party (LDP). LDP veteran of the House of Councilors Moriyama Mayumi has commented about the obstacles that stand in the way of the careers of women Diet members:[6]

> The LDP knows the power of women as part of the vote-getting mechanism, so its strategy on women is directed at attracting them as voters. They see women only as *objects* of policy, not as partners in the policy-making process [my emphasis]. It's too bad, because women don't have to have men do the thinking for them and do things for them; they have the ability to raise their own voices and create their own policies.

That the LDP politicians do not think of women as equal partners is highlighted by the fact that its female contingent currently serving in the Diet is largely made up of former singers, actresses, and Olympic medalists, that is, women whose appeal is based more on their popularity and physical attractiveness than on their political ability. But the other parties, too, have a proclivity for running television or theater personalities in elections as attractions to fan voter interest.

In a speech in 1989 the minister of agriculture caused a controversy with insensitive remarks about women in politics. He questioned the usefulness of women in the political world, noting that while they had advanced in various other fields of society, they did not have the right instincts to really function in the Diet. He was willing to recognize Prime Minister Margaret Thatcher's success but only because she had a husband and children. He disdained Chairperson Doi because she was not married and had no children, apparently thinking that her qualifications as a politician could only be established after she had proved herself in the traditional roles of mother and wife and that she thus was hardly material for the prime ministership of Japan (male politicians, of course, need not prove themselves as husbands or fathers in order to be recognized by their peers). These comments produced a stream of protests, which the minister sought to stem the following day at a press conference with a pro forma apology. It was clear enough that he spoke for many men who do not welcome the advance of women into politics; as the male critic reporting on the agriculture minister's apology in the July 9th edition of *Yomiuri Shimbun* commented, "Certainly there are a great many men [in Japan today] who agree with [the minister's] remarks." Men do not usually say so explicitly, but the opinion expressed by the words blurted out in an unguarded moment by the agriculture minister—that "women are no use in the arena of politics"—is actually shared not only by LDP dietmen but by Japanese men in general. The real problem is the widespread hypocrisy among both sexes. The men publicly deny that they look down on woman's abilities, and the women privately forgive them for excluding women, feeling that female sex roles do not embrace politics.

The way women are appointed to ministerial posts is also symbolic of the lack of a substantive female role in politics. In the first Kaifu Cabinet formed in August 1989 following the heavy losses suffered by the LDP in the general elections, two women were appointed to ministerial positions for the first time: economic journalist Takahara Sumiko as head of the Economic Planning Agency and veteran politician and ex-bureaucrat Moriyama Mayumi as chief cabinet secretary. Moriyama had been head of the Environment Agency, but when the chief cabinet secretary, Yamashita Tokuo, became involved in a scandal involving illicit affairs with women and was forced to resign, the experienced and unflamboyant Moriyama was chosen in a deliberate LDP strategy to project a clean image. Takahara was chosen, although she had no previous political or administrative experience, after failure of a desperate measure to lure a prominent female novelist to the post. But neither woman had a chance to outgrow her unfamiliarity with her post, for the cabinet was reshuffled after only 10 months; there were no women members in the new lineup. In Kaifu's third cabinet, former actress Santo Akiko was appointed as head of the Science and Technology Agency, but in the subsequent Miyazawa administration lineup there were no women.

Appealing for an extension of her appointment as chief cabinet secretary, Moriyama called the prime minister to task for using professional women politicians as pawns to obtain a stable majority of votes; her anger at her own party's unfair treatment of female politicians was unconcealed. The public's response (both men and women) to Moriyama's protest did nothing to suggest that her efforts had produced a more enlightened electorate: The general reaction was that she was clinging too hard to power and had said too much (for a woman), in violation of the traditionally desirable qualities of women. The newspaper headlines made fun of her protest. This incident illustrates the fact that while the determination to grasp and hold on to power is important for a politician, a broad segment of the public feels that women should not be in the power-mongering business. The incompatibility of role expectations for women politicians makes it practically impossible for women to gain political power.

THE 1989 SHAKE-UP

The July 1989 House of Councilors elections brought women into the limelight as never before in Japanese politics. The leading issue of the campaigns was the newly introduced consumption tax, a problem of very immediate concern for women, who customarily shop daily and are in charge of household finances. For this reason, there was an unusual and brief convergence of political and established roles of women. Half of the seats in the House were, as usual, up for election for six-year terms, and a record 146 female candidates were running. The sex scandal involving Prime Minister Uno aroused female indignation, bringing women to the polls to chastise the ruling party for making such a disreputable character its president. Polls taken just before the elections showed that 34 percent of women were "very concerned about the elections," almost three times the proportion surveyed three years earlier, and that among women in their twenties, who usually do not go to the polls, four times as many as three years earlier, or 23 percent, were "very concerned." Predictions were that the women's vote would determine the outcome of the elections.[7]

The results were basically as predicted, with the number of LDP seats in the upper house drastically reduced, leaving the ruling party without a clear majority. There was, however, a notable increase in the number of female upper house members,[8] enough to set off a media flap about the "age of women" and the advances being made by women in society. In the election for assembly members of the Tokyo city government that were held just before that for the House of Councilors, 17 women were elected (11 of them young women in their thirties and forties), an increase of 8 over the previous assembly, adding to the impression of the growing strength of women in public affairs. The success of the Socialist Party in the Tokyo elections was especially remarkable, with one third of the 36 successful candidates from the party being women.

After the House of Councilors elections, the leader of the Socialist Democratic Party of Japan, Doi Takako, automatically became a candidate for prime minister, the first time a woman had ever been among the nominees for the position. Ultimately, of course, since the LDP held the majority of seats in the lower house, the post of prime minister went to the LDP candidate, Kaifu Toshiki, but, as mentioned earlier, the new cabinet did include two women, at least for a limited period.

Although the impact women had in the routing of the LDP in the upper house election race has to be recognized, their participation in politics appears, from the male point of view, to be only a temporary trend influenced by their "emotional" opposition to the imposition of the consumption tax. In the argument that the growing strength of the anti-LDP drive and the political advances made by women stem only from women's resistance to the consumption tax, a resistance based on their so-called "housekeeper's instincts," we can glimpse the male desire to keep the role of women in politics as close as possible to traditional norms. The convictions that the roles of women and children should be those confined to the home, that women are ill-equipped for theoretical or intellectual work and in any case function only on instinct or whim, and that important political questions are the preserve of men and cannot be left up to women are rooted extremely deeply in the Japanese male psyche. Middle-aged men were especially bitter and disdainful in their criticism of Doi Takako because she had overstepped the permissible bounds of the female stereotype. If their reaction to her is evidence of the extent of male dread of the day women become a substantial presence to be reckoned with in national politics, it will be a long time before these stereotypes change.

At the time of the House of Representatives elections half a year later, in February 1990, the number of women candidates was 66, twice what it had been for the previous election four years earlier. But this time women, who make up more than half of Japan's voters, chose not to tip the balance in favor of major political reform by voting for the opposition and bringing about a change of government. Some said that voters were affected by a peculiarly Japanese sense of balance, which women prize, as if they had collectively calculated that since "the opposition won in the upper house election, the ruling party ought to be allowed to win in the lower house election."

Perhaps unconsciously, women often make political judgments in the traditional mold of the good wife and wise mother role, falling back on old-fashioned remedies. Since olden times in Japan, one way of chastising little boys who constantly got into trouble or misbehaved was to give them a moxa treatment (okyū o sueru), an ancient folk treatment for stiff muscles and other ailments consisting of placing a small mound of dried moxa on the skin and igniting the mound with the glowing tip of a stick of incense; the moxa smolders, stimulating the area, and the surface of the skin is scorched. When children repeated some transgression or other, mothers were apt to threaten them with the promise of this treatment, which adults might have found therapeutic but which children experienced simply as painful. Children might not be able to accept that their behavior was wrong by their own reasoning, but they would soon remember the pain of scorching skin. Similarly, women may have voted for the Socialist Party because they felt the LDP would benefit from the shock treatment; however, they were not prepared to completely overturn the LDP regime and give the reins of government to the political opposition. Thus, women voted for the LDP in the House of Representatives elections knowing that the lesson had been learned while male voters backed the LDP for a different reason, namely, in recognition of the prosperity enjoyed under its stewardship of the government. Here we can observe the traditional "good wife" mentality whereby a wife might severely chide a husband who has had an affair with another woman but then generously forgive him if he recognizes his transgression. This attitude of sternness but willingness to forgive that pervades Japanese society.

While the LDP enjoyed a clear victory at the polls and obtained the stable majority it required, the Socialist Party also gained a much larger number of seats than in the previous election. Most of the other parties suffered a loss of seats, and the unusual number of women elected, as in the previous race, carried forward the steady advance of women. At the center of the advance was party chairperson Doi Takako, first elected to the House of Representatives in 1969, whose presence was so important that the advance of women into politics and the resurgence of the Socialist Party is sometimes called the "Doi Takako phenomenon." Meanwhile, the number of women who were not content just to chastise the ruling party but who wanted to work actively to change the political situation continued to increase.

THE DOI PHENOMENON

For some time there has been a brand of woman known as *genki-jirushi no onna* (see Chapter 1) who does not fit the old stereotype of the unprepossessing female who passively accepts her fate. Today, the world is at last recognizing that these women have ceased to be a negligible minority. They are now what is known as "the ordinary woman *[futsū no onna]*." The champion of the growing ranks of these middle-aged, mostly full-time housewives was the woman who became the first female chairperson of a Japanese political party and of the strongest opposition party, Doi Takako. By profession a scholar of constitutional law, she did not enter politics of her own volition. She, like the majority of women politicians, did not purposefully seek a political career but was recruited by others. There was nothing in her family background that might have influenced her to go into politics. Persistently wooed by the party, Doi had to be persuaded to run for office (thus, her campaign funds were provided by the party and did not come out of her own pocket). She was chosen by the SDPJ as its chairperson in 1986, at a time of crisis, to play the role of sacrificial lamb. Yet Doi's powerfully worded stumping speeches delivered in her distinctive Kansai-dialect twang were enthusiastically received throughout the country during both election campaigns while she was chairperson.

Other than the "Stop the Consumption Tax" drive, it is hard to find any policy of note for which Doi Takako was responsible, and even on that issue she did not propose a specific or workable alternative. Nevertheless, her spell was undeniable. It was said that a campaign speech by Doi could win 10,000 votes, and at election time she flew around the country on a schedule calculated down to the last minute giving speeches backing candidates. Wherever Doi went, her middle-aged women fans called out fondly using her first name, offered her homemade box lunches and other expressions of concern for her well-being, and generally gave her an unqualified welcome. Their backing, however, was not based on support for her policies but on their identification with her as a woman; even the ways they expressed their support showed that she was not viewed as part of the male world of politicians but as a member of their familiar female world. No one knew how to predict how many actual votes would result from Doi's popularity among these women, but in the House of Councilors election the vote for SDPJ candidates shot up unexpectedly. One spokesman said, "We don't know where the votes came from." Even within the party, it was said, some people spoke of the end of the old Socialist party and the founding of the Doi Socialist party.

How did Doi herself overcome the conflict between her identity as a woman and the political challenge she sought outside the traditional roles of women? It happened partly in the course of her selection as party chairperson.

In 1986 the SDPJ had suffered a major defeat. After most of the party leadership resigned to take responsibility for the defeat, there were unexpected difficulties choosing a successor for Chairman Ishibashi Masatsugu, who had led the party for three years. The politician who admits to originating the idea of drafting Doi as chairperson candidly described the atmosphere in the Socialist Party at the time as follows:[9]

> To be perfectly honest, we considered Doi Takako as a "tide-over" (*tsunagi*) figure. Everybody realized that. In the party, they were saying eloquent things about Doi and the ability of women, but when it comes right down to it, the Socialist party is a man's party. To tide things over until a better person appeared, we were basically putting on a show with Chairperson Doi taking care of the interests of women.

In other words, the SDPJ members, predominantly men, were able to tolerate the mismatch between Doi's roles as party chairperson and woman because she was considered temporary.

It was not as if the party anticipated or sought a change in women's consciousness by choosing a woman chairperson. It was simply torn by the chronic struggles between its right-wing and left-wing factions, and Doi surfaced as a neutral alternative. She was the product of compromise and desperation, and Doi herself knew that her supporters considered it a victory if she lasted three months as chairperson. At a gathering of women civil leaders and feminists convened under the banner "The Beginning is Now: Politics for Women" to celebrate Doi's appointment as Japan's first woman party chairperson, a participant asked her what had motivated her to accept the position. "Well, it was because I'm a woman. To run away from this [challenge], I felt, would be a loss of face for me as a woman. That was my real reason . . ." Clearly, she was always conscious of the fact that she was a woman. Her lack of goal orientation at the time she accepted the appointment was as obvious as her passivity in the face of the unprecedented challenge. It is undeniable that the SDPJ, which is said to be even more conservative, old-fashioned, and rigid than the Liberal Democratic party, used Doi as a last-ditch salvage strategy. We are reminded of the old phrase "Komatta toki no kami-danomi [When the going gets tough enough, all you can do is plead with the gods for a miracle]"; that is, in appointing a woman the SDPJ was hoping for a miracle. But Doi, fully aware of that fact, decided to take what advantage she could of the opportunity to further policies for women and back female party candidates running for office. The result of her courageous endeavors was the surge in Socialist Party support, helping it to shed its image as the labor union party and revamp itself as a party championing the causes of women and urban citizens. Her term in office demonstrated the importance of women's votes as well as the very real potential of women participating in politics and the kind of changes they could bring in the fabric of political life if they were a more viable force. In the 1989 upper house elections, 38 percent of men and 36 percent of women voted for the SDPJ, indicating that not only women but also men, especially younger men, had high expectations for the growth of the reborn SDPJ that Doi spearheaded.

How did Doi's supporters resolve the conflict in their role expectations of a woman and of a chairperson? The reasons cited by women for Doi's large following are varied:[10] Some praised her clear way of talking and easy-to-understand idiom; some were inspired by her hopefulness and trustworthiness. Because of her cool, stalwart style; her substantive, articulate speeches; and her large facial features and tall, sturdy, not so very feminine build, some analyzed her popularity as stemming from qualities responsible for the immense popularity among women of all ages of the male-impersonating stars of the famous Takarazuka revue. Perhaps her role was accepted in the same way the women playing male roles on the stage were accepted.

Doi's unbudging position on the consumption tax—"What's no good is *no good* [Dame na mono wa dame]"—was acclaimed by some. Her fans applauded the clarity of this stance. Japanese women have long disdained the wheeling and dealing and clever stratagems of male politics as instances of cheating and corruption. They feel very strongly about the need for clean politics and the settlement of issues in a clear-cut, uncomplicated fashion. But Japanese in general believe that in politics "you have to take the bad with the good" and that making deals is the unwritten rule. Because politicians often find they have to dirty their hands in some way or other in order to survive, many criticized Doi's posture as demonstrating the limitations of female political acumen and her own narrow-mindedness and immaturity as a politician. Even within her own party Doi was often censured for her ignorance of the ABCs of politics. Although she dealt with issues openly, her critics deplored her unwillingness to engage in the behind-the-scenes dealing and manipulations that are part and parcel of Japanese politics. During the Persian Gulf crisis of 1990, for example, when a realistic and immediate reaction was urgently needed, she remained stubbornly opposed on principle to any role by the Japanese Self-Defense Forces and to Japanese participation in the U.N. peacekeeping organization. Because of that failure, many voters lost hope in the SDPJ, leading to major setbacks in the April 1991 local elections and ultimately to Doi's resignation the following July.

Other reasons voters identified with Doi are precisely that she is ordinary, that is, not a beauty (although she is not particularly homely, either); that she is of middle-class intelligentsia origin (the daughter of a physician); and that she is not a member of any elite group (she is a graduate of the old and respected Christian university in Kyoto, Doshisha, not of the vaunted University of Tokyo). Still other traits endeared her to the ordinary man and woman in the street, among them her flair for *karaoke* singing (her favorite is the old Sinatra song "I Did It My Way") and her enjoyment of the working man's pastime of *pachinko* (pinball). With her large proportions, low voice, and confident carriage, she demonstrated traits one step removed from the usual Japanese stereotype of feminism.

Many wondered whether Doi Takako would be the first and last of her kind, but she is by no means an anomaly. Among all the policies for women that have been hammered out in the wake of the U.N. Decade of Women, those directed at furthering women's involvement in politics lag behind the most seriously. Doi made an important contribution as a role model who gave the Joans of Arc in various other walks of life the courage to take up the struggle against the evils of the male-dominated society. Doi did not have any concrete policies to speak of, save opposition to the consumption tax and encouragement of women in national politics, with which she might have appealed to women. In fact, her appeal seems to have been that she did not in most cases take a hard stand on specific policies, assuming instead a flexible stance that satisfied women voters.

Hashimoto Osamu, a writer known for his accurate portrayals of the attitudes of women in their forties and fifties, wrote about Doi and those who follow in her footsteps in an article entitled "*Mina 'Doi Takako' ni natchatta* [Everyone's Turned into Doi Takakos]," which reveals the tremendous impact she had on her supporters:

> When Doi Takako became Chairperson of the Socialist Party, I confess I really didn't think she was a particularly bright person. . . . After all, there is some question as to whether she has the ability to formulate viable policies.
>
> However, there was one thing that did change after Doi became chairperson, and that is that all the ordinary women in their forties and fifties *[obasan]* who had kept quiet and sat on their hands in the past began to emerge, like so many Doi Takakos.
>
> What has changed is that all these ladies are now coming out of the woodwork, so to speak, and are putting their leadership abilities to work, inspired by the confidence that "if Doi Takako can do it, so can I."[11]

Despite the claims made for equality of the sexes in the postwar Constitution, women have so far had to be content with secondary status. The appearance of Doi as female head of a basically male party was epochal, and her presence had considerable impact in various spheres. Just about that time, opportunities arose for women to become active in society through the consumer and antipollution movements and the need for the kind of volunteer work that is considered part of the traditional female role was proliferating; thus, the number of women in the first postwar generation who were gaining experience and increased confidence thereby was steadily increasing. Inspired to action by Doi's example, they discovered through their involvement in local activities the political power they had possessed all along.

Another result of Doi's experience has been her impact as a role model in the education of children. All the politicians who appeared on television up until her appointment as chairperson were men. After Dio's nearly five years as party chief, she projected a visibility that will ensure that today's children find nothing unusual in seeing a woman in such a post. In Noda Akiko's youth, equality of the sexes meant that the men took the top position and women stood alongside them in the secondary position; Akiko's children may not necessarily be bound by that convention.

THE TRADITIONAL CAMP

It must also be said that there are, in addition to men, many women, mainly of the older generations, who find the "Doi Takako phenomenon" decidedly distasteful. For them, woman's place is in the home, and they feel a clear conflict when women emerge as politicians. They think that women do not even need to be concerned with the complexities of politics, that all they have to do is consult their husbands or friends and vote as they are advised. This is the pattern of political behavior consistent with traditional sex roles, but it also says something about the fundamental nature of voter attitude in Japan, in which individuals do not see themselves as directly responsible for the quality of their political leadership. There are still quite a few women who

continue to prefer ignorance, believing that something as compli-
cated and "dirty" as politics is simply beyond their comprehension as well as their domain.

The traditional view of women as inferior to men tends to be
deeply internalized, especially among older men and among the
wives of these men. One such example is Nobuyo, an urban
woman 65 years of age. Nobuyo's attitude toward politics might
be summed up as follows: "Nothing changes much regardless of
who's in charge. Whatever they do in politics doesn't make much
difference anyway, does it?" By claiming that she has no interest
in the world of politics and by distancing herself from it, she
denies that women have equal responsibility with men in politics
and shows that she has no interest in the redefinition of
traditional roles. A 1990 public opinion poll showed that 81
percent of men and only 60 percent of women were interested in
politics.[12] Among women, political consciousness changes markedly according to age, peaking between 40 and 59 and falling
quite low when they are in their twenties and in their sixties and
older. The number of women age 60 and over who are uninterested in politics surpasses those who are interested.

Women like Nobuyo do not necessarily welcome the advances
of women in the world of politics, for their vision is limited to the
realities of the status quo, namely, the male-dominated system
and the absence of women of high caliber to combat it. Nobuyo is
convinced that politics requires a kind of broad perspective and
knowledge of the ways of the world that women (as far as she
knows) do not have. Women are serious, she notes, but there are
some issues upon which they tend to be inflexible (like pacifism)
for emotional reasons, which makes them, she feels, unsuitable
for politics. And Nobuyo saw what happened to Doi Takako
during the ups and downs of the party during her chair-
personship—how she glowed at the beginning and how her face
changed as time went on, becoming hard and tense, "as if she'd
ceased being a woman." And Nobuyo is generally skeptical of
the ability of the growing number of women in political office,
saying, "They're just taking advantage of the boom." She does
not feel women are suited to politics, and the reason stems from
her feeling that politics is a different, quite alien, world. Far from
seeing her vote as an opportunity to express her own ideas on
politics, she considers going to the polls simply a civic duty. It is
apparent that she does not link that action to the politicians who

are elected and what they do in office. Involvement in political causes or local movements such as anti-pollution campaigns, or those for improvement of the urban environment, seems to her not quite suitable to what she considers her social station as the wife of a elite corporate executive.

Actually, this spectator-like attitude is a very common phenomenon not only among women but among many men as well. A very large number of voters have no idea what politicians are doing, or where, after they are elected. Their detachment can be seen as evolving from the relative affluence and economic growth Japan has enjoyed, the widespread trust the people have in the national civil service, and the apparently unshakable control of the government by the conservatives for so many years. Political interest and active voting sharply mounted when living and economic conditions were bad and urgent issues were at stake.

Another element of the traditionalist view is the image of politics as ugly and dirty. The major strengths politicians are expected to have are (1) the ability to move or influence people, (2) the ability to cling tenaciously to power, (3) negotiating and bargaining skill, and (4) the ability to collect funds. In the Japanese mind the first quality may be admired but the others, especially the fourth, are considered suspect if not downright vulgar. From long ago, the open discussion of money was avoided in polite society, and people held to the belief that government was supposed to be conducted on the Confucian principles of enlightened rule, not by the politics of influence and popular participation. Traditionalists believe that people of real virtue do not cling to power, that they are honest and do not make deals, and that they are not besmirched by matters of money. The history of party politics and the development of democracy in Japan goes back only to the 1890s and has unfolded in this deeply entrenched moral environment.

Reality requires that politicians have fund-raising ability and skill at bargaining and making compromises; the notion that politics is a dirty business derives from the age-old suspicion of these traits. It is said that politicians have to be able to take the good with the bad. They have to be magnanimous, willing to close their eyes to a certain degree of underhanded dealing (lack of preciseness and ambiguity here being a merit), and able to cope realistically with the complex conditions that result from a web of vested interests. In politics, a person with such traits is considered mature and sophisticated, while a person who champions ideals or just causes on principle is made to look naive and childish by comparison. Thus, women, who are newcomers to the political world, tend to be uncharacteristically rigid, righteous, and unwilling to compromise for the sake of political survival, and to have difficulty competing with male politicians' skill and unscrupulousness in negotiating deals with little consideration for principle or justice. Many people are convinced that women will therefore never be successful in the world of money grubbing and behind-the-scenes dealing that is Japanese politics. Politics, they say, operates on standards different from those of daily life, and women, with their "housekeeper's instincts" (frugal, honest, caring, etc.), do not know how to function on such a double standard. Under these circumstances, women are not much motivated to redefine their roles to include politics. They seem, rather, to actively avoid involvement, emphasizing their lack of aptitude for and interest in politics.

THE "MADONNAS" AND THEIR SUCCESSORS

There was much discussion over whether the advances by women in politics, particularly in the 1989 election, represented simply an evanescent phenomenon or a permanent shift. Since these advances came at a time when the possibility had surfaced that the SDPJ might acquire the strength to challenge the dominance of the conservative LDP forces and take over the reins of government, some suggested that women might provide the key to change. But in the years since that election it does not seem that women have really gained the power necessary to effect change in Japanese politics. It is even less likely that people have become accustomed to the idea of women embracing any role in political life beyond that of voter.

Yet most female opinion leaders believe the political advances attained by women represent an irreversible current of change. As Doi Takako has described it, "The mountain has moved." Moriyama Mayumi, who began her career in the bureaucracy and moved from chief of the Women and Minors Bureau of the Ministry of Labor to become a member of the House of Councilors, said, "We could feel the explosive dynamism of women building from five or six years back. The magma reached boiling point and has already begun to flow. Yes, the mountain is being shaken. It looks as if politics, that final fortress of male chauvinism, is being besieged."[13]

The next question is whether the 45 women elected to the Diet in the 1989 and 1990 elections (the lower house has 512 seats, the upper house 252 seats) have actually been able to change Japanese politics. We must realize that these women did not become politicians in order to address the problems of sexual inequality or because they are necessarily unhappy with women's established roles. Nor did they set out deliberately to obtain revenge against men or to compete with them on male territory. Although a few female Diet members have had long careers in politics—including Doi, Moriyama, and Santo—most (31 of the 46) are first-timers in the Diet. Moreover, 17 of them are women who won in the proportional voting district elections for the upper house, elections in which voters do not write in the name of an individual candidate but vote for the party of their choice. Thus, these candidates gained seats from their ranking position on the party ballot.

Many of the female Diet members, especially those in the SDPJ, were women without any particular interest in politics until Doi persuaded them to become candidates, and many never dreamed they would actually be elected. Having been persuaded to enter political life, their ambivalence about taking a role in politics was settled for them, somewhat mitigating their own feeling of responsibility. Until they suddenly found themselves victorious, they had done nothing to prepare themselves for holding a seat in the national legislature, not even such basic tasks as reading the charter of the SDPJ or studying the definition of socialism. They and most of their fellow newcomer Diet members are complete amateurs when it comes to politics, and they have frequently found themselves in bewildering circumstances both during and after the elections.

The innocent path by which these women came into the limelight caused the male-dominated media to dub them "Madonnas," even though the meaning—reflecting the Japanese penchant for sometimes arbitrarily co-opting English words for a particular context and usage—is not completely clear. (As described in Chapter 5, Japanese men seem to display a yearning for maternal images throughout their lives. Is it possible that they unconsciously wanted to be infants cradled in the arms of these

"Virgin Mary" politicians?) It is certain, however, that there are many men who do not welcome the advance of women into politics. There was a rash of sensational journalism—with headlines like "Ritual of the Witches" and "These Women Will Ruin Japan"—warning of the perils awaiting Japanese politics if amateur women with their housekeeper's instinct became too powerful. The determination of men to preserve their monopoly on the domain of national politics was all too manifest. Some of the articles portraying the private lives of specific new female members of the Diet were derisive and downright mean, clearly meant to discourage and destroy their impulse to participate in national politics.

For their part, the newcomer dietwomen declared that they were determined "to talk about politics in the ordinary way ordinary people think";[14] they felt strongly that politics, which had become such a dirty, ugly process in the hands of men, could be cleansed by women, and they wanted to treat politics within this traditional view. What they could actually accomplish, they soon discovered, was very little. Their ideas did not mesh with what the professional dietmen considered important. The women were elected, but the party did not have any concrete plan to utilize their skills and appeared not to expect anything in particular from them. The women saw that they, like women hired in corporate offices to brighten up the scenery as "flowers of the office," were essentially no more than "flowers of the party." In an interview one year after the election one newcomer dietwoman said, "The party leaders are not good at looking after us or helping us learn the ropes." The crux of the problem is that the party does not expect (perhaps it does not want) these women to be active members of the Diet, and the women, as amateurs, have neither the necessary know-how nor any models to learn from.

Since the new dietwomen did not receive proper orientation about how politicians should behave in the Diet, sometimes their very commonsense behavior, though not conforming to Diet convention, has opened the ground for new rules, for what could be called the feminization of the Diet. For example, it was customary not to applaud the statements of members of other parties, no matter how much they might merit it. If the new women members thought someone had said something praise-worthy, however, they applauded, not knowing about the custom; today this nonpartisan gesture of praise has become acceptable.

Nevertheless, many of the customs attached to the political system of Japan, observed over the decades because it was a domain of men, have not changed in the slightest. One example is the round of parties held at the end of each year to solidify ties and affirm solidarity, occasions that involve considerable drinking of sake and beer. One dietwoman, former Olympic medalist Ono Kiyoko, attended 30 parties from the end of December 1990 through the early part of January 1991, paying her respects to influential colleagues and supporters of the party, participating in toasts, and then moving on to the next party (at a rate of four or five a day). Ono, who was not elected on a proportional representation ballot, has to stump individually for every vote she gets. In order to win the coming election, she has to visit as many gatherings of voters as she can and leave a favorable impression among as wide a swath of the electorate as possible.[15]

CHANGING POLITICAL ATTITUDES

In 1991 women accounted for more than half, by a margin of 2.75 million, of the eligible Japanese electorate, and since 1968 the voting rate for women has consistently been higher than that for men both in national elections and in local elections for governor or metropolitan mayor. It would appear from these data that women are more aware than men of the importance of the vote, but unfortunately, the results of surveys on reasons for voting indicate that the high figure mainly reflects women's strong sense of their civic obligation to vote.

The nature of women's political awareness has been defined in the past basically as follows: a general inclination not to support one particular party firmly but to venture support more passively; a tendency to take an active stand on issues traditionally identified with women—namely, those relating to war, peace, pollution, prices and consumer concerns (housekeepers' issues), and other phenomena involving questions of the quality of life—but to show little interest in other political policies; a reluctance to clearly oppose or support particular issues; and comparatively little basic knowledge or understanding of the political process.

This fundamental trend in female political consciousness has continued basically unchanged for the past 20 years for traditionalists like Takashima Nobuyo in spite of the pervasive maturation of women's roles in other spheres. On the other hand, the attitude of some women toward the participation of their sex in politics *has* changed, most visibly in the first postwar generation of women. In February 1992, the Feminist Assemblymen's Federation (made up of 70 national and local government representatives, including 5 men) resolved to pursue action aimed at instituting membership quotas of 30 percent for women in each prefectural assembly. Nevertheless, the hope for such quotas for the national Diet is still quite remote.

In a survey conducted in 1987, more than 60 percent of women stated that they thought "more women should move into the field of politics."[16] Among women, those who thought the number of women in politics "should not become greater" was approximately 16 percent; among men, 26 percent. By age group, the men and women most supportive of the advance of women into politics were those in their thirties, with more than 60 percent of men and more than 70 percent of women of this age-group expressing this opinion. Those who thought more women should "not enter politics" were primarily women over fifty (with 20 percent of this group offering this opinion); among women in their thirties the figure for the latter response was under 10 percent.

Although level of interest in politics does not fluctuate much for men by generation, women's interest rises and falls with age in a mesa-shaped curve with the top leveling off between the thirties and forties, meaning that this age group represents the key segment of the female electorate that must be appealed to in elections. Nevertheless, the survey showed that about 60 percent of women in their thirties and forties (and more than 50 percent for all women) "do not think politics reflects women's opinions," indicating the feeling among many women that politics is basically leaving women behind. This sort of dissatisfaction is stimulating political activity among some women of this generation, and the changes in 1989 that seemed the harbingers of the "age of women" reflect this growing attitude. The election of that year showed for the first time that women were casting votes not out of duty but with the clear intention to change the current of politics. This was a truly remarkable event in the history of female political behavior in Japan.

Unlike other areas, such as the home and workplace, where the sex roles of women have rapidly changed with broad and significant implications for society as a whole, the preserve of national politics seems unlikely to be the venue of dramatic new roles for women in the near future. Indeed, women continue to place their confidence in Japan's highly regarded civil servants (the bureaucracy), trusting that they will run the country properly regardless of the ups and downs of the legislature. They do not even consider political policy as an instrument for achieving better conditions for women.

Because of women's reluctance to become involved in politics, it is unlikely that the corrupt practices widespread in Japanese politics will be done away with. Women may not care to involve themselves in large numbers in national politics, but it is still possible that, as occurred in the case of the appointment of chairperson Doi, they might suddenly be thrust into the political limelight. There is little evidence, however, to suggest that female politicians with real power or leadership ability will soon emerge.

9

FULFILLMENT THROUGH ACTIVISM

Women may have made few inroads into national politics and their convictions and needs may be little reflected in the running of national government, but on the local level they are a significant force in the formation of policy. They occupy a substantial number of seats in prefectural and municipal assemblies, are active as leaders and organizers of citizen's movements, and are concerned backers of environmental and welfare movements.

Although political activity was not part of the woman's role in traditional society and was frowned upon by husbands and society in general, women today are beginning to enter political life and to be involved in local political activities, gradually incorporating this new dimension into the fabric of their female roles. In fact, political decision-making ability is required of women in many aspects of their daily lives—in neighborhood relations, in PTA activities, and in workplaces. In this sense, they have far more opportunities than ever before to have the experiences of bargaining, negotiating with persons of conflicting interests, and struggling for power or advantage.

242

FULL-TIME ACTIVIST HOUSEWIVES

The many women who have become active in citizens' movements at the grass-roots level form a vigorous force that is reversing some of the trends in local politics. Housewives, typically among the first postwar generation women (born between 1946–1955) and well established in their roles as wife and mother, often become so interested in activities outside the home that they cease to be "full-time housewives [sengyō shufu]" and become "full-time activist housewives [katsudō sengyō shufu]." These women have emerged as an important political and social force.

In Chapter 6 we observed the factors that prompted an increasing number of women (of the first postwar generation, in particular) to seek employment and fulfillment outside the home: basic household expenses can be covered by the husband's salary, making salaried employment for the wife optional; the women are well educated; usually, there are only one or two children to be raised; the nuclear structure of family allows housewife autonomy; and the women have almost invariably had some working experience after graduating from high school or college. We noted that their husbands, who are in their working prime, put in long hours at work, only returning home late at night, and that they do not interfere in any way with their wife's daytime activities. These same conditions have led women who do not wish to pursue careers or part-time jobs to resolve their dissatisfactions through a steady process of trial and error in the practical context of the conditions in which they find themselves. In the process their roles have been redefined, and many have become virtually full-time activists for some sort of social cause.

Roughly 10 percent of the suburban women whose energies are not channeled into outside employment have become part of the swelling citizen or consumer movements that have arisen in the attempt to make politics more responsive to civic concerns. Activist women are those who are capable of performing beyond their roles in caring for home and children but may live in residential districts remote from possible places of employment or find it difficult to locate work that can be sustained in conjunction with their household obligations. Political involvement offers one way for these women, who are in some ways outsiders in modern society, to assert their identities and attain a healthy source of fulfillment in their lives. Notably, they tend to be members of the first postwar generation, women who experienced the tumultuous days of the late 1960s on university campuses. Partly because of that experience, they are conscious of social issues and willing to assert their convictions. Their sensitivity to social issues may stem from the sense of betrayal they feel because so many of their male peers who spearheaded the antiestablishment student movement in the sixties became salaried workers in elite enterprises and were completely incorporated into the establishment.

The leaders of all kinds of local campaigns and movements tend to be drawn from this pool of activist housewives. Because women are responsible for routine shopping, and meal preparation, and the health of family members, they tend to be particularly concerned about the effects of additives and chemicals used in foods, the safety of household products, and other matters relating to daily health. For example, the Chernobyl nuclear power plant accident caused some women, concerned about radiation poisoning, to join the movement opposing the building of nuclear power plants in Japan, and women responded to a movement opposing the destruction of a wooded area in the city of Zushi where the U.S. Army planned to build dependents' housing. They have organized drives to encourage the use of biodegradable detergents, to recycle empty milk cartons, and to further other causes for the protection of the environment.

As these citizen's movements gain momentum, often their leaders realize that the only way to make sure their ideas and causes are reflected in local politics is for one of their number to run for election to the local assembly or for mayor. Their activism may even lead them to support a member for election to the national Diet.

Housewives (mostly middle-aged or older women) who consider their role as being limited to that of good wife and good mother within the home tend to fear that political activity might damage their husband's position in society. They are inordinately wary of participation in any sort of consumer drive or other civic movement. The more dynamic type of housewife, mainly of the first postwar generation, who feels a compelling need to get out and do something about the problems she sees around her, has a totally different attitude: ''My husband is so preoccupied with his work at the company that he can't possibly get involved in civic activities; I'll do his share of the campaigning, too."

NEW ORGANIZATIONAL STRUCTURE

The groups formed by these activist housewives are notable because their organizational structure is quite different from that of traditional groups, which are organized around vertical relationships. They are linked by bonds that do not fit into the framework of human relationships common to a vertical society, as analyzed by social anthropologist Nakane Chie.[1] Until now groups for Japanese women were primarily pyramid-like vertical structures where the status and roles of the women were based on the rank or family status of their husbands. This organizational form meant that rank was quite clear-cut but had nothing to do with the women's abilities, personal preferences, or availability of time. Activist housewives' groups, however, are formed spontaneously on the individual volition of the members and have no relation to their husband's work or social status. The line separating group members (insiders) and nonmembers (outsiders) shifts as women join, leave, or rejoin the group at their own convenience. Some women leave activist groups temporarily in order to support their children's efforts to study for the highly competitive junior high or senior high school entrance examinations but then return when their time opens up again. Another feature of these groups is that officers are considered more as organizers than as persons of authority or high status. Vertical ranking is generally rejected, in other words, except where it can be a convenience, and the members are linked by horizontal ties.

These groups work to make their needs and concerns heard in society, and their members derive pleasure and fulfillment from banding together to achieve a specific goal. The majority of members are wives of company employees, but the tacit rule in their groups is that their husband's place of employment and rank are irrelevant to their activity within the group. In other words, although these women may be benefiting from the support of their husbands, they are also conscious of their independence and individuality. It is significant that the majority of activist housewives are members of the first postwar generation of women who were educated under the democratic system. They seem likely to be instrumental in the overhauling of the efficient but restrictive and stifling structure of Japan's traditional vertical society.

The organizations women form along these lines are extremely diverse and include everything from campaigns to get a representative of their group elected to political office (as we shall see in a case study later in this chapter) to such widely divergent bodies as a study group of self-supportive day care and groups devoted to networking "to revive mind and body" or to "transcend the institutions of marriage." Roughly clustered, these groups fall into three categories—the mutual help type, the problem-solving type, and the information exchange type—but, as one analyst has pointed out, the activities of all three types of groups are carried forward by four types of women: (1) the idea-generating type; (2) the strong, durable type; (3) the patient, one-step-at-a-time, goal-conscious type; and the (4) optimistic, indomitable type who encourages members when they feel discouraged or defeated.[2] In this way, the division of labor that sustains these groups is based on the personal traits of the members.

DYNAMISM AT THE GRASS-ROOTS LEVEL

The new activity of women in the political realm is exemplified by the Kanagawa Network Proxy Movement, the political arm of a local chapter of the Seikatsu Club (literally, the Daily Life Club) in Kanagawa prefecture.[3] The Seikatsu Club is a nationwide consumer chain that distributes food products as well as apparel, household goods, and sundries to some 160,000 member households throughout the country through local cooperatives. The club carries merchandise selected with a particular concern for quality, and since its prices tend to be somewhat higher than those of some of the other large cooperatives, its members tend to be housewives of relatively well-off households who do not have to work to maintain a comfortable standard of living.

The Seikatsu Club was first proposed and started by a male youth activist who noticed the need for political activity closely linked to the concerns of daily life. From the beginning the enterprise focused on housewives, and its development depended heavily on their initiative. Like other cooperatives, the Seikatsu Club uses the group ordering and purchase system; its goal, however, is not simply the pursuit of economic efficiency but, rather, the creation of a system linking consumers directly to producers. Thus, the club seeks change in the present mass production–mass consumption economic system, as well as in the political system that rests on it. In the process, it is hoped that housewives who were previously swallowed up in the system of urban consumption will be transformed into civic activists who see themselves as concerned community members (seikatsu shimin).

Many of the members are not interested in or are ignorant of the purposes for which the group was initially organized. Being practical, they were motivated to join by their desire to obtain safe and healthful foods. Once they are members, the women take turns serving on their district committees; these responsibilities offer opportunities for learning about environmental and agricultural issues related to food and diet. There are observation tours to growers' and producers' operations and thus a chance for direct exchange between producer and consumer. Members may also hold membership drives involving door-to-door calls as well as exhibitions and special sales. All these experiences help broaden the women's understanding of the workings of society and the economy. It is out of movements like this that many activist housewives realize the need for direct links between politics and community life (seikatsu no ba) and emerge as civic activists or candidates for political office. Thus, the Seikatsu Club has actively functioned to support and encourage those from the pool of well-educated housewives of the middle class who are interested in social activities and have time, economic leeway, drive, and a willingness to redefine their role as women.

Although Japan's political parties may have produced the present token handful of national Diet "Madonnas" as the result of a last-ditch election strategy, they have no intention of yielding any portion of their monopoly on politics to women. The Kanagawa Network Proxy Movement, the pioneer effort of a local chapter of the Seikatsu Club to put up one of its members for political office, was a focus of considerable attention in the 1991 local elections in the prefecture.

The Seikatsu Club had started a drive to get housewives to abandon use of synthetic, water-polluting detergents. Although it gained many supporters, the leaders realized that the movement's effectiveness would be limited with only the cooperative as backing. That realization led them to decide to run a cooperative representative for election to the Kawasaki municipal assembly in 1983. The candidate was elected. In the municipal elections of 1987 the Kanagawa Network backed 15 candidates, 9 of whom were successfully elected. Satō Eiko, whose story appears in this chapter, was among the women elected to the city assembly at that time.

The Kanagawa Network Proxy Movement has 30 chapters throughout the Kanagawa prefecture. All of its candidates are married women in their thirties and forties, full-time housewives with children. They have no connections with big business or established political parties. The campaigns are supported entirely through donations by other housewives and from the proceeds of volunteer work. The membership of the network is not organized vertically but horizontally. The members make a point of calling their candidate a proxy (dairinin) rather than a representative (daihyō), a term that connotes vertical rank. The group decided that their proxy could serve up to two terms (eight years); this diverges from the established pattern among most assemblymen, who cling tenaciously to their positions and try to stay in office as long as possible and even try to cultivate their sons as successors to the post. We can see that these women have redefined the role of women to include political activism. In the process, they are rejecting the corrupt practices and power mongering of male-centered politics and are struggling to prove that clean politics is workable.

Now let us look at a few cases of women who are active as candidates for their municipal assembly and who are members of the Wakaba Shimin Kaigi (Wakaba Citizens' Council), the largest of the 30 chapters of the Kanagawa Network Proxy Movement. (The names of groups and individuals in this chapter have been changed except for the Kanagawa Network Proxy Movement.) Their stories reveal a great deal about the significance of the recent political activities of housewives and how they have successfully redefined the roles of women.

Since 1987, the Wakaba Citizens' Council has supported the

political activities of city assemblywoman Satō Eiko. In the 1991 local elections it decided to put up two additional candidates for the city assembly. Its 280 members have held study meetings, observation tours, and lectures on environmental problems, natural resources, welfare services, education, food, and peace; they have conducted signature-gathering campaigns and demonstrations and have worked to attain concrete results in line with the policies Satō advocates in the assembly. They realized that it was difficult to get their ideas reflected in actual policy with only one member in office and knew it would be difficult for a small group like themselves to support three candidates for office. There was dismay and opposition from among the members to the idea of attempting to increase the number of assembly members backed by the group so soon. Its self-declared intention was to offer alternatives to the solutions of the big political parties to issues involving daily life, alternatives that reflected their commitment to the idea that "small is beautiful." Some members argued, "Trying to expand and play the doubling and tripling game is a male idea. We should not be overambitious but do what we can on the scale we are capable of." (This slow but steady strategy on a small scale was also used by the women entrepreneurs described in Chapter 7.) The members who worked for the Wakaba Citizens' Council on a daily basis feared that the burden of the campaigning might become too great for them and might produce friction in their private lives (i.e., challenges to their roles as wife and mother). A look at the profiles of the three candidates and of one of their supporters offers concrete insight into the workings of this movement.

Satō Eiko, 44, the wife of a pharmaceutical company employee, is short in stature (about 5 feet tall) and attractive, with prominent features. She has two high school–age daughters, and they live in a public housing complex. Satō graduated from a college of pharmacy and met her husband after finding a job at the pharmaceutical firm where he still works. She resigned after the birth of her first child. Among the women her age in the apartment complex her refreshing, cheery personality stands out; she wears bright-colored clothing and has a clear, ringing voice. Of the four types of women described earlier, Satō falls into the category of the optimistic, indomitable type. She says, "Before I became active as a committee member and director in the cooperative, I was just like any ordinary housewife; I knew nothing about the dangers of food additives and used chemical detergents without batting an eye." When she introduces herself, she emphasizes that she is not one of those "awesome assembly- men but an ordinary housewife like everybody else." By empha- sizing that she is playing along with traditional sex roles, she manages to mute the resistance of even some women to a female politician. Satō has been able to survive as city assemblywoman, in spite of the strong tendency in this society to "hammer in any nail that sticks out" (and she does represent an anomaly in many ways), because she is skilled in the techniques of maintaining human relationships. She was able to win in the previous election, despite the fact that the Seikatsu Club had no political record to show for itself, because she had served actively in a number of posts in the cooperative itself and was familiar with the feelings and circumstances of its members. She has adopted the strategy of stressing her trustworthy and reliable personality rather than her stand on particular issues. Here again, policies and principles are relegated to secondary importance.

Hata Mitsuko, a candidate for the prefectural assembly, is 40 years old. A graduate of a prestigious women's university, she is an English teacher and is skilled in the art of capturing the attention of a large audience. An "idea-generating" type of woman, Hata has exercised strong leadership as a representative of the Wakaba Citizens' Council and has spearheaded its activi- ties. Like Satō, she has an urbane maturity, stylish looks, and an intelligent manner, all of which makes her an attractive and compelling figure. Married to a company employee, Hata is the mother of two children, in junior high and senior high school. Her family supports her efforts to run for office. Her husband represents a rather unusual example of a man who has already accepted the occupation of politician as a possible female role. Hata claims that she has been successful at brainwashing him, praising him for his progressive, insightful views and mobilizing him as a supporter and adviser. She was a pivotal member in the Seikatsu Club drive to further the city's recycling efforts, as well as in the club's election campaign backing Satō.

The new candidate for the municipal assembly is 45-year-old Yamada Yoshiko. In comparison with the other two women, Yamada's expression is sterner and her speech is somewhat unsteady. No one would have predicted that she might become a candidate, but when it proved difficult to locate an appropriate third candidate, Yamada, as head of the candidate screening committee, ended up being pressed into service. In choosing the candidate, career record and personal commitment were crucial concerns, and Yamada was known for her sense of mission and strong commitment as well as for her exceptionally long experience in cooperative activities. She is a patient, one-step-at-a-time type of person. However, one who is earnest and sincere can sometimes be lacking in the flexibility required to maintain a broad range of human relationships and may lack sensitivity to others, so Yamada's popularity among Seikatsu Club members is not the highest.

For a female candidate the decision to run for office, still considered unusual for a woman, involves many difficult obstacles that men do not face. If her family or relatives are opposed to the idea, if it is looked on with disfavor by her husband's employer, or if her children are still small, stress from conflicting roles may be too great and she may have to give up the idea. On the other hand, there is also the comfort that if she does lose the election, the welfare of her family is not threatened and she can return to her traditional role. Satō was a full-time housewife when she became a candidate. Hata taught English in high school three days a week and had to quit when she became a candidate. She lost ¥60,000 per month in income, but she considered her candidacy a natural extension of her contributions to the movement. In describing her feelings when she was chosen to run on behalf of the group, Hata said, "Well, if I lost, I thought, I simply lost. I could just go back to my involvement in the civic movement." Male candidates usually cannot afford that luxury.

Among the Wakaba Citizens' Council supporters of the candidates for election is Takayama Toshiko, 38. She has three children, the oldest of which is a sixth grader, and her husband is a company employee three years older than she. After graduating from the university, Toshiko worked for a time in a large trading firm but quit upon marriage. She had no previous experience in political activities and had joined the Seikatsu Club thinking it might help her feed her children better, more healthful foods. She became more involved with the club by consulting with the city on the safety of foods and making inquiries at the sanitation laboratories. Says Toshiko:

> When my oldest child was small, I knew nothing about the dangers of artificial food colorings, chemical detergents, and agricultural chemicals. Who knows what damage my ignorance did to him. Me? Political activist? I never think of it as anything of much note. I'm just an ordinary mother involved in local activities of residents. I think that's the way most of us see ourselves.

Here again, we notice a woman's emphasis on being "ordinary," just like everybody else, and her stress on her role as mother rather than on herself as an individual.

Each day during the election campaign, after putting her youngest daughter on the bus to kindergarten at 8:30, Toshiko hangs up the laundry, does a perfunctory tidying up, and then lugs a bag full of papers to her car for the 10-minute drive to the Wakaba Citizens' Council office. At noon, she goes back home to take in the laundry and the bedding and prepare the children's afternoon snack, to be left on the kitchen table when she returns to work at the office. The office is a 40-square meter room in a large apartment complex. In addition to the office desks, copy machine, and meeting table, there are piles of unsold bazaar merchandise, boxes of biodegradable detergent, and pamphlets. Once there are 10 people sitting around the table, it becomes impossible to move.

Toshiko's cohorts are all women like herself, housewives with small children still in kindergarten or primary school. Together they work to strengthen the candidate's supporters' association (kōenkai), plan her speeches, write and reproduce handbills, make the rounds of the district in loudspeaker-equipped cars advertising the candidate's name, put up posters, raise funds through bazaars, and so on. They may have to spend many days in a row in the office, letting their housekeeping chores slide. Even if they stay home, they find themselves glued to the telephone. Declaring that she can't stand politics ("nor elections either!"), Toshiko insists she's not involved in politics and that what she is contributing to is the citizens' movement, a perfectly "acceptable" role for a woman. When work is so demanding that she has to go out at night also, her husband complains and admonishes her to keep her outside activities within reasonable (by his standards) bounds. Through 15 years of married life, Toshiko has learned how far she can go without causing her husband's grumbling to turn into a real explosion, and she cleverly balances the demands of the movement with the needs and expectations of her family. She does not discuss her activist involvement much with her husband or argue over which stand is right. Rather than provoke an argument in which she might be the loser, she adopts a strategy of nonconfrontation in which she can be sure to win inconspicuously, that is, accomplish what she wants to do. As she says quite clearly: "The family is the most important. I have to make sure everybody is healthy and father goes cheerfully to work, or the household would fall apart."

Toshiko has confidence in her contribution to the functioning and welfare of the household. She makes enough money from her part-time work correcting papers to keep her supplied with funds for her movement involvement. The household is supported on her husband's salary, but Toshiko does not consider herself totally dependent on her husband. As she says, "Sure, we couldn't live without my husband's income, but you can't run a household on just money. If I weren't here in the household, nothing would get done. And I look after Grandmother's [her elderly mother-in-law] needs as well."

The election funds for the three candidates include funds saved from Satō's stipend as assembly member over her four-year term, donations, proceeds from sales at bazaars, and supporters' association dues; moreover, the council's expenses do not include reimbursement to workers since all members of the movement are volunteers. The council's motto is that it should be possible for anyone to become a candidate without having to shoulder the financial burden individually. This is especially important in order for women to participate in politics. During the two-week final campaign period, the three candidates decided to wear coordinated, brightly colored suits (in yellow, orange, and purple), and they bore the cost for the clothing themselves. The supporters discussed whether the association could assume the cost of the suits, but it was decided to wait until after the campaign and pay for them if there was still money left in the till.

Each candidate has an election office with a staff of about 15 members in charge of public relations, accounts, administrative work, and campaign speeches. To man the loudspeaker-equipped campaign car there are navigators with a detailed knowledge of the district's streets, drivers, and "nightingales," women who work the microphone in three daily shifts as the car canvasses the city, calling out the candidate's name and asking for support. By the end of the campaign a total of some 324 people had contributed their time and effort. To sustain the efforts of these people, volunteers prepared about 70 lunch and supper meals a day, which were also delivered to the families of the candidates. In contrast to men, women political activists have had to demonstrate their ability to perform the roles of house-wife, wife, and mother as well. The campaign covered the cost of ingredients for the dishes prepared, but there was no remunera-tion for preparation costs and time. Each woman worked in the way that suited her abilities and convenience best: Some pre-pared meals and brought them to the office, some handled the dishwashing at the office, and so on. Before the election, ques-tionnaires with a "volunteer job list" were handed out, and members were requested to participate on a self-motivated basis. The job list included such tasks as putting up posters, writing addresses on postcards at the office, calling friends and acquaint-ances to ask for support, and taking turns during the two-week preelection period with train station duty (about 10 housewives gathered every morning between 7:00 and 8:00 and every evening between 6:00 and 7:00 at the train stations in the district to appeal to businessmen and commuters on their way to and from work).

In this campaign many movement members were first-timers when it came to electioneering, and most of them say they simply threw themselves into their work, hardly knowing whether they were doing the right thing or not. "It was very exciting, especially as we gradually became more and more determined to win as the days went by. We've all changed through this experience. There were some who used to be quiet, unassertive types, but even they'd be shouting at the top of their lungs the moment they got hold of the election car microphone!" reports Toshiko. It is experiences like this that help housewives gradually gain confi-dence and realize what they can do, and the changes and redefinition of their roles are greatly facilitated by the fact that they are acting together. We also see that the behavior of these women was not initially goal oriented; in Japanese fashion, their sense of commitment gradually evolved in the process of their participation, rather than being something they felt prior to involvement.

Toshiko's husband thought political campaigning did not conform to a woman's role and was critical of his wife's enthusiasm at first, but when she invited Hata and Yamada to dinner and introduced them to him, she says he changed his mind completely. Apparently impressed with the two, he encouraged them and has been completely supportive ever since. Compared to the first election in 1987, there are in the current campaign (1991), Toshiko says, more men contributing their time as drivers and back-up team members at the candidates' speeches.

Still, not all husbands are cooperative. Many of the women say they practically exhaust themselves in the process of making sure that their husbands will not be displeased by their participation in the campaign; they take special pains to fix proper meals and attend to all their phone calls before the men get home. In cases where husbands are uncooperative or opposed to their wife's activities, it is often a blessing when they are away or temporarily stationed in a different city. Of the 15-member staff of Satō's campaign headquarters, 4 of the women had husbands posted away from home, and this allowed them to commit themselves completely to their work. Some housewives with part-time jobs took time off during the campaign period so that they could devote more time to helping. The husbands of Satō and Hata did not take time off from work but contributed their time on weekends as drivers of campaign cars.

What makes these housewives practically abandon their households and children and throw themselves, as if they were returning to their student days, into election campaigning with such fervor? The strong desire to secure a greater voice in local politics for women cannot be the only reason. While cautioning each other that "it's going to be a hard race and we may lose," these women seem to be thoroughly enjoying themselves.

Toshiko absorbed herself completely in the campaign. Her day, like that of all the other members, might go like this: After spending an hour at the train station in the early morning bowing and calling out to passing commuters, she gets into the campaign car and puts in stints at the microphone and as navigator. After lunch she works the phones at the office asking for votes. Then she again takes up her post at the train station in time for the evening return rush. She then helps with preparations for a lecture meeting starting at 8:00 P.M. and checks the campaign car course for the following day.

Toshiko admits that there were days when she did not get back home until midnight. She and her cohorts seem to be enjoying themselves, totally enthralled by the possibility that they might be able, by their own efforts, to make real changes in society. Arriving on the scene to help, their husbands find their enthusiasm mystifying. "What makes these ladies so full of energy?" they wonder. Some men say these women don't really have any conscious political goal: "It's just that they haven't had any way to express themselves, so the election has become their arena of self-expression." These men are partly right (about the lack of specific political goals), but apparently they cannot understand that women are trying to redefine their roles.

It would indeed be a mistake if women involved themselves in election campaigns solely as a means of self-expression. Seeking to do more than just cast their vote, many participate by working in campaign cars and offices, and those activities could become an end in themselves. Unless women's roles are expanded to include being effective in politics, the significance of what they have accomplished (e.g., working to get candidates elected) will be limited. In Japan election campaigns begin roughly two weeks before voting day. Husbands may take a tolerant view of their wife's devoting all her waking hours to politics if it lasts only two weeks, but if politics were a career that affected her daily activities all year round, that might be quite a different story. What really matters is how political activism affects a woman's daily life even after the election.

After the votes were counted, Satō and Hata had won but Yamada had lost. Yamada was undiscouraged and is determined to try again in the next election four years hence. The Wakaba Citizens' Council, however, has made no plans for the next election.

HARVEST OF THE ELECTION EXPERIENCE

After Satō became a municipal assembly member four years ago, she began to introduce into assembly debate concrete issues related to daily life that had not been dealt with before on the political level, issues like corporal punishment in the schools, the use of chlorine disinfectants in preparing cabbage for school lunches, the experimental collection of separated garbage, and programs for home care of the elderly. Faced with these proposals representing the concerns and perspectives of housewives on matters of daily living, male assemblymen gave Satō a hard time: "That's a problem for the PTA"; "There'd be no need for that if women were at home like they ought to be." All the same, Satō's four-year term has changed the impression women had of politics and has made local politics seem much closer to their lives. The number of women who are speaking up and taking an active interest in community-building concerns is increasing. Not so long ago they tended to be passive spectators; for example, if asked to join a signature-collecting drive, they might have demurred, fearing that they would never know how their signature might be used or feeling they had to get their husband's consent. Now these same women will read the contents of the petition carefully, and if they are interested in what is being proposed, they will take a conscientious attitude, saying they'll show the petition to their husband and get signatures from the whole family.

Participation in an election campaign provides an experience of dramatic attitudinal change. By working closely with a candidate, finding that they see eye to eye with her, and taking an active part in the collective endeavor of the election race, women realize that the activities of assembly members and the assembly itself are not as remote as they once thought but in fact are very closely linked to their daily lives. One movement member said she feared at first that her friends and neighbors might look upon her activities in an unfavorable light, but after the election she received unexpectedly encouraging comments like "I'm glad to hear your candidate won" or "I want you to know I voted for your candidate." Moreover, in presenting the issues and describing what the movement is seeking to do when they ask others for support of their candidate, these women are gradually gaining a deepened political consciousness.

Most movement members say a campaign is half excitement and half very hard work, but those who are involved for the first time are more apt to emphasize the enjoyment and excitement. There is a tendency among many of the women to think of the campaign as an event, like some sport or game, that derives its excitement from an experience at a given point in time. They may also be so completely taken with the delight of having their candidate win that they don't consider the real target of the movement. Nevertheless, these women have discovered that they are much more powerful than they previously thought; their experiences have shown them what they can accomplish if they try. We may surmise that the impact this newly discovered confidence will have on women will be considerable.

Another attraction of politics is that it offers a glowing new opportunity for reemployment for well-educated housewives over thirty who no longer seek self-realization through a professional career. The Kanagawa Network Proxy Movement is one that ensures that candidates will not be handicapped by a lack of financial independence, which is a built-in weak point for housewives. The candidate actually undertakes very little financial burden. The salary a proxy receives as an assembly member is controlled by the network, so even if a member becomes the movement's proxy, her income is not large (although it is an improvement over the self-imposed burden of a volunteer); being a proxy is both the extension of a member's previous activities and a step toward financial autonomy. As long as it remains relatively difficult for middle-aged women to find work that accommodates the demands of family and home, political involvement in the form described here may offer an appealing employment alternative.

TOWARD FULLER PARTICIPATION IN POLITICS

Most Seikatsu Club members initially become involved in politics because of their concern about a single issue very closely connected with their daily lives, such as the safety of foods, children's education, or the presence of environmental hazards. In the course of learning about a particular problem and participating in a movement to remedy it, they quickly realize how many related problems and issues exist.

Women's priorities and areas of concern also change with each shift to a new phase of life. For example, a woman who joined the Wakaba Citizens' Council out of concern for the quality of school lunches will eventually encounter new issues when her children move on to junior high school and face stricter school rules, corporal punishment, and educational practices with very limited flexibility for both teachers and students. She will become aware of the contradictions in the political system that underlie the problems of the current educational system and its rules. As women themselves grow older, they may see in the problems connected with nursing care for elderly parents and in their concerns associated with their own old age the urgent need to deal with issues like the maldistribution of wealth and the country's welfare policy. They have opportunities to learn not only about problems of their own locality but also about the global environment and international affairs, and they may find that they have to organize and present their own thoughts on these subjects. As a general tendency, these women do not seek to become specialists on a given subject but to learn more about and analyze all kinds of problems that strike them as important. These women are sure to be more widely involved in politics from now on.

Meanwhile, most men continue to be profoundly critical of these activist women. Because the core of the Kanagawa Network Proxy Movement is a group of women from the middle stratum of society who enjoy the luxuries of time and financial security, many critics dismiss the movement as a temporary phenomenon and insist that these women can only go so far. All the same, the movement—which has succeeded in part because it is spear-headed by these well-off housewives—has accomplished much in letting fresh air into the heretofore hermetically sealed male world of politics. Its significance lies in its effectiveness not only in arousing political awareness among women but also in bringing some feminine qualities to bear in politics and in making it more accessible to ordinary citizens.

Since the movement has decided that the proxy shall serve no more than two terms or eight years, there is criticism that its members will never be anything more than amateurs in politics. This new movement, however, has introduced a new kind of bond—a horizontal one—into Japan's traditionally vertical so-cial structure, and this new structure is becoming increasingly stronger. It may be said that while men are looking the other way, women are becoming the agents of change in Japanese society. Although the gap between grass-roots politics and national politics is great, these trends that are transforming politics on the local level will eventually spread and have an important impact on national politics as well. The participation of women in politics is at the very least contributing to the cleaning up of the money-tainted world of traditional politics.

The women of the first postwar generation who are involved in grass-roots political movements have, on the whole, successfully redefined their roles as women by combining their roles as wife and mother with the citizen's movement. Their husbands, however, continue to define the roles of women along traditional lines and therefore continue to regard politics as a man's world. In order to avoid conflict with their husbands, the vast majority of these women invest great effort in carrying on both roles with equal virtuosity so that they will not displease their husbands. It will probably be another ten years or more before women will be able to participate in politics freely, without having to exert themselves to show that they are not neglecting traditional roles.

THE WOMEN'S MOVEMENT IN JAPAN

The women's movement is usually not considered part of the citizens' movements we have been examining. Abroad, Japanese women are often asked whether their country has a women's movement. In answering this question we always struggle with what is meant by this expression. If it means a movement for social change led by women for the purpose of eliminating discrimination based on sex, then Japan does indeed have a women's movement (and one that can be traced back to the 1880s). Admittedly, however, its impact has been extremely limited.

In the 1960s, publication in the United States of *The Feminine Mystique* sparked controversy in the media over the growing women's liberation movement.[4] In Japan a number of small groups were created by nameless women in different parts of the country; among the better known of these groups were the Group *Tatakau Onna* [Group for Fighting Women] and *Chūpiren* [Federation of Women for Abortion and the Pill]. But Japan was still a totally male-controlled society at the time, and any moves that smacked of women's liberation were quickly targeted, lambasted, and belittled by the male-dominated mass media. The vehemence of those attacks may actually have derived from the growing realization among men of the justification for the women's liberation movement—or at least of the tremendous impact it would definitely have on their lives. Perhaps they thought to douse what flames had appeared before the conflagration got out of control.

The radical strategies and strong language used by some women's groups were partly responsible for the generally negative image of women's liberation that developed in Japan in this early phase, since they were totally alien to the traditional role of women. For example, in response to the request of a woman incensed by her husband's infidelity, representatives of Chūpiren wearing pink helmets gathered in front of the office building where the husband worked and denounced his misconduct through a loudspeaker. Given the importance of the concepts of honor and shame in Japanese culture, it is not difficult to imagine the extremity of his embarrassment. This strategy of personal attacks, in addition to the smugness and inflammatory nature of the pronouncements of groups like Chūpiren, inevitably meant that few people, male or female, were inclined to take them seriously.

Of course, there is no doubt that the radicals had good reason for adopting behavior that was so unquestionably extreme. We may conjecture that because of the rigidity of the conformist, vertically structured Japanese society (unlike societies in which being different is considered a positive trait), those who were determined to assert themselves in ways that went against society's norms and traditional sex roles had to place themselves completely outside the mainstream, since they believed that they would never be appreciated by the mainstream, and had to prepare to accept the worst at its hands. By recognizing this reality and making themselves heretics in their own society, these women were able to engage in actions rejecting the traditional myths of womanhood. Indeed, we may presume that their aim was to arouse the antipathy of society. Flagrant behavior must also have seemed necessary at the time to draw attention to an otherwise small and completely powerless group. Whatever their motivations, the sensational actions of these groups were widely covered in the media, resulting in an extremely negative image being attached to the women's liberation movement and feminists as a whole (as the frustrated, hysterical, and inconsistent shoutings of a bunch of abnormal and unattractive women). When the United Nations Decade for Women began in 1975, the banner of the women's movement was taken up by members of the mainstream, led by governmental agencies involved with women's issues, and with this the so-called women's liberation movement in Japan passed into oblivion.

The Decade for Women helped to call attention to women's issues generally and heighten awareness among Japanese as a whole. When the just-opened National Women's Education Center hosted the first international conference on women organized by the International Group for the Study of Women (of which I was then chairperson) in 1978, it was favorably and widely reported in the media, contributing greatly to the credibility of the new field of women's studies. Women's groups of various kinds subsequently proliferated throughout Japan. The participants of some of these groups call themselves feminists or women activists, but many others do not necessarily identify with the women's movement (they see themselves simply as members of groups dedicated to some specific purpose or cause but not to the reform of social norms or structure). These groups range in size from tiny clusters of only 5 or 6 members to movements of 200 or more. So far, there is no organization on the scale of America's National Organization of Women (NOW), and without such a national coordinating group the women's movement in Japan tends to lack power and solidarity.

A further feature of the Japanese women's movement is that until now it has been virtually without political links. The Constitution of postwar Japan, unlike that of the United States, guarantees equality of the sexes as well as the equal right of men and women to participate in politics. Although, of course, the facts belie these guarantees, it is not the laws that are the obstacle to their realization. Japanese women may have been lucky in this regard, but, by the same token, they were also deprived of the experience of fighting for and winning equal rights by their own efforts. Women activists did not have to join forces in order to put pressure on the political system or cooperate with politicians in order to attain the goal of sexual equality guaranteed under the Constitution. This is the primary reason the women's movement in Japan is relatively weak and does not seek the cooperation of politicians.

The economic prosperity Japan has enjoyed since the 1970s, moreover, has also prevented the women's movement from articulating clear-cut goals. If women are the targets of danger or oppression, the target is clear enough, and history has shown that in such cases Japanese women can exercise tremendous power. Today, however, they tend to be reactive; rather than setting their own goals and forming movements to attain them, they mainly take up already-existing issues, such as deterioration of the environment or political corruption, and mobilize themselves in response.

Many of the women's movement groups share the same characteristics, such as the tendency to serve simply as voices of opposition (in the absence of sufficient mass support for a full-fledged political movement). Movements that become identified with "women's issues" (like opposition to a revision of the Eugenic Protection Act that would change its liberal abortion rights provisions), regardless of how important they might be, invariably lose credibility and become targets of suspicion (especially among men). This loss of credibility has crippled what efforts have been ventured by the groups against treatment of women as sex objects, groups supporting legalized abortion, and groups against nuclear power plants. Outside the mainstream, such groups can accomplish little.

Women's groups seem attached to their separate identities. The well-educated urban women who make up most of their members tend to form close-knit societies with built-in psychological barriers against outsiders; these societies make no effort to unite with other groups, such as labor unions or rural women's groups, by which means they might increase their impact on society and politics. The reason such groups remain very small is to preserve their identity. Although they are considered to be activists (i.e., one step closer to the mainstream than radicals), their aim is usually improvement of the status quo rather than attack on the establishment. As an example, members of a group against treatment of women as sex objects demonstrate at railroad or other companies, demanding the withdrawal of certain sexist advertisements, but they do not engage in boycott strategies.

Those who are active in the women's movement generally come from families that were understanding and liberal. Among the first postwar generation, as a matter of fact, this was a prerequisite for them to get to a university in the first place, for the days when most families actively encouraged their daughters to attend college had not yet arrived. Because of this family background, they were prompted to join the student movement while at school, and their activities were not opposed by their parents. Once having had that experience of dropping out of the mainstream, these women probably became active in women's groups quite naturally.

The handicap these progeny of Japanese liberalism suffer is that their background prevented them from making friends and acquaintances in the establishment (government or big business) and, by extension, from being able to effect change in business practices or government policies that might accommodate the needs of women or lift their status. The fragmented, individualistic nature of the movement can also be interpreted in a positive way, however. As long as they are outside the mainstream, activist women are free to exercise their originality and options for alternative ways of doing things, eschewing the rigid seniority-ranked and power-oriented structures of male organizations and traditional women's groups. But as long as they remain outside the mainstream of policy-making processes, their messages will not be heard. Unlike in the United States, where interest groups can lobby directly with legislators, in Japan policies are usually made through government committees or councils made up of opinion leaders and influential persons (i.e., members of the mainstream); thus, it is difficult for the women's movement to attain or exercise real power to accomplish its goals.

10

DIRECTIONS OF CHANGE

The profound changes now taking place among Japanese women represent no less than a quiet revolution. They constitute an irreversible transformation at the very roots of attitudes and lifestyles in Japanese society. In the tide of change engulfing women's roles throughout the world, what we are seeing in Japan is more than simply the ripples of what happens in the United States, contrary to what some have observed. As I have attempted to demonstrate, in the foregoing chapters we must question the often-heard line that Japanese women "lag behind" women in the United States and Europe. The Japanese attachment to equality in the long term in relations between the sexes seems as firm as American demands for here-and-now equality. For the time being, Japanese women have made equality based on mutual dependence acceptable and workable.[1]

Having come this far, a number of tasks and challenges confront Japanese women. How they will cope is closely related to the reaction and response of men. What do Japanese men and women hope for in their lives in the years to come? This chapter focuses on the directions of change in the attitudes and behavior of Japanese women, although it is by no means clear, because of their inclination to take the pragmatic path rather than one guided by principles, which way current trends may lead.

EXPECTATIONS AND ASPIRATIONS

General assessment surveys show that both male and female attitudes toward women's roles have substantively changed over the past 15 years and that male understanding and sympathy toward women's desire for expanded roles is beginning to grow. Men have become somewhat more cooperative as far as housework and childrearing are concerned, and a consensus is taking shape on the societal level regarding the general trend of change in women's lives.[2] Meanwhile, Japanese women do not enjoy even the level of participation in politics and national decision making of women in the United States and Europe, and their advance into other bastions of male dominance, such as management of large corporations, has been slow. This situation is not likely to change rapidly, for the Japanese women's movement has not been particularly active and women appear to be enjoying lives that are richer and more fulfilling than those of men.[3] In fact, Japanese women today see their lives and social status in a generally positive light, and this leads us to conclude that the pace of change will continue to be slow and that no radical movement will emerge.

The reason for the high level of satisfaction among Japanese women has a great deal to do with how they perceive themselves. In the United States it is generally considered desirable for persons to set clearly articulated goals for themselves and work toward those goals. This goal-oriented behavior contrasts sharply with the role-directed behavior of Japanese. In their endeavor to improve their status in society, American women also tend to set for themselves a clear target and to determine their actions in accordance with that target. This approach has provided momentum for the women's movement and has led to the passage of important new laws for women in the United States, but, as discussed earlier, the dynamics of legislative change have had a very different history in Japan. Its merits and achievements notwithstanding, the goal-oriented appraoch is one in which, from the Japanese point of view, the gap between actual results and the target is always all too obvious, bringing dissatisfaction and anger that further stir the forces for renewal and reform.

In understanding the behavior of women, it helps to recognize that Japanese people, not just women, tend to act not so much *for the sake of* something as *because of* something; that is, Japanese are *reactive* with respect to the status quo rather than *proactive* with respect to the future. For Japanese, an action is no more than one step in a desired direction; it is not determined solely by the goal. In the case of the latter, actions are complete of themselves. The reactive pattern of behavior is the rule among Japanese women, and a significant result of this approach is that they tend to look back frequently at their situation at a previous stage to see how far they have come. This action almost invariably reveals that progress was made and lends itself to at least a modicum of satisfaction. The progress is especially visible at a time when women's lives are undergoing quite rapid changes and when the environment surrounding women not only of the first postwar generation but of all generations has improved far beyond that of men.

Indeed, the environment for many diligent, serious-minded male company employees in Japan has markedly worsened, with one of the most vicious results being the threat of death from overwork *(karōshi)*. Moreover, the benefits of the affluence brought by the rapid growth economy—leeway to enjoy overseas travel, concerts, and the theater; convenient appliances and other equipment; or fine clothing and other pleasures—are being enjoyed mostly by women. These benefits and pleasures, however, are ones women have won not by their own direct labors but, rather, by standing (with their hands tightly gripping the purse strings) behind the men who labored on the front lines of economic growth. As the wealth of the nation as a whole has increased, the portion that goes to household coffers has grown, and from that portion women have collected what they considered their due.

From now on, however, economic growth will continue to be slow, and the national pie is not expected to grow larger. Under these circumstances, men will certainly awaken to their wife's ability to contribute to household income and will begin not only to count on but to demand that their wife shoulder a significant part of the economic responsibility of maintaining a family. The ranks of women who manage to work, take care of the household, and engage in leisure activities are expected to swell. But women will continue to be reluctant to assume a substantial proportion of the financial burden at the expense of their much-prized freedom. And they are as anxious as ever to elicit greater male involvement in household chores and in the care of children and elderly family members.

While surveys show that women have strong expectations that men will eventually perform some of the tasks traditionally reserved for women, they are apparently not particularly anxious to assume positions of leadership in the traditional realms of men. Men, while they are largely oblivious to the changes currently occurring in women, say they hope women will come to share their responsibilities in the future. And though men would like to be able to participate more freely in community and volunteer activities, women do not necessarily want men's role in the home to supersede their role as "ricewinner."[4] What remains the most unliberated aspect of the mentality of Japanese women is that they still conspire to use men as the worker bees of society.

SEX AND STRENGTH

Up until recently, Japanese women submitted to male dominance in major arenas of society. They considered it their destiny and responsibility to respect and encourage men in order to keep them ambitious, hardworking, and devoted to their jobs. In the early decades of postwar Japan, these women were considered wise and perspicacious. It has long been a rule of female wisdom that men are good for nothing without the support of women. For their part, men have played along with the game, even if they recognized the female stratagems being used against them, and they worked very hard indeed. This game played by mutual consent can be considered one of the driving forces behind Japan's rapid economic growth in the 1960s.

However, among the first postwar generation and the succeeding generations who have been educated under the system that teaches the equality of men and women, there are fewer and fewer women who will play the old game. What we see is that men are still being made the workhorses of society, even though they don't have the full-time support and encouragement of women and are not driven by the necessity to support wholly dependent women and children. As long as women do not intend to work as hard as men and do not courageously assume half of the responsibility, they will be forced either to flatter and nurture the male "worker bees"; feed from their sweat and blood;

and even watch them die of overwork, or to accept the fact that the pie is unlikely to become larger and that they will have to manage with a smaller share.

Today, women are less concerned with keeping men going than with gaining greater companionship from them, and this need is sometimes very difficult for men to fulfill. Younger men tend to be inept at genuine partnership with women. Tenderly reared by attentive mothers, they are often more notable for their gentleness than for their strength of character or body. In fact, women wonder if they will make satisfying partners for female age-mates who are growing stronger physically and psychologically and will continue to do so year by year. Young women are now very well educated and ambitious, and they are not interested in indulged, weak men; they want a partner who is at least as sturdy as they are. The fact that women themselves are growing tougher means a commensurate increase in the need for men of at least equal mental and physical fiber, but the way men have been brought up in recent years has tended to make them bright and well educated, gentle and kind, but vulnerable and spoiled, and this is not enough for today's young women.

From the male point of view, women who are highly educated and well informed are difficult to get along with; it is obvious that they cannot be exploited as they once were. The male dilemma is further accentuated by the fact that women today are put off by the old-style male (like their fathers) of few words who grunts grudging responses to questions and tends to behave in a manner that seems arrogant; they seek a man who is capable of carrying on a pleasant and interesting conversation and of pursuing fulfillment in ways other than work.

The vigor with which the sex industry flourishes in Japan in several media (pornographic comics, telephone sex, videos, and other types of commercial voyeurism), and the large number of sex crimes against preadolescent female victims in recent years, may suggest the stirrings of psychological problems engendered in men who are confused and unmanned by women who are aggressive, desire gratification of their own, know their own minds, and can express themselves clearly.

So how should boys be raised so that they will grow into men strong enough to live up to the demands of the considerably changed brand of female from which they must choose their marriage partner? This is an increasingly important issue. More paternal involvement and greater detachment on the part of mothers is necessary, but the solution will not be easy because a new kind of man is needed and the older generations do not provide adequate role models. Some women in their thirties have arrived at a practical reverse solution by wedding younger, more dependent men who act out the wifely role while they themselves assume the husband's role. Marrying an older woman may be a solution for men reared by overprotective, indulgent mothers, providing them with a spouse who will protect and indulge them as their mothers did, and cases of this kind are expected to grow. Conflict and stress between the sexes is unavoidable, and extramarital affairs and divorce may increase. Still, unless there is a fundamental change in the tendency of Japanese to avoid confrontation and not pursue conflicts to the bitter end, it is unlikely that the divorce rate will rise to the level of that in the United States, for example. A marked increase in the divorce rate would be critical if it led to the undermining of the basic Japanese perception of human relationships as based on long-term trust and therefore had a pervasive impact on society as a whole.

HOMEMAKING AND CHILDREARING

Despite their advance into many spheres of society outside the home, women will continue to consider the home extremely important and the family will continue to play a crucial function in their lives. But the decrease in the number of children, whose presence is key to the maintenance of a nurturing family, to only one or perhaps two and the increasing absence from the home of the fathers as corporate soldiers deployed on the front lines of economic growth (in extreme cases, absent for years on end) have cooled the hearths of Japanese homes. Women are beginning to feel more attracted to the pleasures to be found outside the home and the bonds to be forged with other women than to the traditional domestic arts and matronly wisdom. Younger women following in the footsteps of the first postwar generation are not convinced that they have to suppress their own desires and restrain their own activities in order to maintain the home. How will they go about fulfilling their personal needs while maintaining a warm and nurturing family?

Since maintaining the ideal home requires, above all, time and money, several things are likely to happen: (1) The number of women working in part-time jobs will continue to increase. (2) Women will make their husbands and children get by with fewer household services or will try to mobilize other family members to cooperate in performing household chores. (3) The "time is money" approach will be adopted as women seek to free their time from household tasks by purchasing professional services (and as services come to be purchasable, more people will work in order to increase their incomes). (4) And, as observed in Chapter 9, the household may be strengthened by expanding its variations to include a new type that can accommodate both women's homemaking and community involvement.

There is a growing trend among Japanese women to seek an identity of their very own, one that takes into account both the pressure to maintain a warm and nurturing family life and their urge for self-actualization. Although marriage, childbirth, and childrearing have been held in high esteem as life experiences, a housewife who cannot make decisions for herself, who is uninterested in anything outside her own immediate sphere, and who blames her inability to exercise her talents outside the home on household obligations will increasingly be looked down upon. For the Japanese women of the generation following the first postwar generation, the role of housewife is associated with this sort of strong negative stereotype. This can lead them to reject the very idea of becoming a housewife, and some try to convince themselves that they are not housewives by taking part-time jobs.

Meanwhile, Japanese society continues to hold the role of housewife in high regard, and a woman who is a nurturing mother holding a household together has long been revered. According to a study by Kunihiro Yoko, women in their fifties and older feel confident and affirmed in their identities as professional housewives, but the feelings of those of the postwar generations are mixed.[5] They resist the model of womanhood offered by their mothers, whose lives they see as being overwhelmed by the roles of traditional wife and mother; they wish to become something different. Their mothers are the model of what they do *not* want to be. Although the daughters do become housewives, they regard themselves as something different. Yet they have neither abandoned the routine of housewifery nor sought self-actualization through full-time work. They reject a life that is completely devoted to work or completely devoted to the home. By taking part-time work, they can set themselves apart from women who are "nothing but housewives" and gain satisfaction from the contrast with their lives when they were not working at all; now they can proclaim, "I'm not a housewife, I just do the housework." They defend the gap between themselves and the sophisticated career women unhampered by family responsibilities by asserting their identity as mothers and managers of a warm and nurturing home, confirming therein their contentment.

Symbolic of the desire of women to seek their own identities is the increased number of women who have begun to write their own histories and to keep their own names after marriage. Japan's civil code requires that husband and wife use the same family name. Although it can be the name of either the husband or the wife, in 98 percent of cases women change their name to that of their husband upon marriage. Many women find this requirement distasteful, feeling they have given up something very important of themselves, and are unhappy at having to call themselves by another name. The fact that women have begun to take issue with a once-unquestioned practice is indicative of how Japanese women have begun to seek their own identities as individuals. Reflecting this development, voices from the legal profession as well as from women's groups are calling for the introduction of a system for permitting marriage partners to hold separate names, claiming that it is often disadvantageous for a working woman to change her name after marriage. Responding to these calls, even though they as yet come from quite a small minority of Japanese citizens, the government began to study the issue in the Juridical Reform Council of the Ministry of Justice in 1991. (This preempting of a movement issue is a good example of how the government keeps itself one step ahead of the women's movement.)

THE YOUNGER GENERATION
(BORN BETWEEN 1960 AND 1969)

The attitudes and behavior of the younger generation offer important indicators of the direction of change among women and Japanese society as a whole. For women now in their twenties and early thirties, a major dilemma is that while quite a large number of options are at their disposal, they do not have clearly defined goals or a sense of identity. Filled with the confidence that they can do anything they might try, they fail to concentrate on any one particular goal or endeavor. Later, they end up with the unsettling awareness that there is nothing they can actually do with skill or confidence, causing themselves considerable stress.

Immersed in a flood of information, young women today are often frustrated and confused by the tremendous gap between themselves and the image of the smart, well-dressed, dynamic ideal of urban womanhood they see portrayed in the media. The increase in the number of cases of anorexia and alcoholism, as well as in the rates of cigarette smoking, among women reflects the stresses and frustrations of an age of transition in the roles of women. Because they were generally brought up in affluence and spoiled by a lack of sibling rivalry, young people today do not know how to restrain themselves, how to bide their time, or how to cope with failure; they fear above all the pain of being hurt. Although there are a notable number who seek out counseling or self-awareness seminars or join fundamentalist or mass-movement religions, young women's behavior is generally governed not by principles but by their realistic judgment of gain or loss, comparative advantage, and a preference for the easy way out.

Since the material wants of these women are largely satisfied, they tend to lack the motivation or drive to launch a real revolution, opting instead for a tenuous self-preservation. They take jobs and work for several years, postponing marriage longer than their elder sisters but eventually marrying. Accustomed as they are to luxury, they cannot afford to live on their husband's salary alone. The young men who are their partners, moreover, have come to presume that their wife will contribute to the household coffer. In terms of both responsibility for household income and performance of household chores, there is more sharing for this generation than there is for the first postwar generation who are their parents.

Studies of couples in which the income of the wife is higher than that of the husband show the satisfaction of the wife with her husband to be low.[6] Judging from the increase in quarreling and even physical violence initiated by the wife (which was rare in earlier generations), marital problems are likely to grow more serious. The trend that seems to be taking shape among couples of the younger generation is for the household to rely more on the income of the wife, allowing the husband to consider work from a more relaxed perspective. Once they are no longer totally responsible for household support, men will be freer to pursue careers that suit their own personalities and tastes rather than being constantly concerned with increased income and social status. Concomitantly, women will lose the quite considerable amount of freedom they enjoyed, despite their status as dependents, and their own frustrations will increase.

Although there have been predictions that the birth rate will further decrease and the number of "double income–no kids" (DINKs) families will increase, it seems unlikely that this group will become predominant, although the age at which women bear children may continue to rise.

When women who have once tasted the experience of working on an equal basis with men and have held responsible jobs are forced to interrupt their careers to raise children, they often end up venting their frustrations on their offspring. The very recently increasing cases of parent (mother)-inflicted child abuse in Japan may be a sign of the increasing stresses on women.

The diversification of values and lifestyles is further widening the gaps among women. The well-educated, highly motivated women entering the work force and attaining fulfillment through careers outside the home live in a world apart from that of women whose lifestyle is closer to traditional roles and behavior and who take a more passive, easygoing approach to what they perceive as the satisfying life. It is relatively easy for women of ability to achieve success in work or local politics whereas those without outstanding ability or talent will be pushed further into the corners, a process that will estrange women at the two extremes even more.

MALE MYOPIA

How will Japanese men adapt to the changed status of women, that is, their stronger status in the workplace as well as the home, and to the sight of women enjoying their increased freedom and power? As noted in Chapter 1, there is a considerable perception gap between men and women as far as goals are concerned and with regard to how far women have actually moved into the territories traditionally considered the preserve of men. A man's understanding of the changes in women depends on whether he was reared in the ethos of male superiority or under the educational system espousing sexual equality, whether there is stress or ease between him and the women in his workplace, whether there are women who represent serious rivals close at hand in his working life, and whether his expectations match or are at odds with those of his wife.

Why is it that men, for the most part, seem not to be aware of the new autonomy and freedom women are enjoying—or even when they are, refuse to believe it or appreciate it fully? The main reason may be that they do not have the time or mental leeway to think about it. Smart men might use women's drive and talents to make their own lives easier, such as by shortening working hours to facilitate women's working needs and ultimately reaping the benefits of improved working conditions themselves, but they have yet to do so.

And current male perceptions are by no means the result of women's active efforts to change them. Japanese women know well enough that if they were to aggressively try to change men's attitudes, they would have to face men in direct confrontation, which could be self-defeating if it triggered bitter counterattacks and backlash. Moreover, it is not as if Japanese men have drawn a line indicating how far they will allow women to advance into their territory. As far as Japanese men are concerned, preoccupied as they are with their work, women have suddenly appeared in their territory, practically before they noticed what was happening. Older men (in their forties and older), who lived most of their lives in a world of traditional sex roles, find the new brand of woman harder to understand and deal with and are often perplexed about how to handle them.

The bewilderment of older men (born before 1935) stems from two basic questions, as pointed out by Kobama Itsuo:[7] Do women really want to play the games (e.g., long working hours and after-hours socializing) of the workplace alongside men? What kind of relationship do women want to have with men? The women, for their part, do not state their position clearly on either of these points, issuing contradictory demands and further confusing the men with whom they come in contact. They demand equal treatment in the workplace and other arenas of activity outside the home but are still not prepared to assume equal responsibility. Women still have a way of thrusting tasks they don't want to cope with themselves—like heading the PTA, running the government, fixing the roof—onto men. These contradictions obviously place a brake on the pace of change. Men say they have yielded quite a lot of what was once their exclusive territory—the workplace—to women only to find they are still shut out of most female territory in the home.

In the home, women criticize men for not shouldering their share of child care and then turn around and refuse to admit fathers into the closed circle of intimacy between mother and child. Their dissatisfaction with the marital relationship centers on the lack of communication with their husbands, yet they much prefer to spend time with their girlfriends.

Furthermore, while men have lost many of the privileges they formerly enjoyed under the male-dominated society, they are still expected by both men and women to act masculine—that is, to be protective of women, assume extensive responsibility, handle heavy jobs, and so forth. And men feel that women have opened up new worlds of pleasure and self-improvement for themselves in total disregard of men. In the face of the energy and vitality of their women, men feel left behind, slightly threatened, and even a bit jealous.

Of the older generation, those born before 1930 find the tremendous changes in female roles and male–female relations confusing and beyond their comprehension. The things their own wives do and say are so different from what their own mothers did and said that they often cannot understand what is going on. For them, women and children still fall in one and the same category, and they continue to cling to the belief that society will not function properly if men are not dominant. They remain firmly convinced that though women may have changed, they are still inferior to men and their rightful place is still in the home, caring for husband and children. Many of them take pride in the fact that they do not lift a finger to help with housework and hold the ultimate authority in the home (teishu kanpaku). These men believe they are of an age at which they can cling to traditional values regarding sex roles for the rest of their lives. When they see a young career woman working hard to succeed, they tend to be magnanimous and fatherly, extending a protective arm whenever they can because doing so is part of traditional masculine norms.[8]

Men born between 1941 and 1945 view the advance of women much more coolly. These men carry the heaviest burden in the workplace; they work long hours and are tired out. They don't have much time to relax or to be at home with their families. Their own wives are preoccupied with work, intellectual and artistic pursuits, and the education of their children, and they don't give much attention to them; these men's role expectations of their wives are far from fulfilled. Knowing how their wives can often enjoy great freedom, becoming involved in diverse activities and gaining satisfaction from many friendships, they cannot understand why a woman would want to work when there are so many more enjoyable ways in which she could spend her time. The middle-aged man, resigned that his wife will not confine herself to the traditional sex roles, is still unable to extract himself from them.

The men of the first postwar generation born between 1946 and 1955 have very mixed feelings about the changes in women. They have been educated by the same textbooks as their female peers; they know intellectually that they should not discriminate against women in employment. They can also understand why a woman would want to be active outside the home for other than economic reasons, but they are concerned about who is going to look after the children and certainly have no intention of doing so themselves. They were not brought up with the assumption that a man should assume a share of the household responsibilities (other than as breadwinner), and they believe that they have neither the skills nor the ability to do so. It is not fair, they think, for women to suddenly demand that they cook and clean and change diapers. In the workplace they encounter career women close at hand, though still in small numbers, who must be considered as capable, serious rivals. There are many women in lower-ranking jobs, but the men know that, if given the chance, many of these women can do work that is just as good as and perhaps even better than that done by men. This leads them to see women as a threat, and they don't like having to deal with confident, independent women. Given a man and a woman of equal ability, it will be the woman who stands out and receives more attention, and this, too, they find unfair.

In the home, first postwar generation couples follow the friend–spouse pattern, and the wife wants her husband to behave like a friend. The husband knows in his head what he is supposed to do but is mostly unable to fulfill his wife's expectations, inviting a flood of complaints. Torn between the urge to lean psychologically on the moral strength and care of women and the admonition against such indulgence following the creed of sexual equality, he struggles and vacillates. The popularity of transvestite bars (where men can momentarily forget their masculinity) and the wave of *kitaku kyohi* (phobic inability to go home) syndrome cases are suggestive of the difficulties men are undergoing. These men are not having difficulty at work, but they cannot get along with their families without stress. The home, far from being a refuge for relaxation, becomes an even greater realm of struggle and frustration than the office, making these men ripe for the *kitaku kyohi* syndrome.[9]

Younger men born after 1960 take the changed Japanese woman in stride because they do not have a firmly established knowledge of traditional sex roles. They try to create more "natural," stressless relationships with women. Being natural means not sticking to principles but being flexible, situationally oriented, and practical. For men, relating to women on an equal basis comes quite effortlessly. Having grown up with the "new woman," these men perceive male–female relationships on an equal, comrade-to-comrade basis. For them, women have not changed; they have grown up recognizing the strength of women and are therefore not afraid to be dependent on them or work with them without a sense of superiority. By relating to women just as they do to other men, as work colleagues as well as rivals, they experience much less tension in their relationships with women than with their older brothers. As students, the women often had more energy and verve than the men; in their homes, mothers exercised more power than the often-absent fathers. Having been protectively reared by their mothers, they are accustomed to being looked after by women; depending on them does not injure their masculine pride. Some men are even adept at playing the helpless male whom women want to take care of and coddle. It is not unusual in workplaces for the women to be the ones who have the best ideas and do the best job. Some men, knowing that integrated-track women have passed much more rigorous entrance requirements than those for men, clearly expect the best from these women in terms of performance.

Young men born after 1960 tend to be more individualistic than their elders and to be more concerned about the quality of their life than about competing with others; they think that jobs should be undertaken by those who want to do them, regardless of sex. Rather than feeling threatened by female colleagues, they assert that they have activities outside the workplace they want to pursue, just as women do.

The way younger generation men demonstrate their maleness is not by means of the old pattern of arbitrarily pulling women along with them in the direction they want to go but by making themselves more approachable by women by adopting more of what have heretofore been considered feminine habits (care for personal cleanliness; modest speech; use of polite, as opposed to gruff, language; awareness of the feelings of others; thoughtful and considerate behavior). Unlike the men of the first postwar generation, these young men don't argue that men and women *ought* to be equal; their attention focuses, rather, on acting in accordance with their spontaneous feelings. They state clearly that they want to marry a woman who is working and cite two main reasons: It's too great a responsibility to have a wife who is just sitting at home waiting for a husband's return, and the only way to enjoy a comfortable, affluent life is for the wife to work and add her salary to the household coffer. Because of this latter expectation, younger wives no longer enjoy the freedom of their elder sisters and mothers, who had the option of *not* working.

In addition to differences in male reactions to the changes in women by age, there are differences related to a man's social class. In the case of the first postwar generation, there is relatively more resistance among men of the elite to allow their wives to work and to willingly contribute (other than monetarily) to housework or childrearing. Among working men who have opted out of the promotion track, on the other hand, many know the blessing of the income their wife brings home, and already we are seeing some changes over past male work patterns as men excuse themselves from working late by saying, "My wife has overtime tonight, so I have to get back and take care of the kids." Men who place the demands of their families ahead of the demands of their employers are growing more numerous.

The disparity in economic status between households in which the wife works and those where she does not is bound to grow. Men are likely to become even more choosy about their marriage partner, taking into consideration their partner's earning power, just as women have been doing for a long time, in addition to her other qualities.

In households where both husband and wife work and the wife has a well-paying job, the work status of the husband tends to be lower and fewer men are in management positions, regardless of whether or not they have elite academic credentials, than in households where the wife's income is low or where she is a full-time housewife.[10] We may surmise from these findings that when the wife earns a substantial income, husbands, realizing that they do not have to put up with overstressful, exhausting jobs and that they can take life a little easier, pursue work they like rather than clinging to the promotion-oriented track. Relying on their wives, they can free themselves from the work-centered lifestyle that has long been male destiny in Japan. Well-paid working wives have allowed their husbands to achieve a greater measure of freedom and a more humane view of work.

BALANCE, PRAGMATISM, ENDURANCE

Amid these changes, Japanese young women will probably tend to take things relatively easy, somehow managing to maintain a balance between work, family, and leisure without trying or hoping to achieve 100 percent in any one realm, as aptly expressed by a 26-year-old woman quoted in a recently published weekly journal:[11]

> The important thing is to know your own limits and not be embarrassed about them. Life is an endurance race. There are times when you have to move quickly, but most of the time you have to maintain a steady, slow pace or you can't keep going. I am married and hope to have children, but I don't intend to try to be the perfect mother, wife, and professional. I am often asked by others since I married how I can possibly manage both work and home. I manage by cutting corners both on the job and at home. I accept that. . . . Instead of trying hard both on the job and in the home, and suffering alone when it doesn't go well, you just have

to change your attitude. I believe in taking the natural road in everything I do. There's no need either to revolt or to do the impossible.

Most Japanese women, while admiring American women for persistently demanding equality with men, cannot help but deeply sympathize with the American women they observe who are waging what looks like a losing battle to live up to the lofty ideal of the woman who is active professionally and culturally and still manages to be a good mother, wife, and community member. The Japanese woman thinks that it must be very stressful to try to achieve so much, all at once, and all alone and that no human being can expect to perform all assigned roles with equal energy and virtuosity. She believes that if one can achieve a workable balance among one's various roles, that is sufficient. This attitude is not likely to change.

What is the reason for the lack of a perfectionist attitude among Japanese women? Perhaps it has something to do with the culture's religious beliefs: If human beings instinctively seek to make themselves resemble as much as possible the ideal represented by the god or gods they worship in their culture, then in societies with a monotheistic, Judeo-Christian tradition, that ideal is of the omnipotent individual. In the case of Japan, where ancient indigenous animism, Buddhism, and Confucianism are part of the religious culture, the realm of the divine is divided up among innumerable deities (so that different shrines must be visited to pray, for example, for success in love or in academic achievement or in job hunting). In this culture, no one god is expected to take care of everything, and human beings are likewise thought, as a matter of course, to have unique strengths and weaknesses. Those very individual weaknesses are what makes it necessary for people to help each other and to cooperate; they provide the basis of interdependence and equality in a human society built on division of labor. Perhaps the ideal of the individual as the all-knowing and all-powerful god precludes the recognition of the need for division of labor. In this age of 80-year life spans, we all face a period when we will inevitably be dependent upon others; thus, this perception of equality based on mutual dependence will become ever more important from the point of view of basic human dignity.

The profound changes in Japanese society centering around

the inner transformation of women can indeed be interpreted as a revolution, the impact of which pervades society and is irreversible. Japanese society is rapidly being pluralized, and in the process discrimination on the relatively clear lines of sex has not come to a head in outright conflict. Instead, evaluations have begun to shift to focus on individual differences and merit. In this context, common ground is increasingly being found between men and women on the basis of ability and experience, while ties based solely on same-sex membership may be eroding. In Japan, where conflict and confrontation are avoided, where realism and pragmatism are highly prized, and where evaluations are based on a long-term perspective, interdependence among individuals will, we can assume, continue to be viewed affirmatively.

Standing on principle—for example, with respect to equal treatment in the workplace—can be important, but Japanese also feel it can be confining as far as the attainment of happiness for the individual is concerned. They often feel that living according to principle forces human beings into unnatural behavior. The path to a goal through the complexities of human society, they sense, is not necessarily linear but one that winds and twists along the way.

The autonomy and separation of activity between the sexes that has prevailed thus far in Japan will probably weaken, but the mutual reliance through division of labor and the evaluation of equality by diverse criteria seem destined to put down ever-firmer roots as the culture shifts away from the work-centered ethos and provides the basis for a new, inimitably Japanese approach to equality between men and women.

NOTES

CHAPTER 1   MYTHS AND REALITIES

1.   Inamori Kazuo, "Nedayashi no shisō, kyōsei no shisō" [The common denominators of existence and coexistence], *Voice* (April 1992): 176–191.

2.   For example, the chairman of Mitsubishi Heavy Industries and deputy chairman of the Federation of Economic Organizations (Keidanren), Iida Yōtaro, wrote in the April 1992 issue of the mass-circulation monthly *Bungei shunjū* an article entitled "Gaikokujin ni wakaru seiji o" [Toward politics comprehensible to foreigners] as follows: "A man whose wife is on the verge of leaving home is unlikely to be able to perform well on his job. Only if he has a stable family, can a man achieve his true potential" (pp. 106–111). Of course, this is true of a woman as well.

3.   *Josei no kurashi to shigoto ni kasuru yoron chōsa* [Opinion poll on women's lives and work], Prime Minister's Office, November 1991.

4.   See Nakane Chie, *Japanese Society* (London: Weidenfeld & Nicolson, 1970).

5.   For example, among the winners of the very prestigious Akutagawa Prize for literature between 1983 and 1992 were 9 men and 10 women, and similar figures can be found for other important literary prizes in recent years.

6.   See Sylvia Anne Hewlett, *A Lesser Life* (New York: Warner Books, 1986), 45.

7.   A male nurse's aide was denied a job at a nursing home purportedly to protect the privacy of its mainly female patients. The Ohio Civil Rights Commission upheld his sex-bias claim and ordered the nursing home to hire him. The U.S. Supreme Court supported the ruling in a decision on March 2, 1992.

8.   Hakuhōdō Seikatsu Sōgō Kenkyūjo, *Kyūjūnendai kazoku* [Families in the 1990s] (Tokyo: Hakuhōdō Seikatsu Sōgō Kenkyūjo, 1989).

9.   A wife refers to her husband as the master (*shujin*), and a husband refers to his wife as the manager (*kanai*) of the house.

10.   Japanese law states that a woman may obtain an abortion of her own

283

free will if she believes she is unable to support the child. Article 14, Paragraph 1–4, of the Eugenic Protection Act (1948) states that abortions may be sought in "cases where the continuation of pregnancy or giving birth is feared to seriously harm the mother's health due to physiological or economic reasons."

11. According to the U.N. definition, in which the proportion of people over 65 is between 7 and 14 percent of the population.

12. On the labor shortage see, for example, Koyō Shokugyō Sōgō Kenkyūjo [National Institute of Employment and Vocational Research], *Joshi rōryoku no shinjidai* [The female workforce enters a new age] (Tokyo: Tokyo Daigaku Shuppankai, 1987), 6.

CHAPTER 2   THE STORY OF AKIKO

1. Figures for women on weekdays. See Shimojima Kuniko, "Nimannin no shufu seikatsu Jikan shirabe" [A study of use of time among 20,000 housewives in Japan] *Fujin no Tomo* (April 1990) 48. Japan National Broadcasting (NHK) also provides survey data on housework, but since their categories have not remained consistent throughout the years, I rely on the *Fujin no Tomo* data.

2. Ruth Benedict, *The Chrysanthemum and the Sword* (New York: Houghton Mifflin, 1946).

3. Japan's public pension system began around 1940, and the current national pension system was enacted in 1986. The funds come from national health insurance payments, national treasury funds, and interest on accumulated funds. The wife of a salaried worker automatically becomes eligible when her husband joins, and she can collect payments even if she is divorced. For persons joining at age 35, payments begin at age 60 for men and at age 57 for women (though this is soon to change also to 60). In addition to national pension payments, a retired salary worker receives payments from his or her corporate pension plan. As of spring 1992, a retired couple receives a total of ¥120,884 per month in national pension funds and ¥212,892 in welfare pension funds, for a total of ¥333,776 (approx. $2,765) per month.

4. Kyodo Tsushin [Kyodo News Service], "Gendai Shakai to Sei" Committee: Ishikawa Hiroyoshi, Saito Shigeo, and Wagatsuma Hiroshi, *Nihonjin no sei* [The Japanese and sex] (Tokyo: Bungei Shunjusha, 1984), p. 220.

CHAPTER 3   MARRIAGE AND THE FAMILY

1. From a survey of 7,000 readers conducted by the popular women's monthly magazine *More* (February 1991).

2. Kokusai Josei Gakkai Singuru Wūman Kenkyūhan [Task Force on Single Women, International Group for the Study of Women, *Jitsuzō*

Repōto: *Singuru Wūman* [A real-life report: The single woman] (Tokyo: Yūhikaku, 1988), 232.

3. Tanimura Shiho, *Kekkon shinai kamo shirenai shōkōgun* [The "I-may-not-marry" syndrome] (Tokyo: Shufunotomo, 1990), 51–52.

4. *Josei ni kansuru yoron chōsa* [Survey on women] Prime Minister's Office, 1990.

5. *Dai-9ji shussanryoku chōsa* [9th survey on childbearing], Ministry of Welfare, 1987).

6. Nakura Kazuhiko, *Imidasu* (Tokyo: Asahi Shimbunsha, 1990), 1064.

7. Kashima Takashi, *Otoko to onna kawaru rikigaku* [Men and women, changing dynamics] (Tokyo: Iwanami Shoten, 1989), 103.

8. Itamoto Yōko, "Advice to the Lonely: Marriage is Self-Affirmation," *Japan Echo* 15 (Special Issue, 1988): 34–40.

9. Virginia Slims Report, *Josei ishiki chōsa: Nichibei hikaku* [Survey on women's attitudes: A U.S.–Japan comparison] (Tokyo: Virginia Slims Repoto Jikko Iinkai, 1990).

10. Arlie Hochschild with Anne Machung, *Second Shift* (New York: Viking Penguin, 1989).

11. Hakuhōdō Seikatsu Sōgō Kenkyūjo. *Kyūjūnenban seikatsu teiten* [Panel attitude surveys on lifestyles] (Tokyo: Hakuhōdō Seikatsu Sōgō Kenkyūjo, 1990).

12. Seventy percent of Japanese women have a very detailed knowledge of their husband's income and a further 25 percent have a fairly good idea, but less than 20 percent of husbands of women who work outside the home know anything about their wife's income. Over 30 percent know almost nothing about it. Among husbands whose wife makes at least 60 percent of the husband's income, a greater number know more about their wife's income. Hakuhōdō Seikatsu Sōgō Kenkyūjo, 1989.

13. Ibid.

14. Seimei Hoken Bunka Center, *Josei no seikatsu ishiki ni kansuru chōsa* [Survey on women's attitudes toward life] (Tokyo: Seimei Hōken Bunka Center, 1987).

15. *Kazoku/katei ni kansuru yoron chōsa, Sōrifu 1986* [Public opinion survey on the family] (Tokyo: Prime Minister's Office, 1986).

16. *Tsuma ga nozomu kyūjitsu no teishuzō* [What a woman wants a husband to do on his holidays], a survey conducted in 1988 and published in *Ankēto dēta bukku '90* [1990 questionnaire data handbook] (Tokyo: Nihon Nōritsu Kyōkai, 1990).

17. Kokusai Josei Gakkai, ed., "Josei to shakai: Betty Freidan kōen kiroku" [Women and society: Lecture by Betty Friedan] in *Katei no kōzō* [The structure of the family] (Tokyo: PHP Institute, 1981), 62.

CHAPTER 4 COMMUNICATION AND CRISIS

1. *Asahi Shimbun*, "Tēma Danwashitsu" [Reader Dialogue Column] *Kazoku* [The family], Vol. 2 (Tokyo: Asahi Sonorama, 1988), 118.

2. Iwao Sumiko, "Zai-Bei Nikkei kigyō de hataraku Amerikajin joshi shain (howaito karā) no fuman to kaizensaku" [Dissatisfaction of American white-collar women working for Japanese corporations in the United States and measures for solution of the problems], Report for the Matsushita Kokusai Zaidan [Matsushita International Foundation], 1991.

3. For example, Ogura Kazuo, Tōzai Bunka Masatsu [Cultural friction between East and West] (Tokyo: Chūō Kōronsha, 1990).

4. This behavior is commonly observed. For further reading, see, for example, Sugawara Mariko, Shinkazoku no jidai [The age of the "new family"] (Tokyo: Chūkō Shinsho, 1987), 46.

5. See Kobama Itsuo, Otoko wa doko ni iru no ka [Where are the men?] (Tokyo: Sōshisha, 1990), 252, and Furuya Kazuo, Tsumatachi no teinen sengen [Declaration of retirement from housewifery] (Tokyo: Kōdansha, 1989), 29.

6. Hakuhōdō Seikatsu Sōgō Kenkyūjo, Kyujunendai kazoku [Families in the 1990s] (Tokyo: Hakuhodo Seikatsu Sōgō Kenkyūjo, 1989).

7. Ministry of Labor figures, 1987.

8. Iwao Sumiko, Saito Hiroko, and Fukutomi Mamoru, eds., Tanshin funin [Commuting marriage] (Tokyo: Yūhikaku, 1991).

9. Ibid. The questionnaire asked what the respondent thought should happen "if the wife is offered a very good job in another city." The largest percentage of respondents in both Japan and the United States responded that "the wife should turn down the job" (Japanese women 56 percent, men 63 percent; American women 42 percent, men 47 percent); the figures reflect the greater weight attached in the United States than in Japan to the wife's career. In Japan, a fairly large number of women and men, 38 percent and 30 percent, respectively, supported wife-alone transfer, choosing the option, "The wife should take the new job and move there, and they should get together whenever they can on weekends, holidays and vacations." This was the least chosen option among Americans (women, 6 percent; men, 7 percent), who preferred instead that "the husband should quit his job, relocate with his wife and try to get another job in the new place" (women, 29 percent; men, 28 percent).

10. My discussion here relies primarily on two sources: the 1990 VSR Survey, giving comparative data on Japanese and American women, and a Japanese book published in 1984 entitled Sei: Tsumatachi no messēgi [Sex: Messages from wives], by a women's group called Group for Wives [Grupu Waifu], which has put out a bimonthly magazine based on letters from readers since 1963. The group conducts reader surveys from time to time on various issues. The book cited here focuses on such a survey on sex conducted in 1983 among 261 women. The sample is small and the educational level of respondents is somewhat higher than the national average, but the responses provide the unprocessed and frank voices of many women.

11. Grupu Waifu [Group for Wives], Sei: Tsumatachi no messegi [Sex: Messages from wives] (Tokyo: Michi Shobō, 1984). The age when

women have their first premarital sex experience with men other than their future husband seems to be moving downward, roughly a year each decade. Based on the Group for Wives study (1984), for those born before World War II it was 21.5 years; for the first postwar generation born between 1946 and 1955, 20 years; and for those born between 1956 and 1965, 19 years. The youngest age reported was 16, and none reported having had intercourse in their early teens. More recent surveys of teenagers show that the age is even lower today, the average being 15 for boys and 14 for girls. More than half of high school students have had intercourse. Cases of pregnancy among senior high school girls (ages 15–18) and the difficulties and traumas they face have been reported in the mass media, but teenagers made up only 6 percent of women who had abortions performed in 1989 (28,000 cases).

12. Ibid., 33.

13. Ibid., 172.

14. Ibid., 171.

15. Amino Yoshihiko, *Nihon no rekishi o yominaosu* [Re-reading Japanese history] (Tokyo: Chikuma Shobō, 1991).

16. "Ichiokusō koishitai jidai: Nihonjin no ren'aikan o kiru" [The age when 1 billion want to fall in love: Probing the Japanese idea of falling in love], *Asahi jānaru* (January 10, 1992), 3–10.

17. Under the Meiji civil code which prevailed until the end of World War II, the basic unit of society was the *ie*, or household. The head of the household, who was as a rule male, exercised unchallengable authority over the lives of all family members. Women (wives) were seen primarily in terms of their role as bearers of male offspring who would carry on the family line and assume the responsibilities of family head. Women exercised no authority over marriage, divorce, or inheritance. The *ie* as part of the legal system was abolished in 1947.

18. "Ichiokusō koishitai jidai." This statement refers to remarks by Kishida Shū in the dialogue with Umehara Takeshi which constitutes this article.

19. See *Kazoku*, Vol. 2 (cf. note 1). These feelings are clearly expressed in many of the letters received from Asahi Shimbun readers, such as those quoted on pp. 83 and 131.

20. *UN Demographic Yearbook*, 1989.

21. *Statistical Abstract of the United States 1991* (Washington, D.C. U.S. Department of Commerce, Economics and Statistics Administration, Bureau of the Census, 1991).

22. *Kazoku*, Vol. 2, 217.

23. Fukushima Mizuho, "Sei ni tsuite hanashiaeru fūfu to hanashiaenai fūfu no sa" [The difference between couples who can discuss sex and those who cannot] *Croissant* (January 1991), 46–47.

24. Yamashita Katsutoshi, *Sayonara, anata* [Goodbye, dear] (Tokyo: Asahi Shimbunsha, 1984), 209.

25. *Kazoku*, Vol. 2, 500.

26. Bandō Mariko, *Nihon no josei dētabanku* [Databank on Japanese

women] (Tokyo: Ministry of Finance Publishing Office, 1992).

27. Atsumi Masako, "Kekkon/rikon no genjitsu" [The realities of mar-
    riage and divorce], in *Jurisuto sōgō tokushū: Josei no genzai to shōrai* [The
    Jurist feature issue: Women today and tomorrow] (Tokyo: Yūhikaku,
    1985), 201–206.
28. Ministry of Welfare, *Jinko dotai tōkei* [Demographic statistics] (Tokyo:
    Ministry of Welfare, 1978).
29. See Furuya Kazuo, *Tsumatachi no teinen sengen* [Declaration of retire-
    ment from housewifery] (Tokyo: Kōdansha, 1989) for stories of
    couples whose lives are rocked by the retirement of the husband.

CHAPTER 5   MOTHERHOOD AND THE HOME

1. It must be noted that this belief is the result in part of national
    propaganda—the slogan *"umeyo fuyaseyo* [conceive and multiply]"—
    and the high child mortality rate of prewar times.
2. If this figure seems low, it should be pointed out that it covers only
    tuition. Most Japanese universities are nonresidential, so living costs
    must be considered separately. The average tuition for a private
    university is ¥1,080,000 and for a public university ¥605,600.
3. Prime Minister's Office, *Kazoku/katei ni kansuru yoron chōsa* [Survey on
    the family] (Tokyo: Prime Minister's Office, 1986).
4. Hakuhōdō Seikatsu Sōgō Kinkyūjo, *Kyujunendai kazoku* [Families in
    the 1990s] (Tokyo: Hakuhōdō Seikatsu Sōgō Kenkyūjo, 1989).
5. Prime Minister's Office Survey, 1986.
6. For example: *"Baka na ko o motaba, kaji yori tsurai* [A stupid child is a
    worse catastrophe than a fire]" and *"Haji wa ie no yamai* [Shame is the
    ruin of the family]".
7. Saimon Fumi, *Ren'ai ron* [On infatuation and love] (Tokyo: PHP
    Institute, 1990), 62.
8. Prime Minister's Office Survey, 1986.
9. Hakuhōdō Seikatsu Sōgō Kenkyūjo, *Kyūjūnendai kazoku*.
10. General Affairs Agency, Statistics Bureau, *Rōdōryoku chōsa tokubetsu
    chōsa* [Special survey on the labor force] (Tokyo: General Affairs
    Agency, 1990) for Japanese figures. For American figures, see *Statisti-
    cal Abstract of the United States 1991* (Washington, D.C.: U.S. Depart-
    ment of Commerce, Economics and Statistics Administration, Bureau
    of the Census, 1991).
11. See Sylvia Anne Hewlett, *A Lesser Life* (New York: Warner Books,
    1986).
12. Ministry of Health and Welfare, 1983 figures.
13. Tomobataraki Kazoku Kenkyukai [Research Group on Working Cou-
    ples], *DEWKs no kurashi ni tsuite no chōsa* [Survey on the lives of
    double-earner-with kids couples] (Tokyo: Tomobataraki Kazoku
    Kenkyūkai, 1990).
14. Iwao Sumiko and Sugiyama Meiko (eds.), *Hataraku hahaoya no jidai:
    Kodomo e no eikyō o kangaeru* [The age of working mothers: The effect of

mothers' working on children] (Tokyo: Nihon Hōsō Shuppan Kyokai, 1984).

15. As pointed out by many analysts including Ueno Chizuko in *Mazakon shōnen no matsuro* [The fate of teenagers with mother complexes] (Nagoya: Shingaku Kenkyūsha, 1986, 54.

16. Merry White, *The Japanese Educational Challenge* (New York: Free Press, 1987), esp. pp. 140–50.

17. Ueno Chizuko, *Mazakon shonen no matsuro.*

18. Narabayashi Hiroshi Interview, *Croissant* (January 1991), 66–67.

CHAPTER 6   WORK AS OPTION

1. *Heisei gannen joshi koyō kanri chōsa* [1989 survey on female employment management], Ministry of Labor, Nov. 1989 (hereafter Ministry of Labor survey, November 1989).

2. Kyūtoku Shigenori, *Bogenbyō* [Children's illnesses originating in maternal behavior] (Tokyo: Sunmark Shuppan, 1979).

3. I vividly recall in the early 1970s that I was the only full-time working mother in my son's public primary school class of 40 children. I felt guilty for not being able to take part in the PTA activities organized by the other mothers, all scheduled in the daytime. Some other mothers worked but were either part-timers or worked in family-run stores along with their husbands, situations that gave them the flexibility to attend PTA meetings and other activities at which a mother's presence had become customary. I was subject to both criticism and envy for having an excuse that freed me from the often burdensome work of PTA committee duty, a great deal of which was mostly procedural. By the late 1970s, however, the situation changed; I was no longer a black sheep. Other mothers began openly to excuse themselves from PTA duties because they were busy with work. In fact, by the early 1980s so many mothers were working that having a job was no longer an adequate excuse for not participating in PTA-organized functions. The speed of these changes has been remarkable, just as it has been in the case of the graying of Japanese society.

4. International Labor Organization, *Yearbook of Labour Statistics* (1984). The percentage of elementary school teachers who are women is 56.2; for junior high school, 38.7; high school, 34.3; junior college, 18.9; four-year university, 8.5 percent (1986 figures).

5. Prime Minister's Office, *Josei ni kansuru yoron chōsa* [Survey on women] (Prime Minister's Office, 1987).

6. Prime Minister's Office, *Fujin mondai ni kansuru kokusai hikaku chōsa* [International comparative study of problems of women] (Prime Minister's Office, 1982).

7. According to figures from a October 1989 Prime Minister's Office survey (*Josei no shokugyō ni kansuru yoron chōsa* [Opinion poll on working women]) (hereafter cited as Prime Minister's Office survey, 1989), nearly 24 percent of women (compared to 28 percent of men)

are "satisfied" with their jobs and 55 percent of women and 52 percent of men are "moderately satisfied" (although these results must be weighed in the context of the trend among Japanese respondents to reply in moderate terms to any question). American women, as reported in a Virginia Slims survey in 1990, indicate a higher percentage of "great personal satisfaction" (37 percent) in their jobs. The major sources of dissatisfaction with their jobs among Japanese women are low pay (49 percent) and not enough holidays (30 percent); among Japanese men the respective figures are 72 percent and 47 percent.

8. Prime Minister's Office survey, 1989.
9. Koyō Shokugyō Sōgō Kenkyūjo [National Institute of Employment and Vocational Research], *Seinen no shokugyō tekiō ni kansuru kokusai hikaku kenkyū* [International study on work adaptability of young people] (Tokyo: Japan Institute of Labor, 1989).
10. Prime Minister's Office survey, 1989.
11. Japanese Institute of Labor, *Pāto taimu rōdō jittai chōsa kenkyū hōkokusho* [Report on a fact-finding study of part-time labor] (Japanese Institute of Labor, 1991).
12. Prime Minister's Office survey, 1989.
13. Sixty percent of both men and women respondents stated that part-time work is more desirable for women who have been out of the work force for several years. The crux of the matter is what kind of work pattern both men and women believe most suitable for women with families. Full-time employment was considered desirable by only 18 percent of women and 16 percent of men, and self-employment thought suitable by 12 percent of women and 9 percent of men, perhaps due to its greater risks and lack of security. Support for part-time employment among women has risen rapidly, by 10 percent over the previous poll conducted in 1983.
14. Ministry of Labor survey, November 1989.
15. Perhaps not surprisingly, the rate of satisfaction among part-time workers is higher than that of regular full-time workers with regard to both "content of the work" and "position and status in the workplace." (From Japanese Institute of Labor 1991, 69.) Sixty-seven percent indicate they wish to continue working part time. The high satisfaction rate can be explained partly by the women's motivations for working in the first place: They will work only under conditions that allow them to go on fulfilling their household duties and responsibilities toward their children.
16. For example, Karel van Wolferen, *The Enigma of Japanese Power: People and Politics in a Stateless Nation* (London: Macmillan, 1989); Kawai Hayao, "Nihon no shinwa ni miru ishi kettei" [Japanese decision-making as seen in its mythology] *AΣteion*, no. 15 (1990), 26–32; and Nakatani Iwao, "Chōbunken kokka Nihon" [Japan: The super power-splintered state] *AΣteion*, no. 15 (1990), 20–25.
17. Ministry of Labor survey, November 1989.
18. Josei Shokugyō Zaidan [Japan Institute of Women's Employment], *A*

Survey on the Employment of New University Graduates (Tokyo: Josei Shokugyō Zaidan, 1987).

19. Ministry of Labor survey, November 1989.

20. Prime Minister's Office survey, 1989.

21. Material in the following paragraph is based on interviews conducted in 1991.

CHAPTER 7 WORK AS PROFESSION

1. Ministry of Labor, "Chingin kōzō kihon tōkei chōsa kekka" [Compiled results of basic statistics on the wage structure] in Koyō Shokugyō Sōgō Kenkyūjo, ed., *Joshi rōdō no shinjidai* (Tokyo: Tokyo Daigaku Shuppankai, 1987), 48–49.

2. From a confidential report prepared by the Seikatsu Dezain Kenkyūjo [Life Design Institute], 1990.

3. Josei Shokugyō Zaidan [Japan Institute of Women's Employment], *Joshi kanrishoku chōsa* [Survey on women in management] (Tokyo: Josei Shokugyō Zaidan, 1989).

4. Arlie Hochschild with Anne Machung, *Second Shift* (New York: Viking Penguin, 1989).

5. Japan Institute of Women's Employment, 1989.

6. Ibid.

7. Ibid.

8. Rōdōshō Fujinkyoku [Ministry of Labor Bureau on Women], *Heisei Gannendo joshi koyō kanri kihon chōsa* [Basic survey on employment management of women] (Tokyo: Ministry of Labor, 1989).

9. "Josei shain no katsuyō jōkyō" [Utilization of female employees] survey by the Tokyo Chūsho Kigyō Tōshi Ikusei Kaisha [Tokyo Small and Medium Enterprise Investment and Growth Company], 1991.

10. Hara Hiroko, Muramatsu Yasuko, and Minami Chie, eds., *Chūshō kigyō no joseitachi: Kei'ei sankakusha to kanrishokusha no jirei kenkyū* [Women in small and medium enterprise: Case studies of women participating in management and in management positions] (Tokyo: Miraisha, 1987).

11. Ishida Hideo, ed., *Josei no jidai: Nihon kigyō to koyō byōdo* [The age of women: Japanese corporations and equal employment] (Tokyo: Kōbundō, 1986).

12. Sugawara Mariko. *Josei kanrishoku no jidai* [The era of female management] (Tokyo: Chikuma Shobo, 1983).

13. Barbara A. Gutek, "Sex and the Workplace," paper presented at the Twenty-Second International Congress of Applied Psychology, Kyoto, 1990.

14. Kashima Takashi, *Otoko to onna kawaru rikigaku* [The changing dynamics of men and women] (Tokyo: Iwanami Shoten, 1989), 35.

15. *Yomiuri shimbun*, February 20, 1992.

16. Based on observations shared by Obayashi Yoshiko, chief researcher at the Hakuhōdō Research Institute.

CHAPTER 8 POLITICS AND NO POWER

1. Prime Minister's Office, *Josei ni kansuru yoron chōsa* [Survey on women] (Tokyo: Prime Minister's Office, 1990). Responses affirming "no interest in politics" came to 39 percent for women (18 percent for men).

2. Unpublished personal diary of Suita Daisaburō, who was Cabinet Secretary in 1945, in the collection of the National Diet Library of Japan.

3. One reason for this is related to the way the electoral system was set up at the time. The double- or triple-entry ballot system in use then is said to have made it relatively easier for female candidates to win (a typical strategy if there were two entries was to make one a woman). The electoral system was revised the following year to institute the single-entry ballot, and under that system, the number of successful female candidates fell to only 15.

4. This rests on three main pillars, known as *jiban, kanban,* and *kaban*. *Jiban* (local support base) means strong roots and political following in the constituency; *kanban* (sign, trademark) means degree of fame; and *kaban* (briefcase) means a fat pocketbook (or more blatantly, money). The political legacy of many of the leaders who carried the ruling party ball for years since the end of the war has been succeeded to in many cases by their sons (or sons-in-law). These younger-generation politicians have enjoyed the singular advantages to be had from inheriting the support base, the name and recognition, as well as the wealth built up over the years by their fathers. Here, women are excluded outright.

5. Based on accounts in Ieta Shōko, *Daigishi no tsumatchi* [The wives of Dietmen] (Tokyo: Bungei Shunju, 1987).

6. Moriyama Mayumi, *Asahi Shimbun*, July 18, 1989.

7. *Mainichi Shimbun,* June 1989 poll.

8. Ten from electoral districts and 12 from proportional representation districts for a total of 22; of members up for election, 12 were women, which meant the number had increased by 10. Added to the 11 women members elected three years earlier, this made a total of 33.

9. *Asahi Shimbun,* July 28, 1990.

10. Tawara Kōtarō, "Doi Takako wo miru onna no 'kawaisa'" [Doi Takako's appeal among women], *Seiron* (January 1991), 42–52.

11. In *Sapio* (Shogakkan), August 10, 1989.

12. Prime Minister's Office survey on women, 1990.

13. Moriyama Mayumi, *Asahi Shimbun*, July 1, 1989.

14. Masuzoe Yōichi, "Onnatachi ga Nihon o tsubusu" [The women will crush Japan], *Seiron* (September 1989), 176–185.

15. See Iwai Tomoaki, "Josei giin o tettei chōsa suru" [Complete survey of women Diet representatives], *Bungei Shunju*, March 1991.

16. Prime Minister's Office survey on women, 1987.

CHAPTER 9 FULFILLMENT THROUGH ACTIVISM

1. See Nakane Chie, *Japanese Society* (London: Weidenfeld & Nicolson, 1970).
2. Fujiwara Fusako, *Nakama-zukuri, kinjozukiai* [Forming groups; Community relations] (Tokyo: Shinchōsha, 1983).
3. Satō Keiko, ed., *Joseitachi no seikatsu nettowāku: Seikatsu Kurabu ni tsudou hitobito* [Networking women: The people who joined the Seikatsu Club] (Tokyo: Bunshindo, 1988).
4. Betty Friedan, *The Feminine Mystique* (New York: Dell Books, 1963).

CHAPTER 10 DIRECTIONS OF CHANGE

1. Many of the sources for material discussed in this chapter are unpublished surveys and research analyses made available to me by government agencies including the Prime Minister's Office and private research institutions. These sources are noncommercial publications. Detailed versions are made available to a limited number of scholars, opinion leaders, and policymakers, and abridged versions are available in public libraries. For these publications, the author and publisher are the same. Most of the newspaper articles quoted in this book do not give a specific byline. Sources such as *Asahi Shimbun* and *Mainichi Shimbun* are Japanese-language newspapers. Information on the younger generation discussed in this chapter is based on a questionnaire survey I conducted among women aged 20–25 and numerous interviews with men and women of various ages. My conclusions have also benefitted from my discussions of issues involving women with many specialists in psychology and women's studies, including Hara Hiroko, Kunihiro Yoko, Ogawa Akira, Kobayashi Yoshiko, Sugawara Mariko, and Kuramori Kyoko.
2. Prime Minister's Office, *Josei no shigoto to seikatsu ni kansuru chōsa* [Survey on women's work and lives] (Tokyo: Prime Minister's Office, November 1991). The survey asked respondents to assess the changes in male and female roles over the past 15 years. We should note that the responses reflect general impressions of society, not necessarily a radical change in personal attitudes or awareness.
3. National surveys conducted every 5 years since 1958 show that while 35 years ago the majority of Japanese women would have liked to be reborn as men (64 percent), the number who wanted to be reborn as women has steadily increased, reaching 59 percent in the latest of the surveys, conducted in 1988. Tōkei Suri Kenkyūjo [Institute of Statistical Mathematics], *Nihonjin no kokuminsei chōsa* [Survey of Japanese national characteristics] (Tokyo: Tōkei Suri Kenkyūjo, 1991).
4. Prime Minister's Office, *Josei no kurashi to shigoto ni kansuru yoron chōsa* [Survey on women's work and lives] (Tokyo: Prime Minister's Office, 1990).
5. Kunihiro Yoko, "Shufu to iu kategorii: Kōgakureki josei no shufu ishiki to shutai keishiki," unpublished master's thesis, Yokohama City

College, 1990, is the source upon which this paragraph is based.

6. Hakuhōdō Seikatsu Sōgō Kenkyūjo, *Kyujunendai kazoku* [Families in the 1990s] (Tokyo: Hakuhōdō Seikatsu Sōgō Kenkyūjo, 1989).

7. Kobama Itsuo, *Otoko doko ni iru no ka* [Where are the men?] (Tokyo: Sōshisha, 1990), 16.

8. See *Kyujunendai kazoku*.

9. Kobama Itsuo, *Otoko doko ni iru no ka*, 223.

10. *Kyujunendai kazoku*.

11. "Josei shain yarimasu: Kigyō senjō ni naritakunai" [I'll be happy to be a working woman, but I won't be a corporate footsoldier], *Asahi jānaru* (February 28, 1992): 19–26.

INDEX